LEGAL FICTIONS IN PRIVATE LAW

Legal fictions are falsehoods that the law knowingly relies on. It is the most bizarre feature of our legal system; we know something is false, and we still assume it. But why do we rely on blatant falsehood? What are the implications of doing so? Should we continue to use fictions, and, if not, what is the alternative? *Legal Fictions in Private Law* answers these questions in an accessible and engaging manner, looking at the history of fictions, the theory of fictions and current fictions from a practical perspective. It proposes a solution to what to do about fictions going forward, and how to decide whether they should be accepted or rejected. It addresses the latest literature and deals with the law in detail. This book is a comprehensive analysis of legal fictions in private law and a blueprint for reform.

Liron Shmilovits, PhD, is a Fellow in Law at Wolfson College, Cambridge. His research interests lie in private law, primarily contract and torts, as well as intellectual property.

Legal Fictions in Private Law

LIRON SHMILOVITS
University of Cambridge

CAMBRIDGE
UNIVERSITY PRESS

CAMBRIDGE
UNIVERSITY PRESS

University Printing House, Cambridge CB2 8BS, United Kingdom

One Liberty Plaza, 20th Floor, New York, NY 10006, USA

477 Williamstown Road, Port Melbourne, VIC 3207, Australia

314–321, 3rd Floor, Plot 3, Splendor Forum, Jasola District Centre, New Delhi – 110025, India

103 Penang Road, #05–06/07, Visioncrest Commercial, Singapore 238467

Cambridge University Press is part of the University of Cambridge.

It furthers the University's mission by disseminating knowledge in the pursuit of education, learning, and research at the highest international levels of excellence.

www.cambridge.org
Information on this title: www.cambridge.org/9781316519479
DOI: 10.1017/9781009023788

First published 2022

A catalogue record for this publication is available from the British Library.

Library of Congress Cataloging-in-Publication Data
NAMES: Shmilovits, Liron, 1987– author.
TITLE: Legal fictions in private law / Liron Shmilovits, University of Cambridge.
DESCRIPTION: Cambridge, United Kingdom ; New York, NY : Cambridge University Press, 2022. | Based on author's thesis (doctoral – University of Cambridge, 2019) issued under title: Deus ex machina : legal fictions in private law. | Includes bibliographical references and index.
IDENTIFIERS: LCCN 2021024853 (print) | LCCN 2021024854 (ebook) | ISBN 9781316519479 (hardback) | ISBN 9781009023788 (ebook)
SUBJECTS: LCSH: Fictions (Law) – England.
CLASSIFICATION: LCC KD703.F53 S56 2022 (print) | LCC KD703.F53 (ebook) | DDC 346.42–dc23
LC record available at https://lccn.loc.gov/2021024853
LC ebook record available at https://lccn.loc.gov/2021024854

ISBN 978-1-316-51947-9 Hardback

To Eliezer and Rivka

Contents

Tables

Acknowledgements

My thanks are due to many helpers:

To my doctoral supervisor, **Professor David Ibbetson**, and doctoral advisor, **Professor Graham Virgo**, for knowledge, patience and wisdom;
To **Nicholas McBride**, who volunteered to read a student's drafts, for generosity;
To **Professor Richard Nolan** and **Professor Paul Mitchell**, my PhD examiners, for forbearance;
To several **anonymous reviewers**, for being tough but fair;
To my **publisher**, for believing in an unknown author;
To my **family**, finally, for unconditional love and unfailing support.

Table of Cases

Abbreviations

Books of Authority

Bl Comm	W Blackstone, *Commentaries on the Laws of England* (Clarendon Press 1765–9)
Co Litt	E Coke, *Commentarie upon Littleton* (London 1628)
Glanvill	R Glanvill, *Treatise on the Laws and Customs of England*
Hale PC	M Hale, *The History of the Pleas of the Crown* (London 1736)

Courts

CA	Court of Appeal of England and Wales
Ch	Chancery Division or, before 1875, Court of Chancery
CP	Court of Common Pleas
HC	High Court of England and Wales
HCA	High Court of Australia
HL	House of Lords
KB	King's Bench Division or, before 1875, Court of King's Bench
PC	Privy Council
QB	Queen's Bench Division or, before 1875, Court of Queen's Bench
SC	Supreme Court of the United Kingdom
SCOTUS	Supreme Court of the United States

Titles of Books

HCLC	AWB Simpson, A *History of the Common Law of Contract* (Clarendon Press 1987)

HFCL	SFC Milsom, *Historical Foundations of the Common Law* (2nd edn, Butterworths 1981)
HILO	DJ Ibbetson, *A Historical Introduction to the Law of Obligations* (OUP 1999)
HLL	AWB Simpson, *A History of the Land Law* (2nd edn, Clarendon Press 1986)
IELH	JH Baker, *Introduction to English Legal History* (5th edn, OUP 2019)
LFTP	Maksymilian Del Mar and William Twining (eds), *Legal Fictions in Theory and Practice* (Springer 2015)
LTB	JH Baker, *The Law's Two Bodies* (OUP 2001)

General Introduction

A legal fiction, for present purposes, is a false assumption a court knowingly relies on. The maxim 'Everybody knows the law' is an example of a legal fiction.[1] As a statement of fact, the maxim is evidently false. Not even lawyers or judges know all the law. And yet courts apply it, as if it were true, with the result that ignorance of the law is no defence.[2] We therefore say that the maxim is a legal fiction.

The griffin dominating the cover of this book is an illustration in both senses of the word. This mythic beast – half lion and half eagle – is neither a mistake nor a lie. It is a *fiction*. It is a known untruth that we accept for certain purposes, such as literature or art. Legendary creatures are more familiar than legal fictions, but legal fictions are more important.

* * *

To better understand our subject, let us consider the case of one Richard Bailey, who, in the year 1800, learned about legal fictions the hard way.[3] His case is particularly illustrative of the maxim that 'Everybody knows the law', for Mr Bailey was not merely ignorant of the law: he could not *possibly* know it. The facts were as follows. In May 1799, Parliament passed an Act that created a new offence.[4] In

1 1 Hale PC, ch 6, 42; 4 Bl Comm, ch 2, V, 27; *Carter v Mclaren & Co* (1870–75) LR 2 Sc 120 (HL) 125 (Lord Chelmsford); *Cooper v Simmons* (1862) 7 Hurl & N 707, 158 ER 654 (Exchequer) 658 (Pollock CB).

2 Today the maxim applies only when a person is accused of wrongdoing. A mistake of law does not bar recovery by a mistaken claimant: *Kleinwort Benson Ltd v Lincoln CC* [1999] 2 AC 349 (HL) 371, 375 (Lord Goff), 405ff (Lord Hope); *Pankhania v Hackney LBC* [2002] EWHC 2441 (Ch), [2002] NPC 123 [57] (Rex Tedd QC).

3 *R v Bailey* (1800) Russ & Ry 1, 168 ER 651 (Crown Cases Reserved).

4 The offence was 'maliciously shooting'. It had originally been enacted by 9 Geo I c 22 (1723) ('Black Act'), s 1. The Act referred to in the main text extended this offence to the high seas: 39 Geo III c 37 (1799).

June 1799, Mr Bailey committed this offence. It so happened that during this period Bailey was on a ship sailing the high seas. It was practically impossible for news of the change in the law to have reached him. That was his defence at trial. But his protestations of ignorance fell on deaf ears. Ignorance was no defence. Everybody knew the law and so did Bailey, who was duly convicted. The punishment for the offence was death.[5]

* * *

Bailey's mortal experience with fictions shows that the subject of our inquiry is not theoretical. Legal fictions decide real cases and affect real people. The fiction may not be real, but the result is as real as life and death. What if the reader should find himself or herself, like Bailey, the victim of a legal fiction?

Even where life and limb are not at risk, the use of fictions in the law raises serious questions. Can legal fictions be justified? Why do we have them? What is to be done about them? These are the questions that animate this work.

Important though they are, these questions are not the only reasons to study legal fictions. After all, these questions are not new. Legal fictions are as old as ancient Rome, where one fiction killed a Roman citizen a moment before he was taken prisoner and another fiction abolished his captivity upon release.[6] Fictions have provoked thinkers throughout the ages – some to fury; others to approbation; none, it seems, to indifference. Hale, Bentham, Fuller, to name a few, weighed into this controversy, each in his time: the Restoration, the Industrial Revolution, the Great Depression. So why indeed, after two millennia, do we ask the same questions?

This brings us to the state of the scholarship. Fictions are seldom treated as a topic in its own right. Just as fictions are incidental to the law, so are they incidental to legal commentary – with few notable exceptions.[7] Fiction scholarship, such as it is, is beset by three challenges. First, scholars have widely divergent definitions of legal fiction. While they appear to discuss the same thing, in truth each refers to a somewhat different device, though by the common label of 'fiction'. These different conceptions of legal fiction, which

[5] Black Act (n 4) s 1.

[6] A captured citizen was considered a slave (of the enemy) and could not own or bequeath property. If he died a captive, his inheritance was saved by *lex Cornelia*, which presumed he had died before capture: Digest 35.2.1.1. If he returned, *postliminium* reinstated him in citizenship and property as if he had not been captured (except property owned by possession): Digest 49.15.5.1; Rules of Ulpian 23.5.

[7] See, for example, Lon L Fuller, *Legal Fictions* (Stanford University Press 1967); Pierre JJ Olivier, *Legal Fictions in Practice and Legal Science* (Rotterdam University Press 1975); and Maksymilian Del Mar and William Twining (eds), LFTP; all of which feature prominently hereunder.

are sometimes implicit, part overlap and part contradict. This breeds confusion and impedes debate (which requires agreement on premises). This work will propose a way out of this house of mirrors.

The second problem with the scholarship is the resolution. It is either too high or too low: a particular fiction under the microscope or philosophical disputations about truth, fact and fiction. There is scarcely anything in between. An analysis of the role of fictions in an area of law is what we need. This work will supply this want.

The third problem is that the literature is strong on theory and weak on practical advice. It is too, dare we say, *academic*. Fiction scholarship is varied, insightful and, for those so-inclined, rewarding in intellectual satisfaction. It has certainly enriched the ensuing pages. But, for all its wealth, it does not answer the real-world questions of what to do about the fictions that exist, and under what circumstances to create new ones. This work will answer these questions.

* * *

This monograph is a study of legal fictions in English private law. The field of inquiry is thus confined to one, albeit broad, area. It is so confined for reasons of practicality, namely time, space and the author's competence.

The aim of this book is to answer a single practical question. Answering this question naturally involves answering many preliminary questions. Yet everything in these pages is directed towards answering the following core question: *Which fictions should we accept and which should we reject?* The answer to this question – the 'Acceptance Test' for fictions – is the thesis of this book.

* * *

I will seek an answer to this core question by doctrinal legal analysis. Unlike many doctrinal projects, my mission is not to come up with a model that *explains existing law*.[8] My approach does not assume an underlying consistency waiting to be discovered. At present, let it be said, there is no set of principles governing fictions. For fiction is the *abandonment* of principle. I wish hereby to offer a *new system* for dealing with legal fictions. This system is designed to be as compatible as possible with existing law, but is emphatically not a reflection of it. I will describe the law, evaluate it and propose reform. The reform is encapsulated in the answer to the core question highlighted above: which fictions to keep and which discard.

[8] Christopher McCrudden, 'Legal Research and the Social Sciences' [2006] LQR 632, 632–4.

The monograph which follows is divided into four substantive chapters in chronological order. Chapter 1 summarises the extraordinary history of legal fictions in English law. Chapter 2 recounts the history of *thought* concerning legal fictions and, arriving at the present, tackles the problem of definition. Chapter 3 analyses contemporary fictions in the light of the preceding chapters. Chapter 4 answers the core question by proposing a test for which fictions to retain and which to abolish.

In the course of this journey, traversed in just over 100,000 words, we will encounter 25 legal fictions, visit several jurisdictions, meet many scholars and take our part in intellectual battles. We will heed the anonymous call to arms in the *Harvard Law Review* that 'the nearly dormant debate over the legal fiction should be reawakened'.[9]

* * *

Incidentally, Mr Bailey was pardoned by George III, on the advice of the judges who had tried him.[10] The law works in mysterious ways.

9 Anonymous, 'Lessons from Abroad: Mathematical, Poetic, and Literary Fictions in the Law' (2002) 115 Harvard LR 2228.

10 *R v Bailey* (n 3) 653.

1

Old Fictions

As readers of plea rolls, we will have long since learned to be skeptical of the facts contained in our documents. Jurisdictional ruses, fictional procedural devices, and other non-traversable tricks are familiar. . . . Sometimes we can find comfort in thinking that the clerk who entered them did not know precisely what they meant either; or we may occasionally seek solace in the possibility – sometimes the sure knowledge – that they meant nothing at all.

Morris Arnold[1]

1.1 INTRODUCTION

The common law is a building whose foundations were laid in the High Middle Ages. Legal fictions may not have been solid or stable enough to be called foundations, but they were certainly building blocks – or at least, as commentators like to say, scaffolding.[2] In hindsight, it seems the law would not have been able to answer the changing needs of society without them.

So great a role did fictions play in the development of the common law[3] that any study of fictions in English law must perforce include a historical dimension. As one historian noted, 'understanding . . . the abuses which Dickens and others decried in the early nineteenth century is impossible without some cognizance of mediaeval forms and the elaborate fictions which came to be

[1] Morris S Arnold, 'Law and Fact in the Medieval Jury Trial: Out of Sight, Out of Mind' (1974) 18 American Journal of Legal History 267, 267.

[2] For example, John Chipman Gray, *The Nature and Sources of the Law* (2nd edn, Macmillan 1921) 35; Lon L Fuller, *Legal Fictions* (Stanford University Press 1967) 70; Michael Lobban, 'Legal Fictions before the Age of Reform' in LFTP, 215.

[3] FW Maitland, *The Forms of Action at Common Law* (AH Chaytor and WJ Whittaker eds, CUP 1965) 79.

based upon them'.[4] This chapter tells the fascinating, and at times strange, story of these fictions.

For our purposes, legal history begins in the twelfth century with the emergence of the common law and ends in the mid-nineteenth century with the abolition of the forms of action. For ease of reference, I will call this period the 'Old System' and fictions that developed under it 'Old Fictions'. The system established by the nineteenth-century reforms is the 'New System', our system. Fictions existing under it are 'New Fictions'.

At the outset, I will set the scene by explaining the procedural conditions that prevailed under the Old System. The most important of these, as far as fictions are concerned, were the writ system, formal pleading and civil juries. I will then look at a selection of Old Fictions, one by one, against the background of these three conditions. I will describe the development of each fiction, how it functioned and how far it effaced the rule that came under its attack. Finally, I will ask how the abolition of the forms of action affected Old Fictions: did they die, survive or metamorphose?

Specifically, this chapter will consider eleven Old Fictions: (1) *dominus remisit curiam*, (2) *vi et armis*, (3) geographical fictions, (4) the bill of Middlesex, (5) the writ of *quominus*, (6) the benefit of clergy, (7) pleading the belly, (8) the common recovery, (9) trover, (10) ejectment and (11) quasi-contract. This is by no means an exhaustive list – such an undertaking would require an entire book. The fictions discussed here are a sample and have been chosen for their diversity. They illuminate different facets of the Old Fiction and help us answer the questions I have posed regarding the development, operation, effect and abolition of Old Fictions.

As we will see, Old Fictions do not submit easily to systematic classification; we attempt a taxonomy at our peril. Nevertheless, it is instructive for our purposes to distinguish between three broad types. The first type is the 'Jurisdictional Fiction'. This fiction does not affect the substance of any action but simply which court the action may be brought in. It is normally used because a litigant wants to avail himself of a procedure which that court offers. The second type is the 'Auxiliary Fiction'. This type of fiction affects the substance of the law but without disturbing its conceptual basis. Auxiliary Fictions are thus mere incantations, legal lip-service, that no lawyer takes seriously as reasons for the result of a case. The third type is the 'Essential Fiction'. This title I bestow on fictions which affect the substance of the law

[4] Margaret Hastings, *The Court of Common Pleas in Fifteenth Century England* (Cornell University Press 1947) 157.

through doctrine. Unlike Auxiliary Fictions, Essential Fictions are seen as a conceptual basis for the result of a case.

It is contended in this chapter that this typology of Old Fictions is the key to understanding how the downfall of the forms of action affected Old Fictions. It is argued that Jurisdictional and Auxiliary Fictions disappeared seamlessly, whereas Essential Fictions survived, even festered. Released from the strait-jacket of the Old System, these Essential Fictions, which had been harmless (if unprincipled) instruments of justice, became obstacles to justice.

1.2 THE PROCEDURAL FRAMEWORK OF THE OLD SYSTEM

1.2.1 *The Writ System*

Henry II is credited by legal historians with the foundation of the common law.[5] But unlike the giants of the legal pantheon – Justinian, Suleiman, Napoleon – the first Plantagenet king was no lawgiver. FW Maitland said of his contribution that 'we may even doubt whether he published any one new rule which we should call a rule of substantive law'.[6] He certainly left posterity no code or treatise.[7] His legacy, which is rightly revered, was administrative: the centralisation of justice in England. Previously, law had depended on local custom and been administered in local assemblies or manor courts.[8] Centralisation was achieved not by laying down the law as such, but by establishing a uniform and effective *procedural* framework for the resolution of disputes.[9] Hence *common* law. This common procedural framework was the writ system.

An original writ was a document, written in Latin, on a strap of parchment, about eleven inches long, folded and sealed with the tip of the great seal of the realm.[10] It was issued by the Chancery in the name of the king and addressed to the sheriff of the relevant county.[11] The writ was a mark of authority and

5 Frederick Pollock and Frederic William Maitland, *The History of English Law before the Time of Edward I*, vol 1 (2nd edn, CUP 1968) 136; GDG Hall (ed), *The Treatise on the Laws and Customs of England Commonly Called Glanvill* (Nelson 1965) xii; William Holdsworth, A *History of English Law*, vol 1 (AL Goodhart and HG Hanbury eds, 7th edn, Methuen, Sweet & Maxwell 1969) 4; IELH, 16.

6 Pollock and Maitland (n 5) 136.

7 The treatise known as *Glanvill* was written during Henry's reign, but it was the work of an unidentified scholar and not attributed to the king: Hall (n 5) xxx–xxxiii, 3.

8 John Hudson, *The Oxford History of the Laws of England*, vol 2 (1st edn, OUP 2012) 276–89.

9 Holdsworth (n 5) 47–53.

10 Hastings (n 4) 158; IELH, 64.

11 The writ of right patent, exceptionally, was addressed to a feudal lord rather than the sheriff.

a symbol of jurisdiction – hence the expression that one's writ does or does not run somewhere.

Certain writs were called 'original', not in the sense of not being copies but because they *originated* an action. The original writ was the claimant's ticket, obtained for a fee, to the royal justice system and had the effect of commencing proceedings. Generally speaking, the writ described the substance of the claim and demanded either compliance or a defence.[12] As such, the writs were the claim forms of medieval England.

Unlike today's claim form – and this is crucial for our purposes – these writs had set wording. The claimant only filled in the blanks: names, places, times, quantities, particulars. Each action had its fixed formula.[13] Thus, if A sought to recover a debt of £20 from B, A would commence proceedings by causing a 'writ of debt' to be issued. It is a testament to the stability of the writ system that the writ of debt was in constant use throughout England for six centuries. During this time, its operative wording barely changed.[14] The following is a sample from 1318:

> Edward, by the grace of God, King of England, Lord of Ireland and Duke of Aquitaine to the sheriff of X, greeting. Command B that justly and without delay he render to A twenty pounds which he owes him and unjustly detains, as he says. And if he does not do so, summon the aforesaid B by good summoners to be before me or my justices at Westminster on the third Sunday after Easter to show why he has not done so. And have there the summoners and this writ. Witness myself at Westminster the eighth day of October in the twelfth year of our reign.[15]

Note that in this entire – somewhat august – statement, the claimant only 'contributed' the names, the place and the amount; the rest was template or administrative detail. Even though other writs (notably the writ known as 'trespass on the case') allowed the claimant greater liberty in framing his case, the writ system was essentially about fixed forms of words that represented actions in law.

And so the law grew around the writs. Each writ was a distinct procedure with its own rules, pre-trial process, mode of trial and defences. Thus emerged the formulary system that has come down to us as 'the forms of action'. As late as 1824, a barrister described the role of writs as follows:

12 The writ of right patent was again exceptional in that it demanded compliance without the option of a defence, but in practice a defence could still be mounted.

13 Trespass on the case was a notable exception: *Bernardeston v Heighlynge* (1344) Baker & Milsom (2nd edn) 381 (KB) 383.

14 For the evolution of the writ of debt, see HCLC, 54–9.

15 Elsa de Haas and GDG Hall (eds), *Selden Society: Early Register of Writs* (Bernard Quaritch 1970) 108, 221.

> An original writ ... is essential to the due institution of the suit. These instruments have consequently had the effect of limiting and defining the right of action itself; and no cases are considered as within the scope of judicial remedy, in the English law, but those to which the language of some known writ is found to apply.... The enumeration of writs, and that of actions, have become, in this manner, identical.[16]

Many a worthy plaintiff lost a case due to choosing the wrong writ – and in borderline or novel cases, the choice was something of a gamble.[17] Such was the nature of a formulary system. As one Chief Justice said, 'We must keep up the boundaries of actions, otherwise we shall introduce the utmost confusion.'[18] Professor Milsom commented that 'law itself was seen as based, not upon elementary ideas, but upon the common law writs ... a range of remedies which had as it were come down from the skies'.[19]

This writ system was partly abolished in the 1830s,[20] finally meeting its quietus in 1852.[21] It gave way to the system we have today, where an action is a concept rather than a form of words or procedure. The period I have herein called the Old System is demarcated by the life of the writ system: from the twelfth century to the mid-nineteenth century.

In a system so dependent on form, legal development often meant deviation from form; or more precisely, turning a blind eye to deviation from form. This is where legal fictions came in. But before we turn to the Old Fictions themselves, I need to describe the two other procedural conditions of the Old System.

1.2.2 *Civil Juries and Formal Pleading*

One of the problems facing any legal system is how to decide questions of fact. In the twelfth century, when the writs made their appearance, several primitive

16 Henry John Stephen, *A Treatise on the Principles of Pleading in Civil Actions* (Joseph Butterworth & Son 1824) 8 (footnotes omitted).

17 The elusive boundary between trespass and case in the eighteenth century was a particular frustration: HFCL, 397–8. Arguably the most famous case in English legal history, *Slade's Case* (1598) 4 Co Rep 92b, 76 ER 1074, was technically about which writ to use: David Ibbetson, 'Sixteenth Century Contract Law: Slade's Case in Context' (1984) 4 OJLS 295, 295.

18 *Reynolds v Clarke* (1724) 1 Strange 634, 93 ER 747, 748 (KB) (Raymond CJKB).

19 HFCL, 309.

20 The forms of action were abolished as distinct procedures when one uniform writ was introduced (in which the form of action was to be named): Uniformity of Process Act 1832 (2 William IV c 39) s 1 (being the preamble); Real Property Limitation Act 1833 (3 & 4 William IV c 27) s 36.

21 Now it was not even necessary to specify the form of action in the uniform writ: Common Law Procedure Act 1852 (15 & 16 Vict c 76) s 3.

modes of trial, or rather of proof,[22] were already well-established. The ordeals of fire and water, as well as wager of law,[23] had been in use since Anglo-Saxon times. Trial by battle had been introduced by the invading Normans.[24] All of these appealed to the supernatural – for it was God who determined the outcome.

The jury began as an administrative inquest rather than a mode of trial. With strong roots in Anglo-Saxon England, Norman kings continued to use the jury, then a self-informing investigative body, to collect information about their subjects. A notable example was the Domesday survey of the 1080s – a countrywide census conducted by investigative juries.[25] As Professor Baker explained, when seeking to collect information as opposed to answering a binary question about guilt, an appeal to Providence would not serve. God could not be asked to count oxen.[26]

In time, the jury came to be prescribed as the mode of trial in original writs, the earliest examples being the writs of *iuris utrum*, *novel disseisin* and *mort d'ancestor*,[27] promulgated by Henry II in 1164, 1166 and 1176, respectively.[28] The jury proved a more effective mode of trial than its superstitious alternatives and by 1300 eclipsed the ordeals[29] and judicial combat.[30] Wager of law remained in use for the writs of debt and detinue, albeit in ceremonial form, until the seventeenth century.[31] It then became practically extinct as debt was supplanted by trespass on the case, in which the defendant could not wage

22 'Trial' suggests formal evaluation of evidence: IELH, 79.

23 In a wager of law, also known as *compurgation*, the defendant would conclusively prove his innocence by swearing to it himself and producing eleven other men who swore to his integrity: Hudson (n 8) 81.

24 Ibid. 81, 84, 303, for fire and water, wager and battle, respectively.

25 IELH, 80.

26 Ibid. 79.

27 Respectively, the writs called a jury to be summoned to decide whether land was held by lay or spiritual tenure, whether the claimant was recently ejected from land, and whether the claimant was the son of the person seised of land on the last day of his life. Ibid. 129, 233, 234. For an example of a writ prescribing trial by jury, see Glanvill, XIII, 33.

28 IELH, 80 fn 10; 1166 is an approximate date.

29 The ordeals were dealt a fatal blow in 1215 when Pope Innocent III forbade the (required) clerical participation in them: Canon 18 of the Fourth Lateran Council.

30 Trial by battle went out of use due to the availability of trial by jury, but was not officially abolished as an alternative to jury trial until 1819 by 59 Geo III c 47, s 2. In 1985, two intrepid Scotsmen unsuccessfully challenged the Lord Advocate to battle, arguing the abolition applied only in England: JH Baker, *Introduction to English Legal History* (4th edn, Butterworths 2002) 74 fn 12.

31 Wager of law became 'an indispensable ceremony, but no more' when the eleven compurgators (those swearing to the integrity of the defendant) were simply strangers hired for a fee by the court porters: JH Baker, 'New Light on Slade's Case' [1971] CLJ 213, 230. As Professor Ibbetson showed, wager of law had fallen into such disrepute that 'a gentleman would not, dared not, wage his law': Ibbetson (n 17) 313.

law.[32] In short, by 1300, the jury was the common and favoured option; by 1700, its triumph was complete.

As Professor Arnold noted, the jury presented a challenge for medieval law: 'With the abolition of the ordeal and the disuse of battle, professional lawyers were forced to confront a device which had not the advantages of infallibility and inscrutability.'[33] The crucial difference between the jury and the archaic modes of proof is that God needs no explanations. If we ask God who has the highest 'right' to certain land, we do not need to explain to God what right means or go into questions of priority. In fact, we do not even have to understand these terms ourselves. We ask an impenetrable question and receive an equally impenetrable answer. But when jurors are asked these questions, they cannot answer them unless the questions are narrowed down and presented in a way that is comprehensible to laymen. Jurors may also be confused or distracted by a fact which is not legally relevant.[34] And so the need arose for a mechanism to disentangle fact from law and direct the jury's attention to the right issue.

Formal pleading, which reached maturity in the thirteenth century, did exactly that. It was a system unique to English law.[35] The aim of pleading was to isolate the 'issue' to be decided by the jury. It was an 'oral altercation, in open court, in presence of the judges'.[36] It worked in the following way. The claimant, via his lawyer, stated his claim, elaborating somewhat on the usually succinct writ. This first move was called the 'declaration'. When the claimant had recited the declaration, the defendant had four options. He could

(1) deny everything (by a plea called a 'general traverse'), putting the claimant to proof before the jury of all the facts on which he relied;
(2) admit some facts and deny others ('special traverse'), putting the claimant to proof of only the denied facts;
(3) admit all the facts but say that they amount to nothing at law ('demurrer'); or
(4) admit all the facts but plead new facts which exculpate the defendant ('confession and avoidance').

When the defendant had made this answer, known as a 'plea', the roles were reversed. Now the claimant replied by one of the same four options. This third move, the reply to the reply, was called 'replication'. The process continued in

32 IELH, 81.
33 Arnold (n 1) 277.
34 HFCL, 83.
35 Stephen (n 16) 145–6.
36 Ibid. 29 (emphasis omitted). By 1400, however, paper pleadings, exchanged by the parties outside court, replaced oral pleadings. Ibid. 32–4.

that manner until some proposition was wholly affirmed by one party and wholly denied by the other. That proposition was designated the 'issue'. The parties were then said to be 'at issue' and the issue was 'joined'. If the issue was of law, the result of a demurrer, it fell to the judges to decide; if the issue was of fact, it fell to the jury.[37]

The advantage of pleas (2) and (4), whereby only some facts or new facts are put in issue, is that the jury's attention is focussed exclusively on the relevant aspect of the case. For example, suppose I am a defendant to a writ of trespass alleging I burnt the claimant's field. I could plead the general traverse (deny everything – option (1) above) and simply tell the jury my side of the story. Or I could plead the special traverse (admit some facts, deny others – option (2) above), admitting that I burnt the field but denying that the field belonged to the claimant. That would conveniently focus the attention of the jury on whether the field belonged to the claimant, not on whether I burnt it. It would eliminate all other factual questions.

I could also, alternatively, demur (raise a legal objection – option (3) above), arguing that my burning of the claimant's field amounts to nothing in law since, hypothetically, the writ trespass did not cover the situation. Finally, I could plead confession and avoidance (admit all facts, add new ones – option (4) above): yes, I did burn the claimant's field, but I did it out of necessity to stop a fire from spreading. In this last plea, too, the jury would only be required to decide on my defence of necessity, it being the only thing in dispute.[38] In fact, the jury would be forbidden from taking into consideration any matter that was not in issue, 'for, it is to try the issue, and that only, that they are summoned'.[39] This means that all facts not in issue do not fall to be proved and cannot be proved. They are just statements hanging in the air.

The result is a system where many facts which appear solemnly on the record never have to be proved and whose truth is therefore neither here nor there, neither true nor false. This is the ideal procedural environment for legal fictions: statements required for form but whose truth is immaterial. If the writ is all-important at the beginning of the litigation, what matters in the end is what has to be proved. The writ has standard text, but if certain words in the writ are agreed by the parties not to be in issue, or cannot be put in issue by judicial policy, these words become *mere form* – that is to say, *fictionalised*.

As a way to define the issue, pleading had the neat and logical appeal of an algorithm. But centuries of rule-making made it byzantine, as the following

37 Stephen (n 16) 30, 73–4.

38 Assuming the plaintiff does not demur or confess and avoid.

39 Stephen (n 16) 107.

example illustrates. The rule against double pleading disallowed pleading more than one matter in respect of a particular demand. In other words, a defendant could only have one defence, not two. It was then decided that 'matter may suffice to make a pleading double though it be ill-pleaded', but not if it was 'immaterial' or only 'necessary inducement to another allegation' or constituting 'an entire point'; unless there were several defendants, in which case the pleadings could be severed, leading to several issues; except, again, that if the several defendants 'once united in a plea, they cannot afterwards sever at the rejoinder'.[40] Such labyrinthine pleading manuals filled treatises.[41]

Forms of pleadings multiplied, becoming very specific, and could be reopened, retracted and amended even after trial, but before judgment, by a variety of motions *in banc*.[42] Many meritorious actions failed because of formal niceties[43] or variance between the pleadings and the proof produced at trial.[44] Pleadings also had to be made in 'due order': first to jurisdiction, then disability, then the declaration, then the writ and finally the action.[45] Importantly, as the rule against double pleading implies, the system whose aim was pinpointing an issue confined the proceedings to a *single* make-or-break issue; the parties could not plead in the alternative.[46] From a mechanism intended to facilitate jury trial, pleading became an arcane art and indeed the focus of litigation. It may come as a shock to modern lawyers that medieval law reports (known as Year Books) focussed on the pleadings, not the judgments.[47] As late as the nineteenth century, pleading was a game of high stakes, often likened to a game of chess – so much so that a case 'may be won or lost by playing some particular move'.[48]

Formal pleading was eventually abolished, along with the forms of action, by a series of reforms beginning with the Common Law Procedure Act 1852[49] and

40 Ibid. 264–77.

41 Ibid. v–viii.

42 For example, motions for a repleader, in arrest of judgment or for judgment *non obstante veredicto*. Ibid. 117–20.

43 For example, it was fatal for a writ of trespass to include a '*cum*' clause (i.e., a special description of the facts): MJ Prichard, '*Scott v. Shepherd* (1773) and the Emergence of the Tort of Negligence', *The Selden Society Lectures 1952–2001* (Selden Society 2003) 6–7.

44 Maitland (n 3) 2.

45 Stephen (n 16) 429.

46 Ibid. 152.

47 JH Baker, 'English Law and the Renaissance' [1985] CLJ 46, 57.

48 Lord Bowen, 'Progress in the Administration of Justice during the Victorian Period', *Select Essays in Anglo-American Legal History*, vol 1 (Little, Brown and Company 1907) 541; see also Hastings (n 4) 211.

49 (15 & 16 Vict c 76) esp ss 42, 46, 49, 50, 51, 62, 64–9, 80, 81, 84; see also Common Law Procedure Act 1854 (17 & 18 Vict c 125) esp ss 79, 97, 98, and Common Law Procedure Act 1860 (23 & 24 Vict c 126) esp ss 26, 27, 37, 38.

culminating in the Judicature Acts of the 1870s.[50] In the former, Parliament specifically enacted that 'All Statements which need not be proved . . . shall be omitted' and that pleadings shall not be contested for any 'Imperfection, Omission, Defect in or Lack of Form'.[51] As Lord Bowen stated: 'It may be asserted without fear of contradiction that it is not *possible* in the year 1887 for an honest litigant in Her Majesty's Supreme Court to be defeated by any mere technicality, any slip, any mistaken step in his litigation.'[52]

In 1854, the same wave of reform struck its first blow against the civil jury by allowing judges, with the consent of both parties, to decide questions of fact.[53] This was the first time in the history of the common law that a judge could determine a fact. Twentieth-century legislation took away the right of a freeborn Englishman to a civil jury – except in cases of fraud, defamation, malicious prosecution and false imprisonment.[54] In 2013, defamation was excised from the list of exceptions.[55] Today, judicial policy (in civil cases) is to refuse jury trial where there is no specific right to it.[56]

1.2.3 *Procedural Framework: An Epilogue*

Throughout the Old System, a period of more than six hundred years, the common law was characterised by strict formalism. However, this formalism was sometimes bypassed by the pleading rules which prevented certain allegations of fact from being tested at trial. One element of the system thus counteracted the other, enabling the substance of actions to change while the form remained unchanged. It is this aspect of the Old Fiction which prompted Sir Henry Maine, in 1861, to define legal fiction as 'any assumption which conceals, or affects to conceal, the fact that a rule of law has undergone alteration its letter remaining unchanged, its operation being modified. . . . The fact is . . . that the law has wholly changed; the fiction is that it remains what it always was.'[57] We will now look at a selection of Old Fictions to learn

50 See esp the Supreme Court of Judicature Act 1875, sch 1; see also Maitland (n 3) 80–1.

51 Common Law Procedure Act 1852 (15 & 16 Vict c 76) ss 49, 50.

52 Lord Bowen (n 48) 541.

53 Common Law Procedure Act 1854 (17 & 18 Vict c 125) s 1.

54 Administration of Justice (Miscellaneous Provisions) Act 1933, s 6, later replaced by Senior Courts Act 1981, s 69, and County Courts Act 1984, s 66. As the cited sections show, even the excepted causes of action are subject to exceptions.

55 Defamation Act 2013, s 11.

56 *Williams v Beesly* [1973] 1 WLR 1295 (HL) 1298 (Lord Diplock).

57 Henry Sumner Maine, *Ancient Law* (first published in 1861, Murray 1930) 32–3; see also Oliver R Mitchell, 'Fictions of the Law: Have They Proved Useful or Detrimental to Its Growth?' (1893) 7 Harvard LR 249, 262; LTB, 35.

how and why they formed and the ways in which they functioned. We will see how Maine's concealed alteration of the law was achieved in practice.

1.3 OLD FICTIONS EXAMINED

1.3.1 Dominus Remisit Curiam

Possibly the earliest legal fiction to enter the common law made its mark on land law. Under customary feudal law, which predated the common law, a lord had jurisdiction to determine claims among his tenants. Henry's writ system gave the tenant a second resort: if the lord failed to 'do right' in the dispute, the tenant could appeal to royal justice by procuring a writ ('of right patent'). In practice, however, tenants preferred to skip their lord's court altogether – that is, to beg royal intervention without bothering with the seignorial court. As a result, the lords lost face and business. So chagrined were the barons by this usurpation of their ancient jurisdiction that one of the demands they forced upon King John in *Magna Carta* was that 'the writ called *praecipe* [e.g., a writ of right patent] shall not in future be issued . . . if a free man could thereby be deprived of . . . his own lord's court'.[58]

But the barons could not halt the march of history – in this case, legal history. These warlike magnates, who had brought the king of England to heel, were at last bested by the English legal fiction. After 1215, it became standard to include a clause in the writ stating that '*dominus remisit curiam suam*' (the lord has waived his court), even if the lord had done no such thing. But neither litigant had any interest in putting the dubious clause in issue during the pleading process. It became mere form and thus the lords' ancient right was lost – the Great Charter notwithstanding.[59] By 1300, the baronial jurisdiction over title to land was obsolete.[60] The legal fiction had made its first impression on English legal history and, in its own way, proved the pen to be mightier than the sword.

In summary, the fiction *dominus remisit curiam* functioned as a pleading which could not be disproved or did not fall to be proved. The aim was to evade clause 34 of the *Magna Carta*, which effectively enjoined that the tenant must exhaust his remedies with the lord before petitioning the king. Hence the motive of the fiction was convenience or efficiency. It was clearly a Jurisdictional Fiction as it did not affect the substance of any action, but

58 Magna Carta (1215 version) s 34.
59 HLL, 35–6.
60 Ibid.

simply the choice of court. The effect of the fiction was to completely dispense with the exhaustion rule. Nothing was left of the old prerequisite for jurisdiction.

1.3.2 Vi et Armis

When the king extended the benefit of royal justice to his subjects, he did not do so indiscriminately. Only causes of sufficient gravity would attract the king's benevolence and be justiciable in his courts. Lesser complaints would continue to be dealt with by local courts.[61] In the field of civil wrongs, the position by the mid-thirteenth century was that a case was of sufficient gravity if it involved 'force and arms' and was committed 'against the king's peace'. Henceforth all trespass writs were issued with the words *vi et armis* and *contra pacem regis*.[62]

While the meaning of the king's peace was vague to begin with, the requirement of force and arms was fairly clear. The problem was that local courts could not entertain trespasses over forty shillings without royal sanction.[63] So, ostensibly, trespasses over forty shillings committed without force and arms had no remedy. This was an intolerable situation and something had to give. Fiction came to the rescue. Claimants, who had little choice, crossed their fingers and brought the standard writ (containing the words '*vi et armis*'), even though the trespass had not been carried out with force and arms. Judges, sympathetic to their predicament, eventually ruled that *vi et armis* had to be pleaded but not proved. A concrete example, one of many, appears in the Year Book for 1304:

> R. brought his writ against J. . . . and said that they came wrongfully with force and arms and cut and carried away the wood of this same R.
>
> *The defendants* pleaded Not guilty.
>
> *The inquest* [i.e., the jury] came and said that they cut his wood, but not with force and arms.
>
> BEREFORD [the judge] therefore adjudged that [R.] should recover his damages etc., and that the defendants should be taken . . . notwithstanding they did not come with force and arms.[64]

In the language of formal pleading, the allegation of force and arms became 'non-traversable': incontestable, incapable of being 'in issue'. And so, from the

61 IELH, 68.
62 Ibid.
63 Ibid.
64 *Anon* (1304) Baker & Milsom (2nd edn) 338; see also SFC Milsom, 'Trespass from Henry III to Edward III: Part I General Writs' [1958] LQR 195, 222; HILO, 45–8, 52–3.

beginning of the fourteenth century, claimants falsely pleaded force and arms as a matter of course, adding for good measure such standard embellishments as 'swords and bows and arrows' (all equally fictitious).[65] Thus was born another Old Fiction – *vi et armis*.[66] It had a long life. Lawyers kept averring force and arms until 1852, when Parliament passed the Common Law Procedure Act,[67] abolishing the forms of action, as aforesaid.

It might be added, by way of comic interlude, that the fiction produced some colourful pleadings in the rich legal phraseology of the time. MJ Prichard, in an influential 1973 lecture, recalled:

> Just two hundred years ago one infant sued another infant for injuries received on the day of the fair in Milborne Port, in Somerset, in October 1770. The action was one of trespass, in which the plaintiff declared that the defendant 'with force and arms, (to wit) with sticks, staves, clubs and fists, made an assault upon the plaintiff . . . and greatly bruised, wounded and ill-treated him, so that his life was greatly despaired of, and then and there, threw, cast and tossed, a lighted squib, consisting of gunpowder and other combustible materials, at and against the said plaintiff, and struck the said plaintiff on the face therewith, and so greatly burnt one of the eyes of the said plaintiff, that the plaintiff underwent and suffered great and excruciating pain and torment for a long time . . . and afterwards wholly lost his said eye.'[68]

Like *dominus remisit curiam*, the *vi et armis* fiction functioned as a pleading which could not be disproved. It should be noted, however, that unlike *dominus remisit curiam*, this Old Fiction did not *completely* dispense with the requirement in question (here force and arms, there exhaustion of remedies). Professor Ibbetson, for example, argues that while the 'blood-chilling lists of weaponry . . . bear no relation whatsoever to reality', the allegation of force and arms still implied minimal 'physical interference' and constituted a 'low threshold test'.[69] Professor Palmer contends that while 'the allegation of force and arms was not literally true', *vi et armis* 'was not fictional but rather a low threshold test'.[70] That is to say, the allegation was not *entirely* fictional. Palmer concludes, '[T]he allegation of force was probably not merely formal, an allegation without either

65 *Taumbes v Skegness* (1312) Baker & Milsom (2nd edn) 339 (CP) 340. But note that while the facts could contradict the writ, the pleadings could not – because the pleadings were formal; they were recorded.

66 HFCL, 289, 292; IELH, 68; HILO, 41 fn 20.

67 s 49.

68 Prichard (n 43) 3; the case is *Scott v Shepherd* (1773) 3 Wils KB 403, 95 ER 1124 (KB).

69 HILO, 41.

70 Robert C Palmer, *English Law in the Age of the Black Death, 1348–1381* (University of North Carolina Press 1993) 159.

meaning or effect on the scope of the action. It seemed rather a test limiting the use of trespass *vi et armis* to factual situations in which the defendant had done forcible wrong.'[71] This shows that fictionalisation does not necessarily denude the pleading in question of all meaning. In the case of *vi et armis*, it entailed the significant relaxation of a requirement, almost to the point of extinction, but not the expurgation of it.

In terms of classification, *vi et armis* was a Jurisdictional Fiction. As Milsom and Baker established, it was simply a jurisdictional limit, a ticket to the royal courts, not an element of the concept of trespass.[72] The motive for this fiction was justice. Without it, as we have observed, some trespasses would fall between the cracks and be without remedy.

1.3.3 *Geographical Fictions*

This is a class of fictions used to commence actions arising beyond the seas or on the sea. This Old Fiction is even more tied to the civil jury than other Old Fictions. It was a rule of the common law that a question of fact had to be tried by a jury summoned from the county in which the cause of action arose.[73] It was impossible to summon juries from foreign lands or the high seas and so trespasses committed in such places could not properly be brought. The legal community, however, thought that a procedural problem should not stand in the way of substantive justice – at least when there was an English connection to justify jurisdiction. As Sir Edward Coke explained in 1628, the solution was more pragmatic than imaginative:

> Note, An obligation made beyond the seas may be sued here in England in what place the plaintiff will. As if it bear date at Bourdeaux in France, it may be alleged to be made in a certain place called Bourdeaux in France, in Islington in the county of Middlesex, and there it shall be tried, for whether there be such a place in Islington or no, is not traversable in that case.[74]

In the mid-1670s, Sir Matthew Hale retrospectively justified this fiction:

> Otherwise there might be a failure of justice; for suppose an Englishman sells his horse to another in France; they both come over to England, [so] that the vendor be without remedy for his money. In France, he cannot sue him

71 Ibid. 163.

72 Milsom, 'Trespass from Henry III to Edward III' (n 64) 195; IELH, 68.

73 IELH, 131; see also Matthew Hale, 'A Disquisition Touching the Jurisdiction of the Common Law and Courts of Admiralty . . . ' in MJ Prichard and DEC Yale (eds), *Hale and Fleetwood on Admiralty Jurisdiction*, vol 108 (Selden Society 1993) 54.

74 Co Litt 261b.

> [because the defendant is not there]. ... Certainly no man can think the Common Law so deficient, especially our Island consisting much in forreign [*sic*] Intercourse, and Journeys and Voyages to forreign Parts, as that it should be destitute of a remedy ... merely upon a supposition of want of cognizance for forreign matters.[75]

To that end, judges condoned what became perhaps the most egregious fiction of the common law. The claimant would falsely plead the foreign act to have taken place in some random place in England and the defendant would be barred from traversing it (i.e., denying the fact in the pleading). By Hale's time, the fiction had been in use for centuries: '[W]e see it upon every day's Experience ... and this is no new device, but very ancient.'[76] It was so simple and yet so effective. It brings to mind Lon Fuller's description of the legal fiction as 'an awkward patch applied to a rent in the law's fabric of theory'.[77]

The case of *Mostyn v Fabrigas* (1775)[78] concerned a trespass on the island of Minorca, then a British possession.[79] The alleged tortfeasor was the governor of the island. The reporter, Cowper, tells us:

> This was an action of trespass, brought in the Court of Common Pleas by Anthony Fabrigas against John Mostyn, for an assault and false imprisonment; in which the plaintiff declared, that the defendant on the first of September, in the year 1771, with force and arms, &c. made an assault upon the said Anthony, *at Minorca, (to wit) at London* aforesaid, in the parish of St. Mary le Bow, in the ward of Cheap, and beat, wounded, and ill-treated him, and then and there imprisoned him, and kept and detained him in prison there for a long time.[80]

The non-traversable falsehood is now a familiar fix – a kind of cure-all in a formalistic system. But note that here the form of the pleading makes the fiction transparent: it begins with the actual place – Minorca – and then asserts that Minorca is in London. In other words, there is no attempt to conceal the fiction; no reticence or bashfulness. This form of pleading stands in contrast to the silent fictions we encountered in *dominus remisit curiam* or *vi et armis*, where there was no way to detect the fiction from the pleadings.[81] The writ and

75 Hale (n 73) 47–8.
76 Ibid. 48.
77 Fuller (n 2) viii.
78 (1775) 1 Cowp 161, 98 ER 1021 (KB); for other examples of geographical fictions, see JH Baker and SFC Milsom, *Sources of English Legal History* (2nd edn, Butterworths 2010) 458 fn 1.
79 The island was conquered by Great Britain in 1708 during the War of the Spanish Succession. British sovereignty was confirmed by Article 11 of the Treaty of Utrecht (1713).
80 *Mostyn v Fabrigas* (n 78) 1021–2 (emphasis added).
81 Professor Baker bemoaned the difficulties legal historians face in identifying silent fictions: LTB, 33–5.

declaration stated that the lord had waived his court, or that the act had been done with force and arms, and there was no hint that it had been otherwise. Here the fiction is obvious on the face of the record. This goes to show just how comfortable with fictions judges and lawyers had grown – no matter how absurd the assertion.

When the defendant in *Mostyn v Fabrigas* had the temerity to challenge the fiction, Lord Mansfield took the bull by the horns:

> [N]o Judge ever thought that when the declaration said in Fort St. George, viz. in Cheapside, that the plaintiff meant it was in Cheapside. It is a fiction of form; every country has its forms, which are invented for the furtherance of justice. . . . I was embarrassed a great while to find . . . counsel for the plaintiff really meant to make a question of it. . . . In sea batteries the plaintiff often lays the injury to have been done in Middlesex, and then proves it to be done a thousand leagues distant on the other side of the Atlantic.[82]

It is worthy of note that geographical fictions were also used by claimants who wanted to avoid the High Court of Admiralty in favour of the common law courts in Westminster. The Admiralty, established in the fourteenth century, was a court in the civilian tradition exercising jurisdiction over the seas. To avoid it, contracts made at sea, for example, could be averred to have been made at the Royal Exchange. This was commonly done by 1600.[83]

Geographical fictions exhibit the characteristics of earlier fictions but in sharper relief. This class of Old Fictions, like the foregoing fictions, functioned as a pleading that could not be disproved. Notice, however, that unlike *dominus remisit curiam*, where the requirement was completely dispensed with, and unlike *vi et armis*, where the requirement was significantly relaxed, here the requirement was generally unchanged. In the ordinary run of cases, questions of fact still had to be tried by juries summoned from the relevant county. It was only in foreign cases that the requirement was (effectively) set aside. In other words, the effect of the fiction was to create an exception to the rule.

Geographical fictions are, without a doubt, Jurisdictional Fictions. No action or remedy was created or changed. The fiction simply enabled actions arising overseas to be brought in English courts. The motive for this fiction, as we have seen from the justifications above, was more than convenience or efficiency. It was justice. Without this fiction, deserving claimants would have been denied a remedy for procedural reasons.

82 *Mostyn v Fabrigas* (n 78) 1030–2.
83 IELH, 133.

1.3.4 *Bill of Middlesex*

This Old Fiction, common by 1500,[84] is harder to explain than the fictions we have already discussed. This is because it involves layer upon layer of procedures. But it is worthwhile to take a glimpse at the tangled web of rules that was the Old System and acquaint ourselves with the world inhabited by lawyers. Besides, the academic interest in this fiction has been great. Marjorie Blatcher went so far as to claim, 'Few legal fictions have attracted as much interest as the bill of Middlesex and none more deservedly, since it was to the manipulation of this bill that the king's bench owed its recovery and hence, to some degree, the common law its future.'[85]

While writs were the primary mode of initiating litigation, it was also possible, from earliest times, to commence proceedings by bill. A bill was a written petition to the king, embodied by the justices of the Court of King's Bench. A bill was better for the plaintiff than an original writ because the bill had no standard text. There was also no issuance fee, as it was written by the plaintiff rather than Chancery clerks.

Understandably, therefore, claimants' lawyers preferred bills to writs. The problem was that bills could hardly ever be used. Generally, an action in the royal courts required an original writ. There were two important exceptions. First, bill procedure could be used for an action which arose in the county where the King's Bench happened to be sitting.[86] Once the King's Bench stopped following the monarch and permanently settled in Westminster in 1421,[87] that county was almost invariably Middlesex.[88] In other words, an action in the King's Bench, arising in Middlesex, could be begun by bill.[89]

The second exception was that bill procedure could be used if the defendant was already in the custody of the King's Bench (usually a prisoner in the Marshalsea prison).[90] This exception applied even to actions, like debt, which were otherwise, by dint of *Magna Carta*, the exclusive province of the Court of Common Pleas.[91] The combination of these two exceptions to writ procedure was the opening the lawyers (who preferred bills) needed.

Suppose I want to recover a debt. As I have said, debt falls in the exclusive jurisdiction of the Common Pleas where bill procedure does not exist.[92] I could

84 Ibid. 48–9.
85 Marjorie Blatcher, *The Court of King's Bench 1450–1550* (Athlone Press 1978) 111.
86 Ibid. 112.
87 IELH, 46.
88 In times of plague the Court would temporarily sit outside Middlesex.
89 IELH, 48.
90 Ibid.; Blatcher (n 85) 116.
91 Magna Carta (1215 version) s 17.
92 Hastings (n 4) 16–19, 170.

go by the book and pay for a writ of debt returnable to the Common Pleas and hope that the defendant will be caught and brought to trial. Or, I could present a bill alleging a fictitious trespass by my debtor in Middlesex. I can do so by bill because the trespass was supposedly in Middlesex. Upon presentation of this bill, my debtor would be arrested and imprisoned in the Marshalsea awaiting trial.[93] This provisional imprisonment was standard procedure in civil actions, effected by a judicial writ called *capias*. Now in the custody of the Court (albeit on false grounds), I can proceed against him, in the genuine action for debt, by *bill*. The action for debt has nothing to do with Middlesex, but it does not matter anymore because the debtor is in custody by virtue of the trespass bill. I then withdraw the trespass bill before it comes to trial, thus ensuring the trespass bill is never exposed as baseless. And *voilà*: I have started an action for debt without a writ, in the wrong court and without a fee.

An additional advantage, which counted more than all the others, is that I would not have to incur the bulk of the legal costs until the defendant's appearance was secured.[94] It was impossible to proceed against an absent defendant.[95] The bill of Middlesex, more than any other fiction, exemplifies the ingenuity of the common lawyers.

Of course, this ploy required the connivance of the judges of the King's Bench in turning a blind eye to the suspicious proliferation of withdrawn trespass bills in Middlesex. But connive in it they did, partly in a drive to attract plaintiffs by offering better procedure than in the Common Pleas.[96] The connivance was made easy by the fact that the fictionalisation process was gradual.[97] In any event, all the chicanery happened outside 'judicial consciousness'.

It may seem unethical to allow people to be imprisoned for a knowingly false allegation, but such interlocutory imprisonment was the procedure in the writ of debt anyway.[98] It made little ethical difference whether the defendant was imprisoned by bill or by writ. More importantly, the imprisonment itself was fictionalised early on when, in a 1452 case, a defendant on bail was deemed to be in constructive custody.[99] Henceforth the debtors would be arrested and released on bail. One fiction propped up another.

93 But note constructive custody; see the text to n 99.

94 For more detail, see Blatcher (n 85) 112–13.

95 A defendant who unjustifiably failed to appear could be outlawed, but that was of no personal benefit to the plaintiff.

96 IELH, 49–50.

97 Blatcher (n 85) ch 7.

98 IELH, 72 fn 70.

99 Blatcher (n 85) 119, citing (1452) YB Mic 31 Hen VI, f 10, pl 15.

To say that the bill of Middlesex, like its fictitious forerunners, was a false *pleading* would be an understatement. The whole action for trespass was fictitious. There was no trespass in Middlesex or anywhere else. As such, the bill of Middlesex was a bolder fiction than its forerunners, which consisted in false incidental pleadings in the course of genuine actions.

Moreover, whereas previous fictions functioned as non-traversable pleadings, the false pleadings in this wholly-false action *were* traversable. No court would ever force a defendant to admit a substantive trespass – as opposed to a jurisdictional condition like force and arms. The false allegation was simply withdrawn before it could be tested. There is perhaps not much in this difference, except that the bill of Middlesex did not depend on formal pleading.

Generally, the motive and reason for the success of this Old Fiction was convenience. As Margaret Hastings summed it up, 'procedure by bill of Middlesex was like the wave of a magician's rod compared to the Common Pleas procedure at its worst'.[100] The rule under attack was the requirement in bill procedure that an action should arise in Middlesex. This rule was completely abrogated. Practically, plaintiffs used the fiction to enjoy the advantages of bill procedure over writ procedure.

It is noteworthy that this fiction was wholly procedural. As a corollary of being so procedural in nature, the fiction was tied to a particular court – the King's Bench. It did not 'work' anywhere else. The substance of no action was affected. Even the availability of actions was not affected. The effect of the fiction was only to expand the availability of bill procedure and end the monopoly of the Common Pleas over certain actions. It was clearly a Jurisdictional Fiction.

Finally, this fiction underscores what we have learned from previous fictions: English courts did not baulk at false allegations, bordering on perjury,[101] so long as they were *formalistic* in nature. So long as there was no substantive injustice, no pleading was too outrageous. It may offend our sense of propriety, but it is heartening to see that the judges, as wedded as they were to formalism, saw it for what it was – just form. They were not mesmerised by the forms or ruled by the forms. They were pragmatic about their merits and demerits. Interestingly, it is in fictions that we see most clearly the distinction between form and substance.

1.3.5 *Writ of* Quominus

This Old Fiction is similar to the bill of Middlesex in its procedural character. Just as the bill of Middlesex was a creature of the procedure of the King's

[100] Hastings (n 4) 26.
[101] The false allegations were unsworn.

Bench, the writ of *quominus* was a creature of Exchequer procedure. The Court of Exchequer,[102] which had grown out of the Chancery in the late twelfth century, was the judicial arm of the treasury. It was primarily concerned with taxation. Generally, its jurisdiction was limited to tax-related claims by or against officers of the Crown. In the fourteenth century, it started hearing debt claims between private citizens (normally the business of the Common Pleas) in situations where the claimant creditor had to recover a private debt *to repay a Crown debt*. Such claims were seen as sufficiently connected with the court's aim of tax collection.[103] The writ used in these three-party cases was called *quominus*.[104]

From the point of view of the claimant creditors, it was highly advantageous to chase private debts in the Exchequer. The procedure in that court, designed for the king's tax collectors, had more teeth than the regular procedure in the Common Pleas. Here was an opening the common lawyers would surely not miss.[105]

All that was necessary to get a private debt claim into the Exchequer was a Crown debt by the claimant. Perhaps encouraged by the King's Bench's acceptance of the bill of Middlesex, lawyers in the Tudor era started alleging fictitious debts to the Crown to take advantage of Exchequer procedure in private debt claims. At first, the judges were unimpressed and thwarted the fiction by allowing the imaginary debt to the Crown to be traversed.[106] Within a century, probably by the Interregnum, the judges relented and the fictitious debt became non-traversable – mere form.[107]

Like many of the Old Fictions we have seen so far, the writ of *quominus* was essentially a non-traversable pleading. Like its cousin, the bill of Middlesex, it was a Jurisdictional Fiction and completely procedural. Its motive was convenience or efficiency. Unlike its cousin, it did depend on formal pleading and did involve a genuine claim (the private debt). The rule it attacked was that only debts that make the Crown debtor less able to pay a Crown debt were within the jurisdiction of the Exchequer. This restriction was completely removed.

102 Not to be confused with the Court of Exchequer Chamber, a name given at various times to different appellate courts: IELH, 147–8.

103 Ibid. 55.

104 Meaning 'so much the less', part of the key assertion in the writ, namely that by reason of the outstanding private debt the claimant was so much the less able to pay his own debt to the king.

105 IELH, 56.

106 Ibid. fn 70, citing *Ragland v Wildgoose* (1581) Saville's 11 (Exchequer) 15.

107 Soon, creditors found an even better Exchequer procedure to recover debts – subpoena. But this too relied on a fictitious Crown debt: IELH, 56.

It is interesting to note that the writ of *quominus* had its origin in a non-fictitious rule of law: that people who owe money to the treasury could recover (in the Court of Exchequer) monies owed to them to the extent that it lessened their ability to pay the treasury. It is only that the factual condition of this rule came to be disregarded. We see this phenomenon of 'prefigurement' in the other fictions as well, although less clearly. Old Fictions were based on, and indeed foreshadowed by, genuine rules whose factual foundation grew weaker and weaker under the pressure of some practical need and eventually partly or wholly gave way. In the bill of Middlesex, for example, the fiction was prefigured by two genuine rules about bill procedure. In time, the factual conditions of the rules evaporated, giving rise to the fiction. The point is that Old Fictions did not appear *ex nihilo*. They were not novel in the sense of being new actions, forms or procedures. Nor were they the product of any systematic intellectual approach. They were simply the well-preserved shells of former rules – fossils.

1.3.6 *Benefit of Clergy*

This fiction is technically outside the scope of this work because it is a fiction of the criminal law. It is included, as useful context, because it shows how far judges were willing to go in using fictions. As Professor Baker wrote, this fiction played a 'bizarre' role in English law.[108] More than any other fiction, old or new, it shows the power of fictions. It was power over life and death.

Suitably for its bizarre future, the birth of the fiction was an ironic twist. The tug of war between Henry II and Thomas Becket, played out from the latter's elevation to the see of Canterbury in 1162 to his assassination in that cathedral in 1170, was fought primarily over the treatment of felonious clergy. The king wanted clerics to be tried and punished by secular courts, whereas the church insisted they had to be dealt with in accordance with Canon law (which was more lenient), in ecclesiastical courts. The murder of Becket by knights loyal to the king, with or without royal sanction, backfired disastrously. Amid international condemnation, Henry was forced to give ground on the very point of the controversy.[109] It was then settled that the clergy would be exempt from capital punishment. If found guilty of a capital offence by a secular court, they would be handed over to the ecclesiastical authorities and face such canonical penalties as penance, imprisonment or defrocking.[110] This was the 'benefit of clergy'.

108 Ibid. 557.
109 The Compromise of Avranches (1172).
110 IELH, 554.

In a practice that would characterise criminal trials in England for centuries, the accused cleric would be tried by jury and, if pronounced guilty, would, before sentence was passed, kneel and claim the benefit of clergy. A church official in attendance, supervised by the judge, would then assess the defendant's clerical status, and either accept or reject him. Rejection often meant death.

In the years following the settlement, judges applied it to the letter. They expected those in holy orders to wear the correct vestments, to be tonsured, to be literate.[111] But as we have so often seen with fictions, that was only an omen of things to come. By 1490, judges had completely abandoned any genuine assessment of clerical status – probably as a way to mitigate the harshness of medieval punishment. Rather than send a man to the gallows for larceny (death was the automatic penalty for many offences), he was declared a clerk and surrendered to the church for milder treatment. Thus a concession reluctantly extended by Henry II to the clergy became, by the time of Henry VII, a general exemption, for laymen, from the law of the land. As FW Maitland observed in a different context, 'By such means our archaic procedure is being adapted to modern times but in an evasory and roundabout way by means of fictions.'[112]

The salient element of this fiction was the reading test. It started as a genuine test of literacy (clergy were expected to be literate), whereby the judge would randomly select a biblical passage for the defendant to read aloud in open court. But it soon degenerated into farce. The judges would always select the same text, namely Psalm 51, and illiterate defendants were expected to have memorised it. Fittingly, the psalm read '*Miserere mei Deus* ... ' (Have mercy upon me, O God ...)[113] and came to be known as the 'neck verse'. The recitation of Latin poetry by illiterate felons, on pain of death,[114] became a symbol of the fiction. This extraordinary ritual, which Blackstone called 'so vain and impious a ceremony',[115] is unparalleled in any other legal system. It bespeaks more clearly than any legal history the role of fictions in English law.

Such was the drama of the fiction that we are not surprised to find it in contemporary drama. In Christopher Marlowe's 1592 play *The Jew of*

111 For a sad illustration, see *R v Henry* (1326) Wilts Record Office, Bruce MS 11, fo, 58v (KB), extracted in LTB, 128–9.

112 Maitland (n 3) 80.

113 The Latin is taken from the Vulgate, in which the psalm is numbered 50. The English is from the King James Version.

114 There is evidence that judges pretended to hear the verse even when the defendant could not actually say it: Baker (n 30) 514.

115 4 Bl Comm, ch 28, 369.

Malta, a villain is said to be 'conning his neck-verse'.[116] A few years later, in 1598, playwright Ben Jonson recited the verse (in real life) to save his own neck, having been found guilty of manslaughter.[117]

In Tudor times, Parliament started to rein in the benefit of clergy by excluding it for certain offences, making them 'non-clergiable'. Thus the benefit of clergy, from a blunt instrument, became a means of distinguishing between offences depending on seriousness or moral culpability. For example, a 1512 statute[118] suppressed the benefit of clergy for *malicious* homicide, incidentally enshrining in law the distinction between murder and manslaughter: manslaughter was clergiable; murder was not.[119] The courts then had to clarify the malice distinction, adding much refinement to criminal law.

Indeed, Parliament used this fiction time and again indirectly to regulate criminal justice. It limited the use of the benefit to once only in the case of laymen[120] (ironically restoring the distinction between laity and clergy sacrificed to create the fiction); introduced branding with a hot iron for 'clergied' criminals, with a judicial discretion to impose a sentence of up to one year's imprisonment[121] (Ben Jonson was branded on the thumb);[122] extended the benefit of clergy to women[123] (an illogicality since women could not be ordained); and allowed transportation (exile to a penal colony) as an alternative to branding of 'clergied' criminals.[124] More strangely, in deciding whether the defendant passed the reading test, the court could take into consideration the defendant's character and the seriousness of the offence.[125] And so criminal law was regulated in large part through the perverse medium of the fiction. The benefit of clergy, the unintended legacy of bloody-minded knights, morphed from an unjust clerical privilege into the main agent of penal reform. In 1827, after six and a half centuries of weird contortions, the benefit of clergy was laid to rest.[126]

116 Act IV, Scene ii.

117 He had killed an actor in a duel: Ian Donaldson, *Ben Jonson: A Life* (OUP 2011) 132–6.

118 4 Hen VIII c 2 (1512).

119 Building upon a similar distinction, enacted earlier, disallowing pardons for intentional homicide: 13 Ric II c 1 (1390) s 2.

120 4 Hen VII c 13 (1489).

121 18 Eliz I c 7 (1575).

122 Probably with the letter M for manslayer: Donaldson (n 117) 136.

123 21 Jac I c 6 (1624); 3 Will & Mar c 9 (1691) s 6.

124 Transportation Act 1718 (4 Geo I c 11).

125 LTB, 39 fn 25.

126 Criminal Law Act 1827 (7 & 8 Geo IV c 28) s 6. The reading test had been abolished by 6 Ann c 9 (1706).

It did not, however, involve a non-traversable pleading. Claiming the benefit after trial took place outside the pleading process – whose purpose, it will be recalled, was to define the issue for trial. In fact, even as a statement, the claim of being a clerk was not incontestable as such. In fact, a test was administered to verify the statement. It is only that the test was a sham. What we have then is not a non-traversable pleading, or even an incontestable statement, but bad evidence. This shows that Old Fictions do not necessarily function as non-traversable pleadings (e.g., *dominus remisit curiam*) or withdrawn pleadings (e.g., bill of Middlesex). The benefit of clergy consisted in the court's conscious acceptance of bad evidence.

Turning to our classification of fictions, the benefit of clergy was an Auxiliary Fiction. It was not a Jurisdictional Fiction because the substance of the law was affected. It was an Auxiliary Fiction as no one considered clerical status, let alone the reading test, to be the real reason for the compassionate treatment of convicted criminals. It was lip service, quite literally. The ostensible preoccupation with religious ordination was an accident of history.

The motive for this fiction was not convenience or efficiency, but justice. As for the effect of the fiction on the law, the original basis of the benefit – clerical immunity – was completely disregarded, with even women found to be of the clergy. The abrogation of the rule was therefore complete. Interestingly, this is the first Old Fiction we have come across that restricts, rather than extends, jurisdiction. By conducting a sham reading test, the court found the defendant to be a clerk and thus outside its sentencing jurisdiction.

The benefit of clergy lends further support to the argument that fictions do not appear *ex nihilo*, but emerge from the existing structures of the law, by hollowing them out. The benefit of clergy had been real. Even the reading test had been real. It was just hollowed out of factual content.

Finally, the benefit of clergy shows that legal fictions can be a means of positive (if tortuous) legal development, to be used by judges and legislators alike.

1.3.7 *Pleading the Belly*

The plea of the belly is the sister-fiction of the benefit of clergy. By the seventeenth century, it served the same purpose of offering an escape from the death penalty. The rule underlying the fiction was that a pregnant woman could not be executed – to spare the unborn child. To claim the immunity, a pregnant woman under sentence of death would 'plead her belly', whereupon a jury of twelve matrons would be convoked. These dozen experts in childbirth would inspect the prisoner and give a verdict whether she was 'quick with child'.[127] If the woman was so found, a stay of execution was given, which often led, by way of pardon, to a commutation of the sentence to transportation.[128]

We have no reason to doubt that the examination by the all-female jury (which is actually of ancient origin[129]) was originally conducted in good faith. However, the statistically improbable number of pregnant convicts, certainly by the seventeenth century, led historians to conclude the examination was spurious in many cases.[130] It would seem that here, too, the factual foundation of a rule was compromised in the interest of policy.

This supposition that the examination had become fictionalised is supported by references to pleading the belly in contemporary fiction (of the literary sort), collated by James Oldham. For example, in Daniel Defoe's novel *Moll Flanders*, published in 1722, the eponymous heroine is told by her fellow inmate in Newgate Prison, 'I pleaded my belly, but I am no more with child than the judge.'[131] Other references abound.[132]

By contrast with the benefit of clergy, neither the finding of pregnancy nor the escape from the death penalty, was a matter of course. Only a proportion of women were found to be pregnant by the matrons and not all of those were pardoned.[133] Those not fortunate enough to be pardoned would be hanged on the next execution day following the birth.[134] What is more arresting is that many women, even in the heyday of the fiction, did not bother pleading the belly. Oldham has found that from 1698 to 1727, '62 percent of all women sentenced to death pleaded pregnancy, and of these, 61 percent were successful before juries of matrons'.[135] The inspection by the matronly jury was not as reliable a fiction as the neck verse. We seem to have a fiction haphazardly applied – which is a creature we encounter for the first time.

Strangely (considering its rationale), but consistently with the benefit of clergy, a woman could only plead the belly once. As Blackstone tells us, 'if she once hath had the benefit of this reprieve and been delivered, and afterwards

[127] James C Oldham, 'On Pleading the Belly' (1985) 6 Criminal Justice History 1, 1, 6.
[128] Ibid. 1, 19–20.
[129] It may be traced to Roman times and medieval England: Ibid. 2–3.
[130] Ibid. 23; IELH, 559.
[131] Daniel Defoe, *The Fortunes and Misfortunes of the Famous Moll Flanders* (David Blewett ed, Penguin 1989) 351.
[132] Oldham (n 127) 22–3.
[133] Ibid. 23.
[134] Ibid. 22.
[135] Ibid. 23.

becomes pregnant again, she shall not be entitled to the benefit of a further respite for that cause'.[136]

Unlike other fictions, pleading the belly was not officially abolished – probably because there was no need to do so. By the nineteenth century, with the advances in medical science, the jury of matrons had fallen into disuse.[137]

Let us summarise the characteristics of this fiction. Pleading the belly did not function as a non-traversable pleading. We have seen that in many cases the jury returned a verdict of 'not pregnant'. We must classify it as a fiction of bad evidence – like its sister fiction, the benefit of clergy. To the extent that it was a fiction, the benefit of the belly was so because of questionable findings of fact by the matrons.

As for the completeness of its effect, we know the fiction was haphazardly applied. The factual foundation of the rule was only weakened, and unpredictably so. Its effect was to undermine the rule but not to obliterate it. Clearly, the benefit of the belly was no more than an Auxiliary Fiction. Feigned pregnancies were not taken seriously as a rational ground for suspending the criminal law. The real reason was compassion. The motive for the acceptance of this fiction was justice – a desire to temper the severity of the criminal law.

1.3.8 *Common Recovery*

The aim of this fiction was to 'break an entail'. An entail was a restriction on the inheritance of land, placed by the grantor. Consider the following example. A has two sons: X, the eldest, and Y. A grants a parcel of land, Blackacre, to Y, on the condition that the land is only heritable by the male descendants of Y and his wife, Z. This is an entail. It means that as long as Y and Z have living male descendants, Blackacre is passed on from generation to generation, from male to male. However, if and when the owner for the time being dies and there is no male of the Y-Z parentage living, the condition cannot be satisfied and Blackacre reverts to the original grantor, A. If by such time A has died, Blackacre reverts to A's heirs, namely first X (his eldest son) and X's heirs. And so, Y does not receive from A an estate in fee simple (a full-blown title), but a curtailed or cut-down estate, known as the *fee tail*. The fee simple remains with the grantor (A and his heirs) as reversioner.

The statute *De Donis Conditionalibus*[138] ('Of Conditional Gifts'), enacted under Edward I in 1285, was aimed at preventing the frustration of entails by

136 4 Bl Comm, ch 31, 394–5.
137 Oldham (n 127) 30.
138 Statute of Westminster II (1285) (13 Edw I c 1) s 1.

the grantee or his heirs, but was poorly drafted.[139] Most significantly, it was unclear how long the entail lasted. After much judicial consideration, the position by the 1420s was that *De Donis* barred the alienation (e.g., sale) of entailed land (for alienation would break the entail) and that the entail lasted so long as there were eligible heirs.[140] This meant that the fee tail was in effect a perpetuity, by which the grantor controlled the land from the grave – potentially forever.

The motivation for the entailment of land was to ensure that the wealth of the family stayed in the family for generations, protecting it against dissipation by reckless descendants (through alienation) and leakage to other families (through female inheritance).

But in the long run, the law abhorred perpetuities. The prospect, theoretically possible, that all land in England could be governed by the dead, unable to be traded, was so ghastly that something had to give. Once again, fiction saved the day. The common recovery, the ultimate entail-breaker,[141] debuted on the plea rolls in 1440, soon after the entail became definitely perpetual.[142] Joseph Biancalana's technical explanation of the common recovery can hardly be improved upon:

> The procedure of a common recovery was fairly simple. Suppose A holds land in fee tail but wishes to grant the land to B and to bar the entail. A grants the land to B and then B brings an action for the land against A in the Court of Common Pleas. A denies B's right and vouches a warrantor[143] who enters into the warranty and defends the action. The grantee-plaintiff, B, pleads against the warrantor, who denies B's right. Either the plaintiff or the warrantor then requests and receives a continuance [i.e., an adjournment]. On the day appointed to resume the case, the warrantor absents himself. The court gives a default judgment for B against A and for A against the defaulting warrantor.[144]

And so the fiction, dubbed the common recovery, was a collusive lawsuit. The purchaser sued the owner in tail for the land. The owner in tail failed to defend

139 Joseph Biancalana, *The Fee Tail and the Common Recovery in Medieval England 1176–1502* (CUP 2001) 87–8.

140 Ibid. 119–21.

141 Less effective methods to break an entail included collateral warranties and fines: Ibid. ch 4.

142 Ibid. 121, 313.

143 '[T]he warranty of land was an obligation, owed to the tenant of certain land [by the grantor], to defend him in his possession of that land against all men. This obligation to warrant was primarily, therefore, an obligation to come into Court, if called upon ("vouched") by the tenant, in order to defend some action brought against him for the possession of that land': SJ Bailey, 'Warranties of Land in the Thirteenth Century' [1944] 8 CLJ 274, 274.

144 Biancalana (n 139) 250.

it. The court awarded the land to the purchaser by default judgment.[145] Collusion on a large scale required judicial acquiescence, but this is exactly what happened by the 1470s.[146]

This fiction, like the benefit of clergy, but now in the private law sphere, does not involve a non-traversable pleading. The pleadings in the purchaser's writ were certainly false, but they were traversable. The defendant owner in tail (or more precisely, his warrantor) simply failed to disprove them. In contrast to the benefit of clergy, however, there was not even bad evidence. In what sense was the common recovery a fiction? This challenges our understanding of Old Fictions. Was it a fiction at all?

On balance, it is more sensible to say that it was. The court knowingly entertained sham proceedings, mounted upon false pleadings (the claimant's ownership of the land), amounting to a conspiracy to disinherit third parties (the heir in tail and the reversioner). It is telling that such collusive suits attracted severe penalties in other contexts.[147] Besides, the fact that all parties involved were happy to say that black was white does not mean it was no fiction to say so. We have now identified a fourth species of the genus Old Fiction, namely collusion. The other three are the non-traversable pleading, the withdrawn pleading and bad evidence.

The motive of this fiction was justice – but in a technical sense. Perpetuities were viewed as fundamentally wrong and unsustainable. Sir Edward Coke called them 'a monstrous brood carved out of mere invention, and never known to the ancient sages of the law. ... At whose solemn funeral I was present, and accompanied the dead to the grave, but mourned not.'[148]

In terms of our classification, the common recovery is best seen as an Auxiliary Fiction. The collusion was countenanced merely as a means to an end – being the prevention of perpetuities. Collusion could not have been the rationale for the outcome of the case.

As for the completeness of its effect, the common recovery was almost comprehensive: it barred all heirs, reversions and remainders, but it did not bar executory devises (an inheritance conditional on a future contingency).[149]

The aim of the fiction was to defeat the statute *De Donis*. It thus stands out as an Old Fiction which does not subvert a rule of common law, or a form of

145 For more, see: Ibid. chs 5, 6.

146 Ibid. 253.

147 See the examples in LTB, 145–59.

148 Baker and Milsom (n 78) 186.

149 Giles Jacob, Thomas Edlyne Tomlins and Thomas Colpitts Granger, *The Law-Dictionary: Explaining the Rise, Progress, and Present State, of the English Law*, vol 1 (4th edn, Clarke 1835), Fine of Lands, I, 1.

action, but an Act of Parliament. Furthermore, the subversion of the Act could hardly be more flagrant. The mischief which the Act had been enacted to stamp out, namely the frustration of entails, was precisely what the fiction achieved. The common recovery thus disturbed the constitutional order. Legal fictions were now used by courts to unmake legislative acts.

On a lighter note, the reader may like to know that the fiction of the common recovery was immortalised in the most iconic scene of Shakespearean theatre. In a churchyard with Horatio, Hamlet holds up a skull and says:

> There's another: why may not that be the skull of a
> lawyer? Where be his quiddities now, his quillets,
> his cases, his tenures, and his tricks? why does he
> suffer this rude knave now to knock him about the
> sconce with a dirty shovel, and will not tell him of
> his action of battery? Hum! This fellow might be
> in's time a great buyer of land, with his statutes,
> his recognizances, his fines, his double vouchers,
> his *recoveries*: is this the fine of his fines, and
> the recovery of his recoveries, to have his fine
> pate full of fine dirt?[150]

1.3.9 *Trover*

It is said that necessity is the mother of invention. This proverb may with all propriety be applied to fictions. Common lawyers were at their most inventive when confronted by some necessity. And for a lawyer, this meant the client's interests. It is a happy consequence, and not an arbitrary one, that the selfish motivations of litigants resulted in gains for the common law. Through the fictionalisation of burdensome rules, the legal system became more convenient (take the bill of Middlesex), more accessible (geographical fictions), more effective (writ of *quominus*), more nuanced (benefit of clergy) and almost certainly fairer (*vi et armis*). This pattern whereby the pursuit of private interests yielded a public dividend repeated itself in the story of trover.

The fiction of trover arose from the shortcomings of the ancient writ of detinue. Alleging that the defendant unjustly detained the claimant's goods, it was meant to be the primary vehicle for the vindication of property in chattels.[151] In reality, it was a 'dismal catalogue of defects'.[152]

150 *Hamlet*, Act V, Scene I (emphasis added).
151 For the text of the writ, see IELH, 583.
152 CHS Fifoot, *History and Sources of the Common Law: Tort and Contract* (Stevens 1949) 102.

Two of these defects are relevant to our discussion.[153] Suppose A lends his horse to B. The horse is not returned and is later found with C. By the thirteenth century, A could sustain an action in detinue against the third party C. The problem was that A had to explain how the horse had come into the hands of C. This explanation was a traversable allegation and imperilled the whole claim.[154] A did not necessarily know by what means, fair or foul, C had acquired the horse from B, or whether there had been intermediate possessors. This requirement of backward tracing was onerous and claimants sought to avoid it.

The second defect of detinue was the unavailability of trial by jury. Instead, this old writ was tried by wager of law. Under this mode of proof, mentioned above, the defendant proved his defence by solemnly swearing to it and producing eleven 'oath-helpers' or 'compurgators', who swore to his integrity.[155] A dishonest defendant who could muster enough support was able to escape liability,[156] if at the risk of his immortal soul.

By 1455, the first problem (of backward tracing) was solved by a blunt fiction. Instead of explaining how C had gotten the horse from B, A alleged that he, A, had casually lost the horse and that C had found and unjustly detained it.[157] B was excised from the narrative. Ironically then, the solution to not knowing how the horse made its way to the defendant was to tell a story that was definitely false. But of course, it was *an* explanation, and for the judges, this was enough. By 1400, the allegation of losing and finding was non-traversable.

The reader may wonder how such a fiction, and indeed the other fictions, could get off the ground in the first place. Was there a trailblazing lawyer who gambled his client's claim on a chance of creating a new fiction (when the false allegation was not yet non-traversable)? How did judges decide to make an allegation non-traversable as a matter of policy? Was there a backroom deal? Was there an invitation or intimation from the bench? These are fascinating questions for the legal historian. Disappointingly, we will probably never know the answers. As Professor Baker said, 'the experiments which preceded the familiar forms, are in some ways the most interesting to the historian, and yet they shade off into the invisible. ...

153 A third defect was that the defendant could return damaged goods without liability. For more, see AWB Simpson, 'The Introduction of the Action on the Case for Conversion' (1959) 75 LQR 364, 364.

154 IELH, 418.

155 Hudson (n 8) 81.

156 Simpson, 'The Introduction of the Action on the Case for Conversion' (n 153) 365.

157 IELH, 419; HILO, 107.

Fictions only surface in the books once they have become widely known and well established. The precise origin of a fictional device is therefore almost always beyond recovery.'[158]

In any event, the courts, from 1400 onwards, did not allow the allegation of losing and finding to be traversed. So was born the fiction of trover – literally 'finding'. Some of its more entertaining manifestations included one plaintiff who lost a ship in London, another who lost a battery of guns and several who misplaced housefuls of furniture and utensils.[159]

The second problem with the writ of detinue (wager of law) was solved when trespass on the case for conversion supplanted detinue as a whole in the Tudor era.[160] This process is of no interest to us, except to say that the trover fiction (the allegation of losing and finding) was copied into the new pleading.[161] Trover thus became part of the tort of conversion.

It has been said (for reasons that space does not permit us to cover) that conversion was also a fiction.[162] If so, the fiction of conversion contained the fiction of trover: a fantastic construction, in both senses of the adjective.

In general terms, trover was a simple non-traversable fiction. Its effect, however, was incomplete. The defendant was allowed to traverse the fiction to show that he had come by the property through some recognised means. The fiction was calibrated to the purpose. That purpose, the motive for the fiction, was justice. For it was unjust that a proprietary action should fail because the claimant could not prove how the defendant had obtained the chattel, unless the defendant could show he had a better claim (in which case the fiction was suspended so that the allegation of losing and finding could be traversed).[163]

Trover was a model Auxiliary Fiction. The story of losing and finding was not a genuine doctrinal ground. It was not seen as the real reason for the decision. It was just meaningless text. So it remained, until the abolition of the fiction by the Common Law Procedure Act 1852.[164] Detinue, incidentally, survived until 1977.[165] Conversion, needless to say, is still alive and well, though recalibrated by Parliament.[166]

158 LTB, 35; see also HFCL, 290.
159 IELH, 424; LTB, 33 fn 3, citing *Arundell v Carye* (1549) KB 27/1149 m 75.
160 Simon Douglas, 'The Nature of Conversion' [2009] CLJ 198, 199–206.
161 IELH, 423; HILO, 108.
162 Douglas (n 160) 203–4, 211.
163 IELH, 425.
164 s 49 (the allegation of losing and finding was to be omitted).
165 Torts (Interference with Goods) Act 1977, s 2(1).
166 Ibid., especially ss 2(2), 3, 11.

1.3.10 *Ejectment*

It was a consequence of the writ system that a body of law grew around the peculiarities of each writ. This sometimes led to illogical inconsistencies between actions that were conceptually similar. The fiction of ejectment owes its origin to such an inconsistency.

Following a change in the law in 1481,[167] lessees could use the highly effective writ of *ejectione firmæ* (a variant of the writ of trespass) to recover a leasehold – that is the land itself – from a squatter. Landlords had no access to this writ and had to use more archaic and dilatory writs to eject a squatter. This Tudor-era anomaly, whereby lessees suddenly found themselves in a better position than landlords, was the incentive for legal ingenuity.

The solution is almost obvious. If the reason the landlord cannot use *ejectione firmæ* is that he is not a lessee, all the landlord has to do is to lease the disputed land to a collaborator who would enter upon the land and be duly ejected by the squatter. The ousted lessee would then have recourse to the writ *ejectione firmæ* as any other lessee in the land. If successful in his suit, the lessee would surrender the lease to the landlord, the true claimant. Thus a landlord would contrive to use the superior writ. The courts approved this practice by 1580 at the latest.[168] What is crucial about this device, in its Elizabethan form, is that there was nothing fictitious about it. A lease was actually granted, the lessee actually entered the land, the defendant did oust the lessee and the lessee really did have a cause of action in trespass against the defendant. In contradistinction to the common recovery, there was no collusion. On the contrary, the defendant (the alleged squatter) had to contest the action or lose the land. In the absence of any fictitious element, we must conclude that the *Elizabethan form* of ejectment was not a fiction.

Professor Sparkes takes a different view. He argues that 'ejectment was fictional in the sense that an artificial lease was used to secure leasehold recovery when the underlying issue was determination of freehold title'.[169] This argument has merit: neither the lessor nor the lessee was genuinely interested in a lease. Nor was the lease ever enjoyed as such by the lessee. It was just a means to an end. However, on balance, it seems to me that the parties' ulterior motives have nothing to do with whether a deed of lease confers a lease or not. If a lease has come into existence – as in the present instance – it should not be downgraded to a fictitious lease; for surely this lease

167 *Pynchemore v Brewyn* (1481) Baker & Milsom (2nd edn) 197 (KB).
168 HLL, 145.
169 Peter Sparkes, 'Ejectment: Three Births and a Funeral' in LFTP, 277.

is as good as any other. This conclusion is consistent with the position this monograph generally takes, to be expounded in the next chapter, namely that fictions should not be *defined* by their motives or effects.

We return to the narrative. As ejectment became increasingly popular in the seventeenth century,[170] the rigmarole of lease, entry and ouster came to be seen as superfluous. It was also unpleasant and potentially dangerous because the lessee had to physically enter the land the defendant occupied and be removed by him.[171] Since the whole charade was merely a means to an end, why not expedite matters by eliminating the need for lease, entry and ouster? At first blocked by legislation against pretended titles,[172] the fictionalisation of ejectment occurred in the early 1650s when the Upper Bench (as the King's Bench was known during the Interregnum) decreed that defendants must 'confess' lease, entry and ouster. In other words, the allegations of lease, entry and ouster became non-traversable.

By 1700, the nominal lessee no longer had to be a real person. He, too, was a means to an end. He became a fictitious party by the standard name of John Doe or the more self-righteous Goodright, Goodtitle, Fairclaim and so forth. And if the ousted lessee was imaginary, why not also imagine a lessee of the defendant as the ejector and call him Richard Roe – or, more pejoratively, Shamtitle, Thrustout, Troublesome or indeed Vice?[173] This second lessee was not essential to the fiction, but he did save the true claimant time and trouble. The appearance of Richard Roe, who was a puppet of the true claimant, was easier to procure than that of a flesh-and-blood defendant (who might be more evasive).[174] The true claimant, the puppeteer, just entered an appearance on Roe's behalf. To seal the deal, this appearance having been entered, the 'attorney' of the imaginary Richard Roe would write to the real defendant, advising him that he, Roe, had been sued and did not intend to defend himself. Then the real defendant intervened in the action as a reversioner and the real case began.[175]

In the 1762 case of *Fairclaim v Shamtitle*, Lord Mansfield said:

> Ejectment is an ingenious fiction for the trial of titles to the possession of land. In form it is a trick between two to dispossess a third by a sham suit and

170 Already in 1601, Coke wrote that 'all titles of lands are for the greatest part tried in Actions of Ejectments': HLL, 146, citing *Alden's Case* (1601) 5 Co Rep 105b.

171 HLL, 146; IELH, 321.

172 32 Henry VIII c 9 (1540).

173 Sparkes (n 169) 281, 286; HLL, 147–8.

174 IELH, 321.

175 HLL, 147–8.

> judgment. The artifice would be criminal, unless the Court converted it into a fair trial between the proper parties.[176]

Jeremy Bentham, typically, was less forgiving:

> A man to whom you let your house for a year – does he at the expiration of the time refuse to quit it? Not a chance will they give you for obtaining possession again of your house, unless you trump up a foolish story about two persons, real or imaginary, one of whom turned the other out of it. This is what you are forced to do, in bringing an action of ejectment.[177]

In the full-fledged version of ejectment, attained in the 1700s, the English fiction reached its apotheosis: an action to try leasehold had become the main common law vehicle to try freehold, every single constitutive element of the action was non-existent (no lease, no entry, no ouster), even the parties were non-existent.

To summarise the characteristics of ejectment, it was a fiction born of convenience, it operated as a non-traversable pleading and its effect was complete. It is the first fiction we can credit as being an Essential Fiction – because the steps that became fictitious (lease, entry, ouster) were the substantive basis for the outcome of the case. The fiction was a convenient shortcut, but conceptually, ejectment remained a vindication of a lessee's possession. The lease, entry and ouster were not mere incantations like the reading test. They actually meant something: a lessee in possession had been ousted. They formed the doctrinal basis for recovery.

The death of this fiction, however, is more interesting for our purposes than its life. The fiction of ejectment was abolished in the bonfire of the fictions that was the Common Law Procedure Act 1852 along with many other fictions – among them *vi et armis*.[178] But whereas *vi et armis* was simply dumped as meaningless text in a writ (that is, the words '*vi et armis*' no longer had to be averred), the fiction of ejectment could not be disposed of so easily. This is because the fiction encompassed an entire action. This action was the primary means to recover land in England. Indeed, an 1833 statute had made it the only permissible real action, with few exceptions.[179] If the fictitious elements of ejectment were simply omitted, as the words '*vi et armis*' were omitted, there would be nothing left of the action – not even parties. And so, in 1852,

[176] (1762) 3 Burr 1290, 97 ER 837 (KB) 1294.

[177] Charles Kay Ogden and Jeremy Bentham, *Bentham's Theory of Fictions* (Kegan Paul 1932) 149–50 fn 1.

[178] Common Law Procedure Act 1852 (15 & 16 Vict c 76) ss 49, 168.

[179] Dower and *quare impedit*: Real Property Limitation Act 1833 (3 & 4 William IV c 27) s 36.

Parliament faced the task of reconstructing an action for the vindication of land ownership on a non-fictitious basis.

The reconstruction proved unimaginative. Statutory ejectment preserved all the substantive aspects of common law ejectment while ditching the fictitious pleadings.[180] Section 221 of the Common Law Procedure Act explicitly incorporated into the new scheme the 'Jurisdiction as heretofore exercised in the Action of Ejectment' and all relevant legislation not inconsistent with the said Act.

In *Butler v Meredith*, an ejectment case decided in 1855, three years after the passage of the Act, Pollock CB said, 'Under the new order of things, which [the Act] has introduced, the action of ejectment is placed . . . on the same footing as when it existed as the mere creature of the Court.'[181] Parke B concurred, 'I feel satisfied that the position of parties under [the Act] is exactly the same as it was before.'[182]

In other words, the action of ejectment was not expunged and built anew, but simply shorn of its disposable elements, namely the fictitious pleadings. In a sense, the fiction's abolition was its ultimate victory, the culmination of the fictionalisation process: originally, in Elizabethan times, lease, entry and ouster had to be carried out; then, from the Interregnum, only pleaded; finally, in the Victorian era, not even pleaded. Thus these steps completely disappeared from the record.

This is a good illustration of the recurring idea in the commentary that fictions are like scaffolding. In the words of John Chipman Gray, which Lon Fuller later endorsed,[183] 'Such fictions are scaffolding – useful, almost necessary, in construction – but, after the building is erected, serving only to obscure it.'[184] Peter Sparkes has recently articulated the concept in the context of ejectment:

> The fiction in ejectment can be seen as scaffolding, a metaphor which implies that a fiction is useful when building a new doctrine out of existing case-law only to achieve redundancy as soon as the construction is complete. While a building under construction is clad in scaffolding the external appearance is an imitation of the final shape, even though the scaffolding carries the purely procedural role of facilitating access to the work by the builders. When work is complete the scaffolding is removed to reveal the true

180 Sparkes (n 169) 288.
181 (1855) 11 Ex 85, 156 ER 755, 757 (Exchequer).
182 Ibid. 758.
183 Fuller (n 2) 70.
184 Gray (n 2) 35.

> shape of the edifice, the substantive doctrine to which the scaffolding provided a path. This is equivalent to the abolition of the fiction.[185]

But herein lies the rub. In simply removing the scaffolding, the Act did not create a new action. The substantive doctrine – a possessory action based on notional entry and ouster – was not abolished. All the Act did was to change the *procedure* for the action. As a result, statutory ejectment did not lie for incorporeal hereditaments, such as an advowson[186] or a *profit-à-prendre*, as these could not be *entered upon*.[187] This is an important point. The claimant no longer had to *plead* lease, entry and ouster, but this doctrinal basis of the action still had to be satisfied notionally. Failure to do so meant the statutory action was unavailable. So much for the abolition of the fiction. FW Maitland's famous saying echoes in our ears: 'The forms of action we have buried but still they rule us from their graves.'[188]

1.3.11 *Quasi-contract*

The story of quasi-contract is another example of a fiction which was officially abolished, but which, Zombie-like, refused to die. Following the watershed case of *Slade v Morley*[189] in 1602, all debts (except by deed[190]) were normally recovered under the writ of *assumpsit*.[191] It was the legacy of *Slade's Case* that the promissory writ of *assumpsit* became the writ most associated with contract.[192] It was promissory because it alleged that the defendant debtor had promised to pay the debt to the claimant creditor. In the contractual context, this promise could be properly implied. To assume a debt is to promise to repay it.

But shortly after *Slade's Case*, for reasons that are beyond the scope of this chapter,[193] plaintiffs adopted a form of pleading in which the promise was subsequent to the contract (rather than implied in it). At this point, the implied promise became a fictitious promise.[194] This fictitious way of pleading *assumpsit* was known as *indebitatus assumpsit*. Literally meaning 'being

185 Sparkes (n 169) 276.
186 A right to appoint a person to an ecclesiastical office.
187 Robert Malcolm Kerr, *An Action at Law* (2nd edn, William Henry Bond 1855) 73.
188 Maitland (n 3) 2.
189 (1602) 4 Co Rep 92b, (1602) 76 ER 1074 (Exchequer Chamber).
190 Still only recoverable by the writ of debt: IELH, 369 fn 1; HILO, 150.
191 IELH, 367.
192 Though actually a variant of trespass.
193 See Ibbetson, 'Slade's Case in Context' (n 17) 315–16.
194 IELH, 370. For more detail, see HCLC, 491–3.

indebted, he promised', these words of the writ encapsulated the fictitious separation between the contract and the subsequent promise.

Now that the promise was fictitious anyway, there was a temptation to use it in non-contractual contexts, where there could not have been any promise, express or implied, coincident or subsequent.[195] One such non-contractual context is what we today call unjust enrichment. Soon enough, the writ of *assumpsit* was doing the work of modern unjust enrichment.[196] To recover money paid to the defendant by mistake – to use the classic example – the claimant would sue in *assumpsit*, alleging that the defendant had promised to pay him the money. The promise was of course made up. It was also more fanciful than the subsequent promise in the contractual context. But it did not matter: the promise was in any case non-traversable. As Lord Atkin retrospectively explained, 'The law, in order to do justice, imputed . . . a promise which alone as forms of action then existed could give the injured person a reasonable remedy.'[197] The *locus classicus* of this fiction is Lord Mansfield's dictum in *Moses v Macferlan* (1760): 'If the defendant be under an obligation, from the ties of natural justice, to refund; the *law implies a debt*, and gives this action, founded in the equity of the plaintiff's case, as it were upon a contract ("quasi ex contractu", as the Roman law expresses it).'[198]

In this quotation, we see the historic entanglement of unjust enrichment with contract. The case was brought on the writ of *assumpsit*, used for contract, meaning the pleading was promissory. Since the fictitious promise was used in *all* contract cases (save deeds), it seemed as though a mistaken payment was recoverable because it was like a contract – and not because the law imposed an obligation. Lawyers thought of the situations we associate with the distinct category of unjust enrichment as analogous to contract; not quite the same as contract, because there was no agreement, but *like* contract – that is, quasi-contract.[199]

It is not immediately obvious why an obligation which springs 'from the ties of natural justice' should in any way resemble a contract, the obligations in which derive from agreement.[200] It is possible that this conflation is simply the

[195] IELH, 386, 393ff.

[196] Ibid. ch 21. For more on the fictional origins of the law of unjust enrichment, see John H Langbein, 'The Later History of Restitution' in WR Cornish and others (eds), *Restitution: Past, Present and Future* (Hart 1998) ch 4.

[197] *United Australia Ltd v Barclays Bank Ltd* [1941] AC 1 (HL) 28; see also HCLC, 490.

[198] (1760) 2 Burr 1005, 97 ER 676 (KB) 678 (emphasis added).

[199] For an interesting discussion of the relationship between quasi-contract and unjust enrichment, see Steve Hedley, 'Implied Contract and Restitution' [2004] CLJ 435.

[200] Cf. Ibid. 436–9.

result of the pleading system: because unjust enrichment cases were framed as promissory actions, they came to be seen in contractual terms.

The operation of the fiction was quite simple. It was a non-traversable pleading, whose effect could be said to be maximal: whenever 'natural justice' demanded a remedy, the fictitious promise obliged.[201] It follows that the motive for this fiction was justice. Importantly, quasi-contract was an Essential Fiction, at least by the nineteenth century. This is because the analogy with contract, or alternatively the promise springing from natural justice, was seen as the rational basis for recovery – even if the promise was known to be fabricated factually speaking.

The conceptual link between unjust enrichment and contract was so strong that when the fiction of the implied promise was abolished by the Common Law Procedure Act 1852,[202] the courts were not soon disabused of it. In fact, Tariq Baloch suggests that far from being abolished, the fiction of quasi-contract thickened, as 'courts would inform their understanding of the indebitatus claims by reference to a *genuine* implied contract'.[203] The 'worst example' of this tendency, according to William Swadling,[204] was the decision of the House of Lords in *Sinclair v Brougham* in 1914.[205] In that case, the claimants had deposited money with a building society pursuant to a loan contract. This contract was declared void for being ultra vires the society's constitution. The claimants sought to recover their deposits in a quasi-contractual action (technically an action for money had and received). Explaining why this action failed, Viscount Haldane LC said:

> [S]o far as proceedings in personam are concerned, the common law of England really recognizes ... only actions of two classes, those founded on contract and those founded on tort. When it speaks of actions arising quasi ex contractu it refers merely to a class of action in theory based on a contract which is imputed to the defendant by a fiction of law. *The fiction can only be set up with effect if such a contract would be valid if it really existed.*[206]

Since the building society in *Sinclair v Brougham* had no power to enter into the loan contract (it being ultra vires its constitution), there could never be any contract, even in theory, and the fiction could not 'be set up with effect'. His Lordship continued:

201 HCLC, 494; IELH, 386ff.
202 s 49 (the implied promise was to be omitted).
203 Tariq A Baloch, *Unjust Enrichment and Contract* (Hart 2009) 40.
204 William Swadling, 'The Fiction of the Constructive Trust' (2011) 64 CLP 399, 403.
205 [1914] AC 398 (HL).
206 Ibid. 415 (emphasis added).

> [T]he law of England cannot . . . impute the fiction of such a promise where it would have been ultra vires to give it. The fiction becomes . . . inapplicable where substantive law . . . makes the defendant incapable of undertaking contractual liability. For to impute a fictitious promise is simply to presume the existence of a state of facts, and the presumption can give rise to no higher right than would result if the facts were actual.[207]

Reading Viscount Haldane's reasons, one might be excused for thinking that the fiction had never been abolished. More, this reasoning betrays a misunderstanding of the fiction of quasi-contract – for the whole point of the fiction is that the promise and contract are not genuine. Even under the forms of action, that golden age of fictions, judges had not fallen into the fallacy of genuine fiction.[208] Like a pathological liar who starts to believe his own lies, post-abolition judges believed a theoretical contract was necessary for recovery. This fallacy, the same we saw in post-abolition ejectment, is the hideous strength of Essential Fictions, which form the doctrinal basis of an action.

Another example of the staying power of the quasi-contract fiction was *Cowern v Neild*,[209] decided by the High Court in 1912. The claimant had bought hay and clover from a business run by a minor. The clover arrived rotten and the hay never arrived at all. The buyer sought to recover the cheque he had given by an action for money had and received. He lost because the minor lacked the capacity to contract and thus no contract could exist in theory to sustain the fiction of quasi-contract.[210] Just as post-abolition ejectment did not lie for incorporeal hereditaments because they could not be entered upon as required by the underlying fiction, so too unjust enrichment did not lie where a contract could not have existed.

It is clear that post-abolition judges did not consider quasi-contract abolished as a matter of substance or doctrine, but simply as a matter of pleading or procedure. The implied promise did not have to be pleaded, but as with lease, entry and ouster in ejectment, the promise continued to exist as the basis of the action. To paraphrase Mark Twain, the report of its death was greatly exaggerated.[211]

By the middle of the twentieth century, the link between contract and unjust enrichment was unravelling. In 1940, with the *Luftwaffe* thundering overhead, Lord Atkin channelled Winston Churchill in the House of Lords:

207 Ibid. 417.
208 Baloch (n 203) 40.
209 [1912] 2 KB 419 (KB).
210 Ibid. 423–4 (Phillimore J).
211 Angela Partington (ed), *Oxford Dictionary of Quotations* (4th revised, OUP 1996) 706.

> These fantastic resemblances of contracts invented in order to meet requirements of the law as to forms of action which have now disappeared should not in these days be allowed to affect actual rights. When these ghosts of the past stand in the path of justice clanking their mediæval chains the proper course for the judge is to pass through them undeterred.[212]

In 1991, the doctrine of quasi-contract was finally jettisoned in favour of a non-fictitious action of unjust enrichment.[213] However, it was not until 2010, in *Haugesund Kommune v Depfa ACS Bank*,[214] that the last vestige of the 'fictitious nexus'[215] between contract and unjust enrichment was finally consigned to oblivion. In a re-enactment of the relevant facts of *Sinclair v Brougham*, Norwegian local authorities borrowed money *ultra vires* their statutory capacity. Departing from *Sinclair v Brougham*, the Court of Appeal upheld the bank's claim in unjust enrichment for the money lent.[216] As Graham Virgo put it:

> The result for the [local authorities] was that they had to make restitution of the money lent. But the result for English law is even more significant: just under 100 years later, this is the final nail in the coffin of *Sinclair* v. *Brougham*.[217]

Indeed, it was the final nail in the coffin of quasi-contract. Now that the law of unjust enrichment was not predicated on an implied contract (which had to be theoretically possible), there was no impediment to restitution in cases of void loans and no denial of just remedies.

What we see in the post-abolition history of quasi-contract is that, even more than ejectment, it resisted retirement for many decades and even gained strength. The Common Law Procedure Act 1852 only succeeded in removing it superficially as a pleading, as a form of action.

1.4 CONCLUSION

Our survey of Old Fictions ends here. We have seen that Old Fictions are not cast from the same mould. Besides being fictions, the similarity between them

212 *United Australia Ltd v Barclays Bank Ltd* (n 197) 29.

213 *Lipkin Gorman v Karpnale Ltd* [1991] 2 AC 548 (HL) 578 (Lord Goff); see also *Westdeutsche Landesbank Girozentrale v Islington LBC* [1996] AC 669 (HL) 710 (Lord Browne-Wilkinson); *Kleinwort Benson Ltd v Lincoln CC* [1999] 2 AC 349 (HL) 373 (Lord Goff).

214 [2010] EWCA Civ 579, [2012] QB 549.

215 *Sempra Metals Ltd (formerly Metallgesellschaft Ltd) v Inland Revenue Commissioners* [2007] UKHL 34, [2008] 1 AC 561 [106] (Lord Nicholls).

216 *Haugesund* (n 214) [87]–[88] (Aikens LJ). The Court of Appeal was able to depart from the House of Lords' decision in *Sinclair* because it understood the House of Lords to have in effect already departed from *Sinclair* in *Westdeutsche* (n 213).

217 Graham Virgo, 'Restitution of Void Loans' [2010] CLJ 447, 449.

TABLE 1.1 *Old Fictions*

Fiction	Type	Manner of operation	Effect on rule	Motive
Dominus remisit curiam	Jurisdictional	Non-traversable pleading	Complete abrogation	Convenience
Vi et armis	Jurisdictional	Non-traversable pleading	Relaxation to a low threshold	Justice
Geographical fictions	Jurisdictional	Non-traversable pleading	Creation of an exception	Justice
Bill of Middlesex	Jurisdictional	Withdrawn pleading	Complete abrogation	Convenience
Writ of *quominus*	Jurisdictional	Non-traversable pleading	Complete abrogation	Convenience
Benefit of clergy	Auxiliary	Bad evidence	Complete abrogation	Justice
Pleading the belly	Auxiliary	Bad evidence	Haphazard application	Justice
Common recovery	Auxiliary	Collusion	Almost complete abrogation	Justice
Trover	Auxiliary	Non-traversable pleading	Partial abrogation	Justice
Ejectment	Essential	Non-traversable pleading	Complete abrogation	Convenience
Quasi-contract	Essential	Non-traversable pleading	Complete abrogation	Justice

is at most a family resemblance. Most Old Fictions operated as non-traversable pleadings, but some relied on bad evidence (benefit of clergy and belly), collusion (common recovery) or withdrawn pleadings (bill of Middlesex). Most Old Fictions completely eradicated the rule they targeted, but some only softened the rule (*vi et armis*) or created an exception to it (geographical fictions). Some Old Fictions were tolerated because they facilitated justice in a formally inflexible system. Others were condoned simply to avoid inconvenience or save money. Table 1.1 above sets out the characteristics of the eleven fictions I have described.

Notwithstanding the versatility of the Old Fiction, it is possible to extrapolate some general conclusions about Old Fictions from these findings about particular Old Fictions. First, Old Fictions did not appear *ex nihilo*. They mostly emerged tentatively, piecemeal, by weakening the factual basis of pre-existing structures. Second, English judges were not afraid of fictions, no matter how ludicrous they might have seemed to a layman. They saw fictions in purely technical, instrumental terms and nothing more. Fictions were thus used to mitigate the rigidity of the forms of action. Fiction was an antidote to formalism – a corrective mechanism that allowed the law to develop in a formalist age.

Third, and perhaps more controversially, for all their inelegance and lack of principle, fictions *under the Old System* tended to be a force for good. They generally made the legal system more just, more nuanced, more accessible, more convenient. As Sir Matthew Hale said in defence of Old Fictions, 'they are but expedients without injuring anybody to bring men to their rights'.[218] The hideous strength of Essential Fictions was a post-abolition, New System phenomenon.

This brings us to the final question, the post-mortem question. What befell the Old Fictions following the death of the forms of action in 1852? It is not surprising that the Jurisdictional Fictions – *dominus remisit curiam*, *vi et armis*, geographical fictions, bill of Middlesex and writ of *quominus* – disappeared without a trace when the writ system and formal pleading were abolished. These Old Fictions were purely procedural. When the procedures went out of use, they too went out of use.

Auxiliary Fictions suffered a similar fate. Although not strictly of procedure, they consisted simply of words that had to be recited with respect to some actions. They were not real reasons for the result of the case. Put differently, they were purely formal. These included such ancient stalwarts as the benefit of clergy and the common recovery – as well as the lesser-known plea of the belly. They, too, went down without a fight when the forms of action vanished.

It was the third type of Old Fiction, the Essential Fiction, that cheated the hangman. When the Common Law Procedure Act 1852 pronounced the death sentence for ejectment and quasi-contract,[219] they did not mount the gallows but instead went underground. There, below the surface, they continued to underpin the action from which they were doctrinally inextricable – inextricable because they had always been the reason for the outcome of the case.

So it was that Essential Fictions lost only their formal manifestations, their outward signs. They receded from the light of day – the pleadings and the writs – deep into the dark heart of doctrine, a grave from which they continued to exert their power over the law above ground. In a sense, they were buried alive.

In ejectment, we have seen that the fiction consisted in the skipping of doctrinally necessary steps. Even when the fiction was removed, the action was still conceived in terms of these steps. When these steps were not possible (e.g.,

[218] Hale (n 73) 24.
[219] ss 49, 168.

entry on an incorporeal hereditament), the action failed despite the formal abolition of the fiction. Similarly, when unjust enrichment was thought of as a quasi-contractual action, the abolition of the implied promise did not mean lawyers stopped looking for theoretically possible contracts. No, the Old Essential Fictions receded into the heart of doctrine, becoming New Fictions.

This metamorphosis from Old to New Fictions is the subject of the next chapter.

2

New Fictions Defined

> It is obvious that a critical evaluation of the fiction as a device of legal thought and expression cannot be undertaken until one has at least attempted an answer to the question: What is a fiction?
>
> Lon L Fuller[1]

2.1 INTRODUCTION

The abolition of the forms of action in the mid-nineteenth century was a seismic shift in the history of English law. Actions now became concepts rather than forms of words or procedures. And if it was an earthquake for the law in general, it was a mass extinction event for legal fictions in particular. We saw in the previous chapter that nearly all fictions – some of which had thrived for centuries – ceased to exist at one statutory swoop. Even the few survivors no longer functioned in the old way; that is to say, as a non-traversable pleading. In fact, that is why these fictions (which I called 'Essential' in the last chapter) survived: by forming a conceptual element of the action they escaped Parliament's purge of 'All Statements which need not be proved.'[2]

The new paradigm, with its conceptual fictions, presents a problem that the Old System did not. Legal philosopher Lon Fuller said that 'it is generally more difficult to say that a given statement is false when it relates purely to legal concepts, than when it relates to extralegal fact'.[3] In the last chapter, we had little reason to doubt whether an Old Fiction was really a fiction[4]

[1] Lon L Fuller, *Legal Fictions* (Stanford University Press 1967) 5.

[2] Common Law Procedure Act 1852 (15 & 16 Vict c 76) ss 49.

[3] Fuller, *Legal Fictions* (n 1) 28.

[4] The Elizabethan phase of ejectment and the common recovery were exceptional in this regard.

(historical accuracy aside[5]). For one thing, the blatancy of many Old Fictions left little to the imagination. For another, their operation was mechanical. The pleading system separated (if artificially at times) law from fact, and pin-pointed which allegations of fact had to be proved. It meant that certain facts were not capable of refutation and were fictions by definition, by the very nature of the system.

Now that we no longer have non-traversable pleadings; now that fictions are conceptual and mixed with the law, identifying fictions is more problematic. It is often difficult to draw a line between legal fictions and intangible legal concepts; between legal fictions and rules; between legal fictions and mistakes; and between legal fictions and the general artificiality of the law. These fine distinctions have bedevilled generations of legal scholars. Lon Fuller devoted a third of his monograph *Legal Fictions* to the question 'What is a legal fiction?'[6] Fully another third of his canonical work was concerned with the awkward position of fictions in a system which is artificial in the sense that it is man-made.

So the challenge raised by the demise of the Old System and the survival of Essential Fictions is this: now that there is no formal system to tell us which allegations are fictitious (by designating them as non-traversable), *we* need to decide what the fictions are. We need a new definition for the New System.

James Stoneking was correct to say that the 'legal fiction often seems to defy definition'.[7] While the research for this book was being carried out, Douglas Lind wrote: 'The paradox of legal fictions begins in a puzzle of definition. Just what is a legal fiction? This simple question yields no easy answer.'[8]

It is argued here that the lack of success which has attended the quest for a definition is partly attributable to an uncompromising approach: that there exists a single, absolute idea of fiction or, as it were, a Platonic form of fiction. This approach, while intellectually seductive, does not capture the nuance of legal argument. It does not do justice to the subtleties of language in which judges couch their reasoning. The alternative approach advanced in this chapter is to define legal fiction as either 'Hard' or 'Soft', and thereby better to understand what goes on in the judgments.

5 The risk of historical inaccuracy is not to be taken lightly. In 1977, John Baker announced the discovery of a case which adjusted the age of the modern trust by about 100 years: JH Baker, 'The Use upon a Use in Equity 1558-1625' (1977) 93 LQR 33, 33ff. For another lucky discovery, see HFCL, 290.

6 Fuller, *Legal Fictions* (n 1) ch 1.

7 James B Stoneking, 'Penumbras and Privacy: A Study of the Use of Fictions in Constitutional Decision-Making' (1984) 87 West Virginia LR 859, 863.

8 Douglas Lind, 'The Pragmatic Value of Legal Fictions' in LFTP, 85.

In short, the aim of this chapter is to clarify the outer boundaries of the term 'legal fiction' and to distinguish between Hard Fictions and Soft Fictions.

This chapter begins with a description of the problem with the current state of the scholarship, followed by a description of the desired solution. I then turn to some common theoretical objections to fictions, before turning to a historical overview of the existing definitions of legal fiction. Next, the definitions of Hard and Soft Fiction are put forward and tested in two contemporary case studies in private law: the reasonable man and *volenti non fit injuria*.

2.2 THE PROBLEM: A LOOSE CONCEPT

We use the term 'legal fiction' familiarly with the confidence that we know what it means. But what does it really signify – except some vague notion of unreality? Does it include strained arguments, counterfactuals, errors, deceptions, absurdities, misnomers?

Commentators have assumed (precariously in my view) that the following are fictions, in whole or in part: companies,[9] trusts,[10] the reasonable man,[11] implied terms,[12] tracing,[13] vicarious liability,[14] 'practical benefit' consideration,[15] absolute Crown ownership of land,[16] hypothetical scenarios[17] and the Crown and the British constitution,[18] to name a few examples. William Swadling, Peter Birks, John Langbein and others have argued that the constructive trust is a fiction because it is not really a trust.[19] The label 'legal fiction' has been

9 Fuller, *Legal Fictions* (n 1) 55; John Chipman Gray, *The Nature and Sources of the Law* (2nd edn, Macmillan 1921) 50–3; Sidney T Miller, 'The Reasons for Some Legal Fictions' (1910) 8 Michigan LR 623, 627; K Scott Hamilton, 'Prolegomenon to Myth and Fiction in Legal Reasoning, Common Law Adjudication and Critical Legal Studies' (1988) 35 Wayne LR 1449, 1458; Frederick Schauer, 'Legal Fictions Revisited' in LFTP, 123.

10 John Gwilliam, 'Legal Fictions – A Critical Analysis' (1975) 8 Victoria U Wellington LR 452, 456; Miller (n 9) 626.

11 Gwilliam (n 10) 455; Victoria Chico, 'Known Unknowns and Unknown Unknowns' (2012) 28 Professional Negligence 162, 171; Geoffrey Samuel, 'Is Law a Fiction' in LFTP, 50.

12 Samuel Williston, 'Liability for Honest Misrepresentation' (1910) 24 Harvard LR 415, 420–1; Samuel (n 11) 51.

13 Derek Whayman, 'Remodelling Knowing Receipt as a Gains-Based Wrong' (2016) 7 JBL 565, 587.

14 Gordon Junor, 'Vicarious Liability – Redefined?' (2016) 24 SLT 125, 125.

15 Janet O'Sullivan, 'In Defence of Foakes v. Beer' (1996) 55 CLJ 219, 227.

16 Gwilliam (n 10) 454.

17 Samuel (n 11) 46–7.

18 LTB, 47–8.

19 William Swadling, 'The Fiction of the Constructive Trust' (2011) 64 Current Legal Problems 399; Peter Birks, 'Fictions Ancient and Modern' in Neil MacCormick and Peter Birks (eds),

applied more generally to 'intellectual sophistication', which causes a 'disconnect between [the law] and the understanding of ordinary men and women'.[20] American writers have expanded the definition even further to include empirically false suppositions (e.g., reliability of eye-witness testimony),[21] discredited legal regimes (e.g., slavery)[22] and complex statutory schemes.[23] Legal philosopher Hans Vaihinger took the matter to the furthest possible extreme arguing that all the law was a fiction.[24]

In the courts, the term is deployed with equal liberality. In two recent decisions, Lord Reed and Lord Hope described a host of hypothetical persons, among them the officious bystander, the right-thinking member of society and the reasonable man as legal fictions.[25] In the Court of Appeal, Arden LJ stated that the 'well-established principle under which … documents constituting a single transaction are read and construed as one document' was a 'legal fiction'.[26] In the High Court, the treatment of past events, found to be more likely than not, as certain was also considered a fiction.[27]

In response to those who spy fictions everywhere, some writers have insisted on a narrow view of fictions, holding that failure to reflect reality is not in itself fictitious;[28] that no matter of law is fictitious;[29] and even that the law is unable to generate a fiction.[30]

And so, opinion is divided: the meaning of legal fiction ranges from all legal thought at one extremity to hardly any law-related thing at the other. As one author recently observed, 'Any reader pursuing the topic will quickly discern

The Legal Mind: Essays for Tony Honoré (Clarendon Press 1986) 84; John H Langbein, 'The Later History of Restitution' in WR Cornish et al. (eds), *Restitution: Past, Present and Future* (Hart 1998) 58; John V Orth, 'Fact & Fiction in the Law of Property' (2007) 11 Green Bag 65, 72–3; Jeremiah Smith, 'Surviving Fictions' (1917) 27 Yale LJ 317, 322–4. For another argument on why certain constructive trusts are not trusts, see Simon Gardner and Emily MacKenzie, *An Introduction to Land Law* (Hart 2015) 173.

20 Philip Harris and Emma McCartney, 'The Harm of Legal Fictions' [2015] Construction LJ 195, 195.

21 Peter J Smith, 'New Legal Fictions' (2006) 95 Georgetown LJ 1435, 1437–8.

22 Nancy J Knauer, 'Legal Fictions and Juristic Truth' (2010) 23 St Thomas LR 1, 26–37.

23 Ibid. 38–48.

24 H Vaihinger, *The Philosophy of 'As If'* (CK Ogden tr, 2nd edn, Routledge & Kegan Paul 1965).

25 *Healthcare at Home Ltd v Common Services Agency for the Scottish Health Service* [2014] UKSC 49, [2014] PTSR 1081 [2] (Lord Reed); *Helow v Secretary of State for the Home Department and another* [2008] UKHL 62, [2008] 1 WLR 2416 [1] (Lord Hope).

26 *Cherry Tree Investments Ltd v Landmain Ltd* [2012] EWCA Civ 736, [2013] Ch 305 [80], [83].

27 *Heneghan v Manchester Dry Docks Ltd* [2014] EWHC 4190 (QB) [26] (Jay J).

28 Knauer (n 22) 42, 47.

29 LTB, 43.

30 Hans Kelsen, 'On the Theory of Juridic Fictions' (Christoph Kletzer tr) in LFTP, 13.

that there is an oscillation in the literature between those who think legal fictions are an illusory category … and those who see legal fictions everywhere.'[31]

How many of the above-mentioned legal concepts, devices or rules are really fictions? When Lord Hoffmann says in *Chartbrook Ltd v Persimmon Homes Ltd* (2009) that in interpreting the terms of a contract there is no 'limit to the amount of red ink or verbal rearrangement or correction which the court is allowed',[32] do we slide into the realm of fiction?

In my view, judges and scholars (with some exceptions) have too broad a conception of fictions. This conception is too broad not only for what I shall define below as the Hard Fiction, but even for its Soft counterpart.

The significance of formulating a definition – the aim of this chapter – is threefold. First, a precise definition for Hard and Soft Fictions would demystify a fraught concept, providing analytical clarity and consistency. In law, language is important. The opening sentence of Sir John Baker's *The Three Languages of the Common Law* reads: 'The development of a body of legal ideas is inseparable from the creation of special legal language.'[33] Later, Professor Baker adds, 'The development of terms of art is of the essence of legal development, and the common law could never have become a distinct body of law without its own distinct language … in which to express its concepts.'[34] It is contended that legal fiction ought to be a term of art.

This leads us to the second benefit of this chapter: the potential for 'legal development'. Just as the law needs terms of art to operate internally, any external academic evaluation of the legal fiction depends on a sound and widely accepted definition.

The third advantage of a precise definition arises from the fact that legal fictions, rightly or wrongly, carry an odour. Thus the classification of a legal concept as fictitious may undermine its legitimacy. Such was the case with quasi-contract[35] and a similar attack has been launched on the constructive

31 Maksymilian Del Mar, 'Introducing Fictions: Examples, Functions, Definitions and Evaluations' in LFTP, ix.

32 *Chartbrook Ltd and another v Persimmon Homes Ltd and another* [2009] UKHL 38, [2009] 1 AC 1101 [25]. This comment apparently alarmed other judges, who subsequently insisted that unambiguous language must be adhered to: *Rainy Sky SA v Kookmin Bank* [2011] UKSC 50, [2011] 1 WLR 2900 [23] (Lord Clarke); *Procter and Gamble Co v Svenska Cellulosa Aktiebolaget SCA* [2012] EWCA Civ 1413 [22] (Moore-Bick LJ).

33 JH Baker, 'The Three Languages of the Common Law' (1997) 43 McGill LJ 5, 5.

34 Ibid. 7.

35 *United Australia Ltd v Barclays Bank Ltd* [1941] AC 1 (HL) 29 (Lord Atkin); Steve Hedley, 'Implied Contract and Restitution' [2004] CLJ 435, 437.

trust.[36] If we conclude that this or that legal concept is *not* fictitious, we can, just by removing the epithet, avoid an argument.

2.3 THE SOLUTION: HARD AND SOFT FICTIONS

The obvious solution to the problem of definition is to suggest a good definition. But in practice that would do no more than add another definition to the pool. It is likely to fare no better than its predecessors and only exacerbate the problem.

The solution proposed here is unique because it takes a more inclusive, yet precise, approach. By offering two original definitions – one 'Hard', one 'Soft' – I aim to make peace between conflicting definitions, without giving up precision. Instead of endlessly arguing about the correct standard, let us recognise two standards of fiction. It is hoped that this solution will be more widely accepted, more likely to take root and end the uncertainty.

Before I commence, one further point needs clarification. The new definition promoted in these pages, including as it does the distinction between Hard and Soft Fictions, does not invalidate alternative definitions. As a matter of English usage, anything which is untrue or fabricated may be called fictitious. The word is flexible enough to sustain any definition which contains invention as an element. The conclusion of this inquiry is not, say, that Bentham's or Fuller's definition is wrong, but that the proposed twin definition is a better analytical tool.

2.4 DO LEGAL FICTIONS EXIST?

The legal fiction is so unsettled a concept that even its existence has been questioned. The first challenge I am called upon to meet, therefore, is to demonstrate that legal fictions exist. Ironic as it may be to prove that fictions are real, and disquieting to the author to doubt the existence of his subject matter, the fragility of the concept must be acknowledged – and dealt with.

The argument against the existence of legal fictions, in a nutshell, is that all law is fictitious and therefore there is no distinction between so-called fictions and the rest of the law. It is the argument from artificiality of law. Below I discuss several intellectual assaults on the legal fiction, each of which is inspired by the argument from artificiality, but in different ways and to different extents. I conclude that these assaults on the fiction do restrict the scope of the concept, but do not destroy its core: some ground is lost to the

36 Swadling (n 19).

assaulting forces, but the citadel holds on. And so the answer to the paradoxical heading of this Section 2.4 is yes, legal fictions exist.

2.4.1 *Vaihinger's Assault*

In his 1911 book, *The Philosophy of As-If*, Professor Hans Vaihinger called for a wholesale re-assessment of fiction in human thought.[37] The German philosopher was not primarily concerned with law. Indeed, Fuller called his 'treatment of the legal fiction exceedingly superficial'.[38] Nevertheless, Vaihinger's radical thesis, if accepted, might have the consequence of expanding the definition of fiction to include – worryingly – all the law.[39]

Vaihinger's thesis, as applied to law by Fuller,[40] may be summarised as follows. All branches of knowledge, including the exact sciences, rely on fictions. Economists assume a market of rational actors and mathematicians use imaginary numbers. Vaihinger attributes this universal reliance on fiction to the fact that fiction is essential to reasoning.[41] We reason by analogy, induction and assimilation – rarely by deduction. When presented with a new thing, we tame it by matching it to something familiar. In this way, we misdescribe the facts and make inexact analogies in order to fit a new case into our existing system of thought.

The writ system we looked at in the previous chapter was, in its own way, a perfect illustration of Vaihinger's theory. New facts had to be shoehorned into existing forms – actually inserted into templates – often by way of fiction. Mistaken payments, for example, were forced into the promissory writ of *assumpsit* by the mediation of the fictitious implied promise. Actions arising overseas were brought within existing procedures by misstating the locality.

The Old System was but an extreme case of a general phenomenon. Whenever a new set of facts presents itself to a lawyer, what does he do? He tries to fit it into the existing legal structures and make analogies with existing cases. Vaihinger says this is how our mind works always. He goes on to say that this process of false analogy – false because no two cases are alike – is endemic, legitimate and inescapable. The point of thinking is not to create an exact picture of reality but to *process* it. This involves oversimplification and mistranslation to familiar terms. To shun fictions is to shun reasoning. Jerome

37 Vaihinger (n 24).
38 Fuller, *Legal Fictions* (n 1) 125.
39 Vaihinger (n 24) 33–5; see also Samuel (n 11).
40 Fuller, *Legal Fictions* (n 1) 93ff.
41 See also Hamilton (n 9) 1480.

Frank, I note in passing, argued along similar lines in *Law and the Modern Mind*.[42]

The breadth of Vaihinger's assault is hard to overstate. Alf Ross said of Vaihinger that '[h]e extends the idea [of fiction] gradually to the point where everything beyond empirically given sense data is taken as fictitious'.[43] We could carry Ross's point even further: to an Idealist philosopher like Berkeley or Kant, sense data too would be fictitious.[44] Christoph Kletzer has also criticised Vaihinger's overinclusion:

> Vaihinger actually ends up arguing that nearly every concept is a fiction. In the 800 pages of his work there seems to be no linguistic construct which he thinks would not benefit from being understood as a fiction. After all he says that every abstract and every general term is a fiction. Now, since every term, even an indexical, has an element of generality, according to Vaihinger every term must have a fictional element. This, however, is clearly proving too much as this generality robs fictions of any explanatory power.[45]

Fuller had reached the same conclusion in the early 1930s: Vaihinger 'proves too much. If everything is "fiction," then the meaning of the word "fiction" has been lost, and "as if" has become simply "is". Indeed . . . if everything is fiction, then this includes Vaihinger's own philosophy.'[46]

What, then, does this mean for the definition of legal fiction? If fiction is understood as the oversimplification of reality for analytical purposes; if all constructs are fictions, surely the law as a whole is implicated. For what is the law if not an oversimplification of reality by rules and constructs that hopelessly aim to answer an infinite variety of circumstances? The law as a whole, then, is a man-made fiction.

Thankfully, lawyers are not philosophers. Even if Vaihinger is right that on some fundamental level all the law is a fiction, we are free to adopt a definition that suits our purposes. Clearly, a definition which covers the entire field has no analytical value. And so, the sting of Vaihinger's assault on fiction is this: if all reasoning involves fiction, if the law is based on fiction, if the law *is* fiction, then how do we meaningfully fish out the 'real' legal fictions from this sea of artificiality? How do we distinguish fiction from non-fiction?

42 Jerome Frank, *Law and the Modern Mind* (Bretano's 1930) 37–40.

43 Alf Ross, 'Legal Fictions' in Graham Hughes (ed), *Reason, Law, and Justice: Essays in Legal Philosophy* (University of London Press 1969) 221.

44 The Idealists believed that all perceived reality was a product of the mind: Bertrand Russell, *The Problems of Philosophy* (2nd edn, OUP 2001) 19.

45 Christoph Kletzer, 'Kelsen on Vaihinger' in LFTP, 24 fn 3.

46 Fuller, *Legal Fictions* (n 1) 123.

2.4.2 *Repelling Vaihinger's Assault*

The artificiality of the law as such must of course be conceded. Positive law is not discovered in the physical world in the same way as the laws of biology or chemistry, but is created by human beings. That said, we can – and should – distinguish between *degrees* of artificiality. There is more nuance in the world than Vaihinger allowed. Much of the disagreement between scholars arises from the fact that the word 'fiction' can be understood in more than one sense. These senses may be ranked in order of stringency – that is, as different *thresholds* for 'fiction'.

At the lowest level, meaning the lowest threshold for 'fiction', we can say that anything which does not perfectly and comprehensively reflect a particular aspect of the physical world is fictitious. According to this understanding, which is really Vaihinger's understanding, even a documentary film is fiction because no film can comprehensively and with perfect precision describe all facets of its subject matter. A threshold that is so low entails, unsurprisingly, that all the law is fictitious. If this is what we mean by 'fiction', then the argument from artificiality succeeds: all the law is artificial so either everything or nothing is fictitious.

An intermediate threshold for fiction is to say that anything which has no parallel, broadly speaking, in the physical world is fictitious. Put differently, anything that we speak of but does not exist in the physical world is fictitious. According to this understanding, corporate personality would be fictitious. It is an invention of the legal mind. In the real world, there is no entity which is independent of the people and things that make up the corporation. If this is what we mean by 'fiction', the situation is much the same; the argument from artificiality still succeeds. The law is a product of the mind; it does not exist in the physical world and so it is all artificial. Either all law is fictitious or none of it is fictitious.

A high threshold for fiction is that only things that *contradict* the physical world are fictitious. This higher standard for fiction requires more than the mere non-existence of the thing in the physical world, but an inconsistency with something that does exist – with a fact – in the physical world. Thus things which have no parallel in the physical world, like corporations, would not be fictitious. Purely legal rules such as 'Thou shalt not kill' cannot be fictitious – because they have no parallel in the physical world which is capable of contradiction. By contrast, the geographical fictions we saw in the last chapter would be fictitious – because to say that Minorca is in London contradicts the physical world. If this is what we mean by 'fiction', the argument from artificiality fails – because not all the law is fictitious. A company is not fictitious. A trust is not fictitious. Rules in general are not fictitious. Only legal statements that contradict facts in the physical world are fictitious. There is now a place for fictions.

In conclusion, the argument from artificiality, here personified by Hans Vaihinger, is effective against the low and intermediate understandings of fiction, but not the more stringent understanding, namely that fiction requires inconsistency with a fact in the physical world. In this monograph, I adhere to the stringent understanding. Hence, for our purposes, legal fictions exist.

2.4.3 *Kelsen's Assault*

If Vaihinger stands for the proposition that all legal thought is fictitious, Professor Hans Kelsen stands for the opposite extreme – that none of the law is fictitious.[47] The Austrian legal theorist granted that statements *about* the law (e.g., jurisprudential theories) could be fictitious.[48] However, as far as the law itself was concerned, it was *unable* to generate a fiction. In Kelsen's words:

> [T]he legislator – and with him everyone applying the law – does not 'think' that the matter were as such, he rather *decrees* whatever he wishes. This is how the 'matters' become actually, i.e. legally, as they are. Within his realm, the legislator is almighty, since his function rests in nothing but his ability to tie certain legal consequences to legal conditions. A fiction of the legislator would thus be as impossible as a fiction of nature itself. After all, the law could only be opposed to itself – i.e. to its own reality. This, however, would be nonsensical.[49]

According to Kelsen, the law is not, as Vaihinger believed, an inaccurate description of reality. It is not a description of reality at all – and ought not to be treated as such. It is an artificial system that has its own inherent validity or truth. Whatever was created by law would share in the general artificiality of the law and be true *as a matter of law*. It follows that legal fictions, which are created by the law, share in the general artificiality of the law; are simply true as a matter of law; and should not be contrasted with the physical world. Hence there are no legal fictions.

2.4.4 *Repelling Kelsen's Assault*

In the first place, it should be pointed out that Kelsen's conception of law as standing apart from the physical world is somewhat unrealistic. Kelsen was more philosopher than lawyer. When one descends from the world of theory to

47 Håkan Gustafsson, 'Fiction of Law' (2010) 41 Rechtstheorie 319, 345–6.

48 Kelsen (n 30) 5; Kletzer (n 45) 26.

49 Kelsen (n 30) 13.

the world of practice, such a purist worldview is difficult to sustain. Let us take the allegations that the defendant entered *vi et armis*, or that Minorca was in London, or that a woman was ordained (for the purposes of benefit of clergy). It would be rather contrived, if not downright wrong, to call these statements purely legal. To say that the location of an island is a point of law merely, and has nothing to do with the physical world, is to stretch the credulity of the most sympathetic reader. To say that ordinary words are to be understood in a non-factual sense is sophistry.[50] As Frederick Schauer said, 'legal language is not, and cannot be, entirely sui generis in all of its words'.[51] One cannot but be reminded of a certain entry from the famous proceedings of the Pickwick Club, as collated by Charles Dickens:

> THE CHAIRMAN was quite sure the honourable Pickwickian would withdraw the expression he had just made use of.
>
> MR. BLOTTON, with all possible respect for the chair, was quite sure he would not.
>
> THE CHAIRMAN felt it his imperative duty to demand of the honourable gentleman, whether he had used the expression which had just escaped him in a common sense.
>
> MR. BLOTTON had no hesitation in saying that he had not – he had used the word in its Pickwickian sense. (Hear, hear.) He was bound to acknowledge that, personally, he entertained the highest regard and esteem for the honourable gentleman; he had merely considered him a humbug in a Pickwickian point of view. (Hear, hear.)
>
> MR. PICKWICK felt much gratified by the fair, candid, and full explanation of his honourable friend. He begged it to be at once understood, that his own observations had been merely intended to bear a Pickwickian construction. (Cheers.)[52]

In the second place, Kelsen's assault is more similar to Vaihinger's than it seems. Although Vaihinger and Kelsen start from opposite extremes – all law is fiction; no law is fiction – they converge in holding all law to be artificial. Vaihinger says it is artificial because it fails to mirror reality. Kelsen says it is artificial because it is not supposed to mirror reality. It is the old argument from artificiality in a different guise. Vaihinger and Kelsen differ in that one says this artificiality means fiction; the other calls it a truth distinct from the truth of the physical world. But, of course, it is the same thing. It is like two

50 For a different rebuttal of Kelsen's theory, see Pierre JJ Olivier, *Legal Fictions in Practice and Legal Science* (Rotterdam University Press 1975) 55–7.

51 Schauer (n 9) 126.

52 Charles Dickens, *The Pickwick Papers* (James Kinsley ed, OUP 1986) 5–6; see also Fuller, *Legal Fictions* (n 1) 21.

men arguing whether *Jane Eyre* is fictitious or exists only in an imaginary world. As the French say, *les extrêmes se touchent* – the extremes meet.

So we return to the same old argument, but now we can attach labels to the possibilities. Either all law is fictitious (as Vaihinger says) or no law is fictitious (as Kelsen says). In either case, how do we isolate legal fictions so as to give them some sensible meaning?

We have already answered this question. We repel Kelsen with the same shield we used against Vaihinger. If we understand fiction as a statement which contradicts a fact in the physical world, then legal fictions are severable from the law in general. This is true even if the law as a whole is artificial in Kelsen's sense of having 'its own reality'.[53]

2.4.5 *The Linguistic Problem*

The refutation of Vaihinger and Kelsen's arguments, for what it is worth, rests on one key idea: a contradiction between words and the physical world. This idea presupposes that words have a static, preordained meaning and, further, that words inherently designate certain objects in the physical world. This set of presuppositions, which we may call 'absolute meaning' for short, may seem unproblematic to most people. After all, what else can 'Minorca is in London' mean except that the Balearic island is in the British capital? Linguists and philosophers, however, regard the assumption of absolute meaning as problematic. This requires some explanation.

It is convenient to begin with Ferdinand de Saussure, who died in 1913. This Swiss linguist is considered by many to be the father of modern linguistics. He saw language as a duality between words and the things they denote. The former he called 'signifiers' and the latter 'signifieds'. Thus the word 'dog' is a signifier whose signified is the four-legged barking mammal. What is interesting about this duality, pointed out de Saussure, is that the bond between signifier and signified is random.[54] As a matter of logic, there is no reason why the word 'dog', rather than the word 'cat', should denote the barking mammal. There is nothing particularly canine about the three letters or sound of 'dog' and nothing more feline about 'cat'. They might as well be reversed. The reason we automatically link certain signifiers with certain signifieds is social convention. This link is historically and socially contingent.[55]

53 Kelsen (n 30) 13.

54 Onomatopoeia is an exception. Words like 'sizzle' or 'drip' sound similar to what they describe. But such words are a small minority.

55 Ferdinand de Saussure, *Course in General Linguistics* (Charles Bally, Albert Sechehaye and Albert Riedlinger eds, Wade Baskin tr, McGraw-Hill 1966) 67–8.

The arbitrariness of the link between signifier and signified is relevant because it threatens the soothing assumption of absolute meaning. For if words have no inherent meaning, if they mean just what we say they mean (which is a circularity), then they can have no absolute meaning; no meaning independent of convention.

We can now bring the discussion back to fictions. The linguistic challenge to the existence of fictions is this: if the meaning of words is anyway determined by convention, pleadings such as 'Minorca is in London' have to be understood in their technical context, as the relevant community (i.e., lawyers) would have understood them. To wit, they should not be read as a rebuff to atlas-makers but as legal jargon.[56] If this is true, there is no contradiction with the physical world, which is irrelevant. Ergo legal fictions do not exist.

This linguistic challenge to the existence of fictions is reminiscent of Kelsen's argument that fictions do not exist because they are true as a matter of law, which is the obverse, as we have seen, of Vaihinger's argument that all thought is fictitious. As stated earlier, I believe that all arguments against the existence of fictions descend from one mother argument: the argument from artificiality. An answer to this argument has already been offered. Nevertheless, it is useful to respond specifically to this descendent of the mother argument, which I have called the 'linguistic argument', and may more fully be called the 'argument from lack of absolute meaning'. It raises the old problem in a new context.

2.4.6 *The Solution to the Linguistic Problem*

In his *Dialogues concerning Natural Religion*, published posthumously in 1779, David Hume delivered this riposte to philosophical scepticism:

> [T]hough a man, in a flush of humour, after intense reflection on the many contradictions and imperfections of human reason, may entirely renounce all belief and opinion; it is impossible for him to persevere in this total scepticism, or make it appear in his conduct for a few hours . . .
>
> Whether your scepticism be as absolute and sincere as you pretend, we shall learn by and by, when the company breaks up: We shall then see, whether you go out at the door or the window; and whether you really doubt, if your body has gravity, or can be injured by its fall.[57]

[56] See e.g., Pierluigi Chiassoni, *Interpretation without Truth* (Springer 2019) 194–5; though Chiassoni does not deny fictions on this account.

[57] Dorothy Coleman (ed), *Hume: Dialogues Concerning Natural Religion* (CUP 2007) 8. The order of the paragraphs has been reversed.

This Scotsman, unusual among philosophers as much for good humour as for lucidity of expression, exposed the flaw of any hard scepticism – it is logically consistent but unsustainable. The same applies to scepticism of the linguistic kind. It may be possible to argue that words have no objective meaning, but it is not possible to *act* accordingly. Whenever we write or converse, we assume that words have the meaning ascribed to them by convention. We assume the *Oxford English Dictionary*. No sophisticated communication would be possible without this assumption. Indeed, scepticism itself cannot be expressed without resort to the very thing it denies.

And so, if any use of language, not least this book, *legitimately and unavoidably* assumes the entire body of linguistic conventions; it follows that this assumption applies to fictions. We cannot selectively apply scepticism only to fictions. 'Cats are deemed to be dogs' should be given its conventional meaning. There is no reason suddenly to depart from conventional meaning when we see a fiction. We cannot explain away the contradiction with the physical world by saying that words have no absolute meaning.

Now it is true that language contains some specialist terms. For example, the word 'consideration' has a legal meaning, which is different from its ordinary meaning. However, this specialist meaning *is part of the body of linguistic conventions*. It does not lie outside or disprove it – otherwise lawyers would not understand each other. Indeed, the *OED* (to take one example) has a legal definition for consideration.[58] The upshot is that a word should be understood in its ordinary sense unless it has a recognised technical meaning in a given context.

It would be far-fetched to suggest that the words in 'Cats are deemed to be dogs' or 'Minorca is in London' have some specialist legal meaning – that 'dog' in this context does not mean dog. I have already quoted Frederick Schauer's observation that 'legal language is not, and cannot be, entirely sui generis in all of its words'.[59] While there are some technical terms (like consideration), lawyers must concede that their language is capable of contradicting the physical world. Hence legal fictions exist – notwithstanding the linguistic problem.

2.4.7 *Fictions and Rules*

Now that I have carved out a place for fictions within the artificiality of the law, I have to deal with subtler challenges to the concept of legal fiction. These relate to the relationship between fictions and rules.

58 JA Simpson and ESC Weiner (eds), *The Oxford English Dictionary*, vol III (2nd edn, Clarendon Press 1989) 769.

59 Schauer (n 9) 126.

2.4.7.1 Can a Rule Be Fictitious?

Let us take the rule that 'Cats are deemed to be dogs for the purposes of pet tax'. It is obviously made up, but seems to me plausible enough as a legal rule. Does this rule represent (or contain) a legal fiction?

Sir John Baker says it does not. In *The Law's Two Bodies*, Baker suggests that so-called fictions often do not make claims about facts but about the legal treatment of these facts.[60] This treatment, Kenneth Campbell agrees, is but a rule with no truth value.[61] And so, if we say that 'Cats are deemed to be dogs for the purposes of pet tax', we are not saying that cats *are* dogs, but only that cats are *treated like* dogs in relation to pet tax.[62] In what sense is this false? It cannot be factually false because it is a statement about the law, not about cats. In Sir John's own words:

> Rules of law cannot be true or false in the factual sense . . . lawyers have often used metaphorical language to describe abstract concepts. For example, husband and wife were deemed to be one person in law, a monk was treated as becoming civilly dead on profession, an abbot and his monks had a corporate legal personality distinct from that of the individuals (who were legally dead), acts of parliament were deemed to have been made on the first day of the session, and so forth. These are often said to be fictions. But they are not really so.[63]

To borrow an example from Fuller,[64] the German Civil Code once provided that '[a]n illegitimate child and its father are not deemed to be related'.[65] Baker would say that to object to this rule on the basis that father and child are biologically related is to miss the point. The law is not saying they are unrelated *in fact*, but that they are unrelated *in the eyes of the law*.

While Baker's view is certainly persuasive, I argue that the better view is that rules of law *can* be fictitious in certain circumstances. Let us reconsider the above examples. If the law treats father and child as unrelated, is this treatment not fictitious in that the law treats them as what they are not? If an Act of Parliament is passed on Friday but is treated as having passed on Monday, is this not a contradiction of reality? And to return to the initial question, if a cat is treated as a dog, is this not a fictitious treatment? There is no relevant difference between treating Minorca as being in London and treating cats as

60 LTB, 45–6.
61 Kenneth Campbell, 'Fulleron Legal Fictions' (1983) 2 Law and Philosophy 339, 351.
62 LTB, 45–6.
63 Ibid. 44 (references omitted).
64 Fuller, *Legal Fictions* (n 1) 30.
65 Formerly BGB §1890.

dogs. The fiction lies precisely in the false treatment: a fact in the physical world is treated as if it is otherwise. This contradiction with reality constitutes a legal fiction.[66] The fact that it forms part of a rule is nothing to the purpose. Indeed, the most notorious fictions, such as geographical fictions, were ultimately rules of law – namely that the location (or whatever) was non-traversable. If we accept that Minorca in London is a fiction (and Baker does),[67] we must also accept that rules can be fictitious and that a rule deeming cats to be dogs is fictitious (or, at least, contains a fiction).[68] In conclusion, a rule of law may be fictitious to the extent that it contradicts a fact.

It may be asked, apropos of this conclusion, whether a rule of law that contradicts another rule of law (rather than a fact) is a legal fiction. If the stringent understanding of fictions advocated above is accepted, the answer is no. Only a contradiction with the physical world can generate a fiction. If two legal rules contradict each other, there is no 'true' or 'false' – because there is no external standard by which to validate or falsify them. There is only a logical inconsistency.

2.4.7.2 Can a Rule Be Fictitious If It Can Be Restated without Resort to Fiction?

It was argued in the previous section that a rule may be fictitious to the extent that it contradicts a fact. But what if the contradiction (i.e., the fiction) can be avoided by way of simple rewording? In such rewording, the fiction disappears but the substance of the rule is unaffected. For example, the rule that 'Cats are deemed to be dogs for the purposes of pet tax' can be rewritten as 'pet tax applies equally to dogs and cats'. The latter formulation cannot be faulted for any contradiction with the physical world. In the American case of *Tyler v Judges of the Court of Registration* (1900), Holmes CJ said:

> [A] ship is not a person. It cannot do a wrong or make a contract. To say that a ship has committed a tort is merely a shorthand way of saying that you have decided to deal with it as if it had committed one, because some man has committed one in fact . . . The contrary view would indicate that you really believed the fiction that a vessel had an independent personality.[69]

The question we need to answer is whether this susceptibility of certain fictitious rules to elimination by re-formulation means these rules are not

66 Subject, of course, to other conditions discussed below.

67 LTB, 33.

68 Fuller reaches the same conclusion by a different route: Fuller, *Legal Fictions* (n 1) 33.

69 175 Mass 71, 77, 55 NE 812, 814 (Massachusetts SC 1900).

fictions, properly speaking. Are these so-to-speak 'avoidable fictions' purely semantic rather than substantive?

Hölder, Eggens and Esser answered the question in the affirmative. For them, fictitious rules were but shorthand or convenient formulations: 'What we usually accept as fictions are mere forms of expression, methods of cross-reference, equalisation.'[70] In the same vein, Kelsen believed that so-called legislative fictions were no more than abbreviations.[71] For to say that 'Cats are deemed to be dogs' is simply to enjoin equal treatment of dogs and cats. The rule, thus understood, does no violence to the physical world. The 'fiction' is not a matter of law, but of language, of phraseology.[72]

Alf Ross put the case against recognising avoidable fictions as true fictions at its most convincing:

> To 'pretend' that A is B is merely an odd way of expressing the thought that, for the purposes of law, A is to be treated as subject to the same rules as apply to B. The oddity is thus exclusively of a linguistic, not a logical, kind . . . it is meaningless to talk of a 'fiction' in this context. . . . There is no falsehood of any kind involved in saying that in a certain context women are to be treated according to the same rules as men.[73]

In my view, this refusal to recognise avoidable fictions as true fictions is misconceived. Ross is correct to say that there is no falsehood in saying that women are to be treated like men. But that is not what the rule under consideration says. The rule under consideration says that women *are* men ('A is B'). The two rules may have the same effect, but they are not the same rule.

As Pierre Olivier cogently argues, the fact that we can arrive at the same outcome by two different legal techniques – one which contradicts reality on its face and another which does not – does not mean the two techniques are the same.[74] Just because I can arrive at the same destination by two routes does not mean the routes are identical. One may be fictitious and the other may not be. To paraphrase Olivier, 'It is fatuous to argue that because the same object can be achieved by the [re-formulation] and the fiction, the fictions we use are not fictions but [re-formulations].'[75]

70 Olivier (n 50) 55.
71 Kelsen (n 30) 10.
72 Olivier (n 50) 52.
73 Ross (n 43) 223.
74 Olivier (n 50) 56. Olivier appears to suggest on p 81 that a deeming provision is not a fiction, but a close reading of pp 56 and 61–2 suggests otherwise (i.e., that Olivier was not thinking of deeming provisions on p 81).
75 Ibid.

Thus the answer to the question posed (Can a rule be fictitious if it can be restated without resort to fiction?) is yes.

The sceptic may retort that my argument, even if valid, is too formalistic. If the proposition 'Cats are deemed to be dogs for the purposes of pet tax' is a fiction but the proposition 'pet tax applies equally to dogs and cats' is not a fiction, does it matter terribly whether something is a fiction? What is the significance of this categorisation when nobody is misled and the facts are not in dispute?

My answer is that it matters a great deal. If we do not strictly distinguish between propositions that contradict reality and propositions that agree with reality, we give up on truth altogether. Once it is conceded that 'Cats are deemed to be dogs' is not a fiction because it is similar to the non-fictitious 'Cats and dogs are treated equally', we lose the right to challenge the most hair-raising contradictions with the physical world. On what ground would English law have abolished geographical fictions, ejectment or quasi-contract? They were all similar to non-fictitious rules ('Minorca is merely treated as being in London for this purpose' etc.)? Why did the grammatical construction matter if everyone who mattered knew the true position? Well, it mattered because those propositions were *false*. If we give up on the simple idea of truth, we surrender so much more – arguably everything.

It is not pedantic or formalistic to insist on the difference between truth and falsehood. It is the keystone of any rigorous approach. For this reason, it is asserted that a rule may be fictitious even if it can be re-formulated in a non-fictitious manner.

2.4.7.3 Is There a Difference between Assertive and Assumptive Fictions?

Lon Fuller distinguishes between two forms of fiction. The assumptive form 'carried a grammatical acknowledgement of its falsity'.[76] Fuller offers as an example the 'as if' construction but deeming provisions would do just as well. 'Cats are to be treated as if they are dogs' or 'Cats are deemed to be dogs' are assumptive fictions. The assertive fiction, by contrast, 'appeared as a statement of fact; its fictitious character was apparent only to the initiate'.[77] Old Fictions were almost invariably of the assertive kind. The defendant was alleged to have entered with force and arms. A trespass was alleged to have occurred in Middlesex. The record made no concession of the falsity of the allegation.

[76] Fuller, *Legal Fictions* (n 1) 36.
[77] Ibid.

Only one initiated into the mysteries of the Old System would know that these statements were not to be taken at face value.

There has therefore been a tendency in some quarters to say that assumptive fictions are not contrary to fact. This is supposedly because they contain an admission of the inconsistency. According to this view, to *deem* cats to be dogs is not a fiction, but to *allege* that cats *are* dogs is a fiction – because only the latter says anything about reality. This tendency has the respectability of old age. In the second century, Gaius 'condemned the kind of fiction which required a lawyer to assert that green was red, but he allowed that the law could resolve to treat green as though green were red'.[78] In his *Institutes*, the Roman jurist says the following of a manifest thief (namely a thief caught in the act):

> The fact that the statute enacts that in [other cases] there is manifest theft causes some writers to say that theft may be manifest by statute or in fact. . . . But the truth is that manifest theft means manifest in fact; for statute can no more turn a thief who is not manifest into a manifest thief than it can turn into a thief one who is not a thief at all, or into an adulterer or homicide one who is neither. . . . What statute can do is simply this: it can make a man liable to a penalty *as if* he had committed theft.[79]

Gaius makes an important distinction between facts and the legal consequence of these facts. However, Fuller rejects the idea that there is any relevant difference between assumptive and assertive fictions:

> It might seem at first glance that we were dealing here with something very fundamental. Indeed, it might be argued that an assumptive fiction (an 'as if' fiction) is not a fiction at all. . . . Yet a closer examination will show that the distinction is one of form merely. The 'supposing that' or 'as if' construction in the assumptive fiction only constitutes a grammatical concession of that which is known anyway, namely, that the statement is false. When we are dealing with statements which are known to be false it is a matter of indifference whether the author adopts a grammatical construction which concedes this falsity, or makes his statement in the form of a statement of fact.[80]

I accept Fuller's argument wholeheartedly. The fiction lies in the false treatment of facts as what they are not. It does not matter if the language of the fiction proclaims or conceals this false treatment.

78 Birks (n 19) 99.

79 *Institutes of Gaius* 3.194; translation from Francis de Zulueta, *The Institutes of Gaius*, vol II (Clarendon Press 1953) 217.

80 Fuller, *Legal Fictions* (n 1) 37.

For the avoidance of doubt, my argument is not that an assumptive formulation and an assertive formulation which have the same effect are actually the same rule. Such a proposition would contradict the previous section. The argument is that they are two separate rules, but both may be fictitious.

2.4.8 *Fictions and Counterfactuals*

Having discussed arguments against the existence of fictions, and then the interplay between fictions and rules, we now come to the relationship between fictions and counterfactuals. A counterfactual, generally defined, is a statement contrary to fact – for example, 'Cats are deemed to be dogs.' Such simple counterfactuals are capable of being fictions, insofar as they contain a contradiction with the physical world. There is nothing new here. The fact that a statement is a counterfactual is neither here nor there. In fact, virtually every fiction is a counterfactual in this sense.

But there is a special kind of counterfactual, which is more problematic. This is the hypothetical counterfactual. For example, 'Had I not missed the bus, I would have made the meeting.' The hypothetical counterfactual is still a statement contrary to fact, but it is a special case of the general definition in that the statement is a conditional supposition. Hypothetical counterfactuals are common in the law. Every negligence case involves one, explicitly or implicitly. A claimant suing in negligence always has to prove, on the balance of probabilities, that the damage would not have occurred had the defendant discharged the duty of care.[81] To answer this question, we need to imagine that the defendant had not been careless and predict what would have happened. This is a hypothetical counterfactual. The interesting question for us is: is this a fiction?

Our gut reaction is probably to say no. But it is not obvious why the answer should be no. Why are counterfactuals in general capable of being fictitious, but hypothetical counterfactuals are not? When entertaining a hypothetical counterfactual, do we not deliberately assume a contradiction with the facts of the physical world? Acts of negligence, like furious driving or selling poisonous food, are facts in the physical world. When knowingly denied, they usually generate a fiction. Why not here?

The reason that hypothetical counterfactuals are not fictions is that they are an attempt to establish what would *really* have happened under different circumstances. They are about discovering facts in the physical world. There

[81] *McWilliams v Sir William Arrol & Co Ltd* [1962] 1 WLR 295 (HL) 301–3 (Viscount Simonds), 305–6 (Lord Reid).

is no falsehood (i.e., there is no contradiction with the physical world) in asking what I would have done, had I missed the bus. It is a bona fide factual inquiry about the physical world. It is categorically different from the undoubted fictions we have encountered. Minorca would not have been in London had the defendant acted differently. In the case, there was no question of it. Nor was Minorca in London a bona fide geographical inquiry. It was not an inquiry of any kind. It was a plain contradiction with the physical world.

In common parlance, too, it is not 'false' to say 'I would have enjoyed the party had I been there.' It is merely a judgement as to what would have happened in the physical world under different circumstances. Hypothetical counterfactuals are not fictions.

2.4.9 *Conclusion*

We began Section 2.4 by posing a life-or-death question for this book: whether the legal fiction exists. In defending the fiction from critics of various colours, it has been argued that the legal fiction does exist in the sense that it contradicts a fact in the physical world. This contradiction often takes the form of falsely treating a fact as what it is not. It is irrelevant that the contradiction is part of a rule, or can be avoided by rewording, or is grammatically acknowledged, or is described as a counterfactual. This is subject to the reservation that hypothetical counterfactuals are not fictions.

2.5 OVERVIEW OF EXISTING DEFINITIONS

Now that we have a reasoned basis for the assumption that our subject matter exists, it is necessary to give it precise shape. All we know at present is that legal fictions contradict the physical world in some sense. In this section, I critically survey existing definitions of legal fiction, and related commentary, with a view to refining the definition. We will find, in Fuller's analysis, the seed of the distinction between Hard and Soft Fictions.

2.5.1 *Plain and Ordinary Meaning*

In a legal context, words such as 'consideration' or 'receiver' have assumed a technical meaning, quite distinct from their ordinary English sense. They have, to borrow a phrase from the tort of passing-off, 'acquired a secondary meaning'.[82] This has not been the fate of the word 'fiction'. Indeed, the subject of our inquiry has no definition in case law or statute and commentators fundamentally disagree on its scope. It is used loosely and inconsistently, within the bounds of its lay meaning.

We therefore begin with the plain and ordinary meaning of the word. *Webster's Dictionary* relevantly defines 'fiction' as 'an intentional fabrication; a convenient assumption that overlooks known facts in order to achieve an immediate goal'.[83] This definition has three core elements: a *falsehood*, which is *intentional* (not a mistake) and *known to be false* (since it 'overlooks known facts').

The *Oxford English Dictionary* generally renders 'fiction' as something 'imaginatively invented; feigned existence, event or state of things; invention as opposed to fact'; and more specifically for our purposes as 'A supposition known to be at variance with fact, but conventionally accepted for some reason of practical convenience, conformity with traditional usage, decorum or the like.'[84] This definition displays the aforementioned core elements of *falsity* and *consciousness* thereof. It omits *intention*, but on reflection, intention is implicit: if a statement is known to be false, its falsity must be intentional.

Kenneth Campbell rightly points out that a statement may be known to be false by some and not others.[85] For example, a party may lead false evidence to mislead the court. To avoid doubt, consciousness henceforth shall mean that the falsity of the statement is shared by the court, the lawyers and the wider legal community, though not necessarily the litigants themselves (who may not be versed in the law or aware of the legal niceties of their case).

I have no interest in developing a definition that falls outside the dictionary definition. My object is precision. What is more, I do not wish to risk the irony of the definition itself being fictitious. I will, therefore, throughout this inquiry, preserve the core elements of the dictionary definition: falsity and consciousness.

The *OED* also provides a legal definition: 'Chiefly applied to those feigned statements of fact which the practice of the courts authorized to be alleged by a plaintiff in order to bring his case within the scope of the law or the jurisdiction of the court, and which the defendant was not allowed to disprove.'[86] *Webster's* technical definition is to the same effect.[87] Such

[82] *Fage UK Ltd v Chobani UK Ltd* [2014] EWCA Civ 5, [2014] ETMR 26 [62] (Kitchin LJ); *Knight v Beyond Properties Pty Ltd* [2007] EWHC 1251 (Ch), [2007] FSR 34 [11] (David Richards J).

[83] Philip Babcock Gove (ed), *Webster's Third International Dictionary of the English Language Unabridged* (Könemann 1993) 844.

[84] Simpson and Weiner (n 58) vol V, 872.

[85] Campbell (n 61) 342.

[86] Simpson and Weiner (n 58) vol V, 872.

[87] Gove (n 83) 844.

procedural definitions seem insufficient. Even under the Old System, not all legal fictions functioned as the non-traversable pleading alluded to in the definition. In a world bereft of formal pleading, it is anachronistic. The definition must be broader than an incontestable pleading.

Specialist dictionaries may offer better legal definitions. *Black's Law Dictionary* speaks of 'an assumption that something is true even though it may not be true, made [especially] in judicial reasoning to alter how a legal rule operates'.[88] Here consciousness is missing. A definition which fails to separate mistakes and lies from fictions is of little analytical value.

Webster's Law Dictionary has 'a court's assumption of a fact known to be untrue in order to fit a case into a category recognized by the law, so that relief can be granted and justice done' and also 'any assumption contrary to fact that is made by the law for reasons of policy or practicality'.[89] Both falsity and consciousness are present, but supplemented by motives and outcome. There is a long tradition of defining fiction by its use or objective dating back to the Roman jurisconsults.[90] It seems unwise to define fictions by their motivations or results. The motivation of judges is often not obvious and the justice of the result may be debatable. If we can define fictions by reference to what they are, and avoid an inquiry into what caused them or what they cause, we should do so.[91] It does not follow that we must be blind to the causes or results of fictions. Indeed, these will be evaluated in subsequent chapters. The point here is that one's view of the justification of a fiction is different from the identification of it. Evaluation is distinct from definition and definition must precede evaluation.

In conclusion, having replaced the dictionaries, we are left with two elements: falsity and consciousness.

2.5.2 *Academic Definitions*

2.5.2.1 Milestones in Anglo-American Thought

Alf Ross claimed that '[t]he legal literature for the most part lacks any explicit definition of fiction'.[92] As Pierre Olivier noted several years later, this was by no

88 Henry Campbell Black, *Black's Law Dictionary* (Bryan A Garner ed, 10th edn, West Group 2000) 1031.

89 James Edward Clapp, *Webster's Dictionary of the Law* (Random House 2000) 267.

90 Olivier (n 50) 9.

91 Indeed, motives are not generally the subject of judicial inquiry in English private law: *Williams v Carwardine* (1833) 4 B & Ad 621, 110 ER 590 (KB) 591 (Patteson J); see also Olivier (n 50) 35.

92 Ross (n 43) 221.

means a new phenomenon: 'Roman jurists never discussed the nature of, or endeavoured to explain or define the legal fiction.'[93] However, as the following whistle-stop tour of academic definitions will show, Ross's was an unduly harsh verdict.

Olivier's criticism of the scholarship was more particular: 'Anglo-American writers do not materially contribute towards a better insight into the structure of the fiction.'[94] This is an uncharitable judgement, but not an incorrect one. This state of affairs is, to my mind, attributable to the pragmatic character of English law. Common lawyers have never had a taste for philosophy. Legal historian Frederick Pollock has said so more than once:

> English lawyers have never taken dogmatic theories of any kind much to heart. Our doctrines get settled either by a gradual process of semi-conscious consent worked out in the solution of particular cases, or by the development, in the same manner, of conflicting tendencies in professional and judicial opinion until at last a decisive practical choice is called for.[95]
>
> No one who is familiar with the English judicial mind will be surprised at the scantiness of positive utterances on a question of this high order of generality.[96]
>
> [M]ediaeval English lawyers were very like their descendants, and would not commit themselves on an abstract question in a general form if they could help it.[97]

Be that as it may, I am concerned here with English private law and accordingly focus on the development of the fiction concept in the common law world.

Writing in the 1590s, Sir Henry Finch proposed, perhaps for the first time in English legal circles, a definition for the now-pervasive fiction: 'A fained construction, which we call a fiction in law, is when in a similitudinary sort the law construeth a thing otherwise than it is.'[98] The examples which follow indicate that presumptions and deeming provisions were included in the definition. Finch could be criticised for failing to distinguish between fiction and error, but such criticism would probably be unjust because 'feigned' implies a deliberate falsification, and hence consciousness, rather than error. Also, the fact that 'the law', as a system, accepts the feigned construction

93 Olivier (n 50) 12.

94 Ibid. 59.

95 Frederick Pollock, 'Has the Common Law Received the Fiction Theory of Corporations?' (1911) 27 LQR 219, 219.

96 Ibid. 221.

97 Ibid. 233.

98 LTB, 41 fn 30, citing Henry Finch, *Law, or a Discourse Thereof* (1759) 66–73.

suggests that no deception is involved, but this is less clear. This is a rudimentary definition, which captures falsity, but fails to adequately pin down the crucial element of consciousness.

In his famous *Commentary upon Littleton*, published in 1628, Sir Edward Coke informs us that '[a] . . . fiction of law shall never worke a wrong or charge to a third person'.[99] In his report of *Mary Portington's Case* (1613), which concerned the fiction of common recovery, Coke pointed out that equity always exists in a fiction of law.[100] Blackstone likewise said, '[T]his maxim is ever invariably observed, that no fiction shall extend to work an injury.'[101] Sir Matthew Hale defended fictions on the same basis, 'For they are but expedients without injuring anybody.'[102] Michael Lobban found numerous cases corroborating this precept.[103] It may be supposed that equity, in the sense of justice, was seen as integral to the fiction.

The better view is that the law refused to *apply* a fiction where it would work an injustice, not that a fiction ceased to be one if its application in a particular case would be unjust. This is consistent with the principle of not defining fictions by their motivation or result.

Bentham gave us at least three definitions, in different parts of his *oeuvre*, all of which captured both falsity and consciousness: 'By fiction . . . understand a false assertion of the privileged kind, and which, though acknowledged to be false, is . . . acted upon, as if true'; more concisely, 'an assumed fact notoriously false'; or more polemically, 'a wilful falsehood, having for its object the stealing legislative power, by and for hands which could not, or durst not, openly claim it'.[104] This last deprecatory definition may with all propriety be applied to the common recovery, which, as I noted in the previous chapter, knowingly subverted the statute *De Donis*. Yet, as a generalisation, it is not true that a legal fiction is, in essence, a usurpation of legislative power. To say so would be to deny the freedom of the common law to develop without legislative sanction. So long as the fiction in question does not interfere with an enactment, the constitutional order is not undone.

99 Co Litt 150a.

100 'Note, reader, *semper in fictione juris subsistit aequitas*': *Mary Portington's Case* (1613) 10 Co Rep 35b (KB) 40. For this and more, see LTB, 55 fn 83.

101 3 Bl Comm 43.

102 Matthew Hale, 'A Disquisition Touching the Jurisdiction of the Common Law and Courts of Admiralty . . . ' in MJ Prichard and DEC Yale (eds), *Hale and Fleetwood on Admiralty Jurisdiction*, vol 108 (Selden Society 1993) 24.

103 Michael Lobban, 'Legal Fictions before the Age of Reform' in LFTP, 210–12.

104 Charles Kay Ogden and Jeremy Bentham, *Bentham's Theory of Fictions* (Routledge 2013) cxvi; C Varga and J Szájer, 'Presumption and Fiction: Means of Legal Technique' [1988] Archiv für Rechts- und Sozialphilosophie 168, 174; Jeremy Bentham, *The Works of Jeremy Bentham*, vol 1 (John Bowring ed, William Tait 1843) 243.

John Austin's definition used different words to express the recurring elements of falsity and consciousness: 'feigning or assuming, "that something that obviously *was*, was *not*; or that something that obviously was *not*, *was*"'.[105]

In *Ancient Law*, first published in 1861, Sir Henry Maine considered legal fictions in the context of social evolution. His treatment of the subject is now famous and looks at the device from a new angle: '[A]ny assumption which conceals, or affects to conceal, the fact that a rule of law has undergone alteration its letter remaining unchanged, its operation being modified. … The fact is … that the law has wholly changed; the fiction is that it remains what it always was.'[106]

For Maine, the key points were legal change and concealment. This definition, while apposite to his analysis of the fiction as a means by which gaps between law and social development can be bridged, is at once too wide and too narrow for our purposes. It is too wide because the 'assumption' is not explicitly false; too narrow because it requires attempted or actual deceit. Few would disagree that it was a fiction for Lord Mansfield to accept that the island of Minorca lay in the parish of St Mary le Bow in London.[107] Yet it is difficult to see how such a blatant fiction could 'conceal, or affect to conceal' anything. The fiction was, to borrow from Lon Fuller, 'a plain falsehood, rendered harmless by its utter incapacity to deceive'.[108] The transparency of the English fictions belies Maine's view that the fiction was somehow a subterfuge – not simply because it was an ineffective subterfuge, but because it was never intended to be one. As Austin said, 'Can it be conceited for a moment, by any reasonable person, that fines and [common] recoveries … ever deceived anybody, or were intended to deceive?'[109] SFC Milsom made the same point, with wonted perspicacity: '[W]ho was to be deceived? Probably nobody. The aim of fictions … is not deception; it is to keep records straight.'[110] Whatever may be said of the fiction, deceitful it is not. For this reason, Maine's element of concealment should not form part of my definition.[111]

In 1907, Roscoe Pound conflated legal fictions with 'spurious interpretation', a practice 'which has done its legitimate work' in a pre-legislative era,

105 John Austin, *Lectures on Jurisprudence or the Philosophy of Positive Law*, vol II (Robert Campbell ed, 5th edn, John Murray 1885) 609.

106 Henry Sumner Maine, *Ancient Law* (first published in 1861, Murray 1930) 32–3.

107 *Mostyn v Fabrigas* (1775) 1 Cowp 161, 98 ER 1021 (KB) 1030–2.

108 Fuller, *Legal Fictions* (n 1) 5; see also ibid. 6.

109 Austin (n 107) 609.

110 SFC Milsom, 'Trespass from Henry III to Edward III: Part I General Writs' (1958) 74 LQR 195, 223.

111 Cf Ross (n 43) 217–18.

but was 'unnecessary and unsuited to a developed system of law'.[112] Spurious interpretation is to 'make, unmake, or remake, and not merely to discover'.[113] In a modern era of legislation, so goes the argument, courts have no need of making or unmaking law.

Regardless of the relative merits of Parliament and judges as lawmakers, it is respectfully submitted that Pound misapprehends the fiction. A *spurious* interpretation is an interpretation which *purports* to be true. It is an argument which fails, or ought not, to convince. Fictions, by contrast, do not purport to be true and fail to convince: their falsity is writ large. The plot of *Wuthering Heights* is not spurious; it is fictitious. That the East Indies are in Islington[114] is not a spurious pleading; it is a fiction.

2.5.2.2 *Lon Fulle*r

During the Great Depression, Professor Lon Fuller published a series of journal articles, really one article in three parts, all under the name 'Legal Fictions'.[115] This trilogy of 1930–1 has become the leading work – surely the most cited work – on legal fictions in the English-speaking world, if not beyond it.[116] One will be hard-pressed to find a work dealing with the concept of legal fiction that does not mention Fuller. In 1967, the articles were re-published in book form, also titled *Legal Fictions*, with an introduction by Fuller and minor amendments. In this monograph, the book is regarded as authoritative and all references to Fuller are to the book.

One need not be interested in legal theory to enjoy Fuller's *Legal Fictions*. To the layman, it is fluent, accessible and persuasive. To the theorist, it is original and insightful. Fuller relies to his advantage on eye-opening analogies. He adds much subtlety and sophistication to an old subject, especially as regards the motives for fictions. Fuller performs the dual service of bringing fictions into the modern world and opening them to a larger audience.

Having said that, the work suffers from a certain disorganisation of thought. There seems to be no common thread as the reader is left with the task of reconciling disjointed ideas. The last chapter is really a commentary on Vaihinger, and it is not clear to what extent Fuller adopts

112 Roscoe Pound, 'Spurious Interpretation' (1907) 7 Columbia LR 379, 382–3.

113 Ibid. 382.

114 Hale (n 102) 51.

115 LL Fuller, 'Legal Fictions' (1930) 25 Illinois LR 363; LL Fuller, 'Legal Fictions' (1930) 25 Illinois LR 513; LL Fuller, 'Legal Fictions' (1930) 25 Illinois LR 877.

116 See e.g., Olivier (n 50) 34–5; Smith (n 21) 1466; Karen Petroski, 'Legal Fictions and the Limits of Legal Language' in LFTP, 132–4 and the references therein.

Vaihinger's far-reaching philosophy. This impressive, if unfocussed, work has no conclusion and no clear thesis. There is a section entitled 'Conclusion',[117] but it is a cryptic reflection on a potential response to Vaihinger. In the end, Fuller offers not a general theory of fictions but a set of useful ideas. It is hard to disagree with Kenneth Campbell's assessment: 'It is difficult to detect an overall thesis. Like Fuller's more famous jurisprudential production, *The Morality of Law*, this book has to be treated as presenting not a full-blown theory, but a series of aperçus. Many of these do not bear examination. Some, however, do.'[118] The following paragraphs will vindicate the last two sentences.

For the present, we are concerned only with Fuller's definition of legal fiction: 'A fiction is either, (1) a statement propounded with a complete or partial consciousness of its falsity, or (2) a false statement recognized as having utility.'[119] The limbs of the definition, it should be stressed, are alternative rather than cumulative. This bipartite definition has proved to be Fuller's most controversial contribution to the debate on fictions. Fuller himself owned that it 'seems . . . to embrace two entirely discordant elements'.[120] His most strident critic was Pierre Olivier, who, before proceeding to demolish the definition, noted it was 'not a happy one'.[121]

2.5.2.2.1 THE FIRST LIMB OF FULLER'S DEFINITION: 'A STATEMENT PROPOUNDED WITH A COMPLETE OR PARTIAL CONSCIOUSNESS OF ITS FALSITY' Olivier argues it was 'not correct' to say that a statement could be propounded with only partial consciousness of its falsity.[122] One is either aware that a statement is false or one is not so aware.[123] For Olivier, there is no grey area, and thus Fuller's first limb is nonsensical. For Fuller, there plainly is a grey area:

> The line between belief and disbelief is frequently blurred. The use of the word 'fiction' does not always imply that the author of the statement positively disbelieved it. It may rather imply the opinion that the author of the statement in question was . . . aware of its inadequacy or partial untruth, although he may have believed it in the sense that he could think of no better way of expressing the idea he had in mind. We have a fiction, then, when the author

117 Fuller, *Legal Fictions* (n 1) 135.
118 Campbell (n 61) 340.
119 Fuller, *Legal Fictions* (n 1) 9.
120 Ibid.
121 Olivier (n 50) 35.
122 Ibid.
123 The discussion of mistake in *Pitt v Holt* [2013] UKSC 26, [2013] 2 AC 108 [104]–[113] (Lord Walker) suggests that awareness of a falsehood is not so simple a matter.

> of the statement either positively disbelieves it, or is partially conscious of its untruth or inadequacy.[124]

It is to be regretted that Fuller did not give an example of the situation he described. I will take the liberty to suggest one. It is possible that in straining a legal rule beyond its intended application, the judge might be assailed by a suspicion that he is entering the twilight zone of fiction, without having 'complete consciousness' – that is, the certainty – of an untruth. For example, if a statute says that 'Cats are deemed to be dogs' and the judge, eager to do justice on the facts, interprets the statute to mean that jaguars are also deemed to be dogs, on the basis that jaguars are feline or 'big cats', the judge may well be 'partially conscious of … untruth or inadequacy'. He will see that he is straining the words to an unreasonable degree or imposing on them an unintended meaning. At the same time, he does not have a complete consciousness of falsehood. Jaguars do belong to the cat family, *felidae*. *Merriam-Webster* defines 'jaguar' as 'a large, powerful cat'.[125] This judge may be said to be in serious doubt as to the truth of his finding, but not in possession of the certainty of it. It will also be appreciated that in this situation the 'truth' itself becomes elusive as 'truth' depends on what construction we adopt and is at the very least contextual. What may be said with confidence is that the judge is proceeding on a strained, or far-fetched, or contrived interpretation. It is either of these adjectives in the definite sense that it departs from the lay understanding, the natural and ordinary meaning, of the statement 'Cats are deemed to be dogs'. No one reading this sentence would think of lions, panthers or jaguars.[126]

Real-world examples may also be found. Delivering the opinion of the Supreme Court of the United States in *Richardson v Marsh*, Scalia J said: 'The rule that juries are presumed to follow their instructions is a pragmatic one, rooted less in the absolute certitude that the presumption is true than in the belief that it represents a reasonable practical accommodation of the interests of the state and the defendant in the criminal justice process.'[127]

Fuller is not wrong to allow for this situation and to describe it as 'partial consciousness' of falsity. Fuller has effectively softened the age-old element of consciousness to include not only the certainty of falsity, but also the awareness of a questionable leap of logic, the consciousness of *serious doubt*. It is

124 Fuller, *Legal Fictions* (n 1) 8.

125 Gove (n 83) 1208.

126 In 2014, Selwyn College, Cambridge allowed its Master to keep a dog on the basis that it was 'a very large cat'.

127 481 US 200, 211, 107 SCt 1702, 1709 (SCOTUS 1987).

narrow-minded for Olivier to censure partial consciousness as some kind of logical heresy. In my view, Fuller's is a more nuanced understanding of judicial reasoning and should not be dismissed as nonsensical. Indeed, the category of Soft Fiction, proposed in Section 2.7 later in this chapter, is inspired by Fuller's ideas (though he never suggested such a thing). The Soft Fiction is the consciousness not of utter falsity, but of a strained, far-fetched or contrived interpretation: the conscious imposition of an unnatural meaning on a rule of law. I shall return to this in due course.

Olivier is, however, correct to point out that 'Fuller's definition is wide enough to include lies, falsehood and deceit.'[128] He then adds, with undisguised disdain, that civilian 'Commentators warned against this error more than six centuries ago.'[129] Of course, making statements with a complete or partial consciousness of their falsity is precisely what a liar does. The point is that the *court* must be conscious of the falsity.[130] Fuller would no doubt have exclaimed, 'Well, of course!' if he had heard this objection, but Olivier is right that Fuller's definition, read literally, is not sufficiently precise.

2.5.2.2.2 SECOND LIMB OF FULLER'S DEFINITION: 'A FALSE STATEMENT RECOGNIZED AS HAVING UTILITY' Olivier castigates this limb as 'extremely vague' and charges that it 'tells us nothing about the construction of the fiction'.[131] Moreover, Olivier continues, 'the statement itself is false, since some fictions exist . . . which are not universally accepted as useful or beneficial – and yet are accepted as fictions'.[132] Kenneth Campbell, who dissected Fuller's definition several years after Olivier, in 1983, was equally harsh:

> Recognised by whom as having utility for whom? If the answer is, recognised by the party relying on it as having utility for him, then once again this fails to distinguish a fiction from any opportunistic lie. If it means recognised by the court as having utility for the person relying on it, then it does not distinguish it from the case where the court appreciates the opportunism of the lie. Does it mean recognised by the court as having general social utility? But surely there can be fictions courts are bound by authority to continue to recognise even though they have outgrown whatever social utility they may once have possessed? So limb (2) of the definition meets an even swifter death than limb (1).[133]

128 Olivier (n 50) 35.
129 Ibid.
130 See also Campbell (n 61) 342.
131 Olivier (n 50) 35.
132 Ibid.
133 Campbell (n 61) 344–5.

Fuller's second limb is bewildering from another angle. Its unqualified simplicity appears to contradict Fuller's statement earlier in his book that 'a fiction is distinguished from a lie by the fact that it is not intended to deceive'.[134] Earlier still he equates fiction with 'a plain falsehood, rendered harmless by its utter incapacity to deceive'.[135] It is likely, given these quotations, that Fuller assumed, in formulating the definition, that the statement is known to be false by the legal community. But any such assumption is far from explicit in either limb of his definition.

Fuller explains the second limb of his definition ('a false statement recognized as having utility') at some length. The burden of the argument is that critics of certain legal devices often call these devices 'fictitious' as opposed to simply 'mistaken', even though they know that the proponents of these devices believe there is nothing untrue about them. In other words, the critics use the term 'fiction' when the element of consciousness is missing. To take a topical example of Fuller's scenario, when William Swadling calls the constructive trust a fiction, he does not imagine that judges and lawyers already know the constructive trust is a fiction.[136] Indeed, he openly acknowledges that '[t]he idea that constructive trusts are genuine trusts is deeply rooted in the English psyche'.[137] This situation is markedly different from geographical fictions, where the entire legal community recognised the factual falsity of the device. According to Fuller's understanding, Swadling calls the constructive trust a fiction, and not simply a mistake, because he recognises that the constructive trust is a falsehood that plays some practical role and has some utility (even if he, Swadling, believes there is a better alternative). Hence Fuller's second limb: 'a false statement recognized as having utility'.

The problem with Fuller's second limb is that, by dropping the crucial element of consciousness, he blurs, if not downright erases, the line between fiction and mistake. The qualification of 'having utility' is too uncertain to draw a new line between fiction and whatever the opposite would now be. And, yet, it cannot be denied that in common parlance the word 'fiction' is used to describe widely-held beliefs the speaker believes to be false. Swadling's use of the term is a case in point and by no means irregular.[138]

134 Fuller, *Legal Fictions* (n 1) 6.

135 Ibid. 5; see also, on the same page, 'a fiction (if the word is to retain any utility) is neither a truthful statement, nor a lie, nor an erroneous conclusion'.

136 Swadling (n 19).

137 Ibid. 433.

138 See e.g., Smith (n 21) 1464 ('fiction' of originalism in constitutional interpretation); Christina Accomando, *The Regulations of Robbers* (Ohio State University Press 2001) 4 ('fiction' of slavery).

In constructing a definition, we face a choice between, on the one hand, a definition which is narrow enough to distinguish between fiction and mistake; and, on the other hand, a definition which is broad enough to accommodate common usage by including widely held but (unconsciously) mistaken beliefs.

My view is that we cannot dispense with the element of consciousness, even if some writers have done so. It is one thing to broaden the understanding of consciousness to include doubt, as discussed in relation to Fuller's first limb. But utterly to eliminate consciousness as an element is a step too far. It does not add nuance to the definition: it destroys it. If fiction simply becomes an entrenched mistake in the law, it will have lost its peculiarity as a legal tool. It will have become no more than an argument somebody disagrees with. This book is about fictions properly so-called, not genuine disagreements.

While we should think twice before adopting a definition somewhat at odds with common usage, it is preferable for a rigorous examination of fictions to say that some people use the term inaccurately than to dilute almost to extinction its own subject matter. It would be better to refer to widely-held but misguided beliefs as myths or misconceptions. The term 'legal fiction' should be reserved for consciously false statements. For these reasons, Fuller's second definition (the alternative second limb) should be rejected.

2.5.2.2.3 THE SECOND LIMB STRIKES AGAIN? Not everyone shares Olivier's (and my) view of the weaknesses of Fuller's second limb. In his recent article, 'New Legal Fictions', Peter J Smith embraces, wittingly or not, Fuller's second limb. Smith's expansive understanding of legal fictions includes empirically false suppositions, such as the reliability of eye-witness testimony or the ability of jurors to follow directions.[139] Unlike Fuller, Smith is explicit in his rejection of the element of consciousness:

> [T]here also are ... important differences between classic legal fictions and new legal fictions. There rarely was any confusion about whether a classic legal fiction had been deployed – as it was not intended to deceive – or what it accomplished. ... For new legal fictions, in contrast, there generally is no recognition of the fact that the premise is false, although the assertions need not consciously be intended to deceive. Indeed, what characterizes most new legal fictions is that the learned reader of the law would not have explicit or implicit indication that the court is simply deeming to be true that about which we know otherwise.[140]

139 Smith (n 21) 1437–8.
140 Ibid. 1470 (footnotes omitted).

It should be noted, parenthetically, that not all of Smith's 'new legal fictions' actually meet his own criteria (as these criteria appear in the passage just quoted). For example, Smith regards the presumption that everybody knows the law as 'a type of new legal fiction'.[141] There is, however, wide recognition among the judiciary that this premise is false. It is not clear why he classifies it as a 'new legal fiction' as opposed to a 'classic legal fiction'.[142]

In any case, Professor Nancy Knauer has penned a comprehensive rebuttal of Smith's 'new legal fictions'. Specifically, Knauer takes issue with Smith on three grounds. First, she says, many of the suppositions (that comprise Smith's 'new legal fictions') are doubtful or debatable, rather than patently false. This is redolent of Fuller's notion of partial consciousness. Second, these suppositions, are valued *for their truth*, not their falsity. Third, if they are indeed erroneous, the cure is to correct them, and there is no value in treating them as fictions.[143] Confusingly, Knauer defends Fuller's definition, even though its second limb favours Smith's approach.[144]

Knauer also resists attempts by other writers to include within the scope of legal fiction discredited legal regimes (such as slavery).[145] The argument is the same: the supposed fictions are actually believed (however erroneously or immorally).

I agree. The flaw, as I see it, in Smith's approach is that he, like Fuller before him (in the second limb), throws consciousness overboard. It is one thing to admit partial consciousness or indifference to the true state of events. To accept as fictitious what is positively believed and valued for its truth is to drive a coach and horses through the definition of legal fiction.

In fairness to Smith, he suggests at various points that judges are aware, or ought to be, of the empirical evidence belying the false suppositions.[146] This introduces an element of consciousness, or at least constructive consciousness, as to the truth of the supposition. Unfortunately, he confirms his thesis is incompatible with my analysis when he declares, 'For new legal fictions, in contrast, there generally is no recognition of the fact that the premise is false.'[147]

141 Ibid. 1459.

142 For the avoidance of doubt, Smith's 'new legal fictions' have nothing to do with the distinction between Old and New Fictions adopted in this monograph. As I explain presently, in my view, Smith's 'new legal fictions' are not fictions at all.

143 Knauer (n 22) 9, 22, 24–5.

144 Ibid. 6 ('I conclude that the appellation of legal fiction is a misnomer and that the integrity of Fuller's classic definition should be retained for its analytic force').

145 Ibid. 26–37.

146 Smith (n 21) 1440, 1476, 1481, 1493.

147 Ibid. 1470.

Even if Smith had maintained consistently that judges should be aware that the premise is empirically false, this awareness would only have *reinforced* the element of consciousness (albeit constructive consciousness). However we look at it, it seems subjective consciousness of falsity, whether partial or complete, is an essential element of the definition.

2.5.2.2.4 LESSONS FROM FULLER To conclude our discussion of Fuller, his definition plainly falls short of the technical, hard conception of the legal fiction accepted in jurisprudential circles. In the first limb, Fuller is not explicit about consciousness on the part of the wider legal community and ambivalent about the degree of consciousness on the part of the court or party making the statement. In the second limb, he discards consciousness altogether in favour of 'utility'.

However, Fuller's very aim was to show that the hard definition was perhaps too narrow: 'it may be questioned whether current usage confines the concept "fiction" within the limits suggested'.[148] Fuller is right that 'fiction' is used in a wider sense than fiction theorists permit, but his more expansive definition, as we have seen, has no clear boundaries. It fails the test of determinacy. It will be suggested below that while the hard definition should not be 'corrupted' by sacrificing consciousness, our imagination is wide enough to sustain, alongside the Hard Fiction, a softer type of fiction, namely the imposition of a consciously-unnatural meaning on a rule of law. This Soft Fiction does not correspond exactly to either of Fuller's limbs, but can be said to be inspired by the borderline situations that exercised the mind of that great thinker.

2.5.2.3 Alf Ross

In 1969, Danish legal philosopher Alf Ross set out his original take on legal fictions in a contribution to an edited book.[149] Ross challenged the near-universal understanding of legal fiction as a consciously false statement. He claimed it was a paradox: if everybody knows it is false, how can judges use it to pretend the law is not changing?[150] We cannot say that no one is deceived by the fiction and at the same time that judges need the fiction to uphold the existing structure or 'keep records straight'.

One possible answer to Ross's paradox is that not 'everybody' knows that the fiction is false. 'Everybody' presumably only includes the legal community. It

148 Fuller, *Legal Fictions* (n 1) 8.
149 Ross (n 43).
150 Ibid. 223–4.

is only the initiated who know how to read between the lines and discount certain statements. Outsiders may believe that the law is not changing.

But the more direct answer to Ross's paradox is that judges (at least English judges) did not pretend the law was not changing.[151] It is evident that Ross was influenced by Maine's idea that fictions were about concealment[152] – a view rejected above. When Milsom said, 'The aim of fictions . . . is not deception; it is to keep records straight',[153] he meant it strictly: the fiction was necessary for form only. The record *had* to contain certain words. There was nothing else to it.

Nobody thought that geographical fictions brought about no change in the law. The judges simply contrived to effect change without fundamentally disturbing the forms of actions, which were the basis of the legal system. The pretence was of form merely. As Professor Baker wrote: 'The books of the law, the judgments, and the outward forms, appear to say one thing, while everyone knows that the law works differently in reality.'[154] Ross's paradox is illusory and rooted in Maine's (misconceived) notion that fictions were intended to genuinely hide changes in the law.

That said, Ross's next insight is most valuable. If fictions are not consciously false statements (to his mind), what are they? Ross argued that fictions were 'posed' statements.[155] That is, statements that are neither asserted nor confirmed. Ross likened posed statements to facts in novels and pleasantries in polite society.[156] The speaker puts them forward without asserting their truth. They may be true but are unreliable. They simply hang in the air. Simon Stern referred to Ross's posed statements as being in 'limbo'.[157]

Of Ross's two analogies (facts in novels and social pleasantries), I think the latter is particularly apt. Pleasantries in polite society have to be said, but no one takes them seriously or much cares about their veracity. When asked by a stranger or an acquaintance about my day, I say that I have had a good day. I could hardly say that I have had a nightmare of a day. Maybe I have in fact had a good day, but my reply is unreliable. In either case, it is not considered dishonest. Nobody expects the truth from such small talk. It just has to be said

151 Ross commented on what I call Hard Fictions and so this discussion only concerns Hard Fictions.
152 Ross (n 43) 217–18, 223.
153 Milsom, 'Trespass from Henry III to Edward III' (n 110) 223.
154 LTB, 33.
155 Ross (n 43) 231.
156 Ibid. 228–31.
157 Simon Stern, 'Legal Fictions and Exclusionary Rules' in LFTP, 158.

for form's sake and the truth is irrelevant. So, too, with fictions: they just have to be stated for form and their truth is irrelevant.

What is the take-home message from Ross's analysis? We already know from our discussion of the existence of fictions that they are false in the sense that they contradict the physical world. I now add, as foreshadowed by Fuller and expounded by Ross, the qualification that the judge and the legal community need not be absolutely conscious that there is a contradiction. Instead, they must be *indifferent to whether there is a contradiction*. A fictitious statement is one whose truth is irrelevant rather than necessarily false. A judge who doubts his finding but proceeds to rely on it anyway is indifferent to its truth, or at least accords it little importance. It is the same indifference which the judges of old showed to the truth of the factual allegations in Old Fictions. They did not know for certain that the defendant had not entered with force and arms (surely on some occasions the defendant had). They just did not care. It was immaterial. The fiction lies in not caring about the facts; not in the absolute knowledge that they are false.[158] As with the exchange of greetings, the truth of the statement does not matter. In short, a legal fiction is the conscious indifference to a contradiction with the physical world.

2.5.2.4 Pierre Olivier

In the adapted reprint of his doctoral thesis, published in 1975, Pierre JJ Olivier gave the world a thorough survey of historical thought regarding the legal fiction.[159] Olivier traced the development of what he called the 'fiction concept' from the legal systems of the ancient Levant, through the Greco-Roman period, to the glossators and the school of Orléans in the Dark Ages, to the post-glossators and post-Enlightenment German, Dutch and Anglo-American jurists. This monograph could not hope to match the scope and detail of Olivier's exegesis – even if there were any benefit in reproducing the material.

We have already consulted Olivier on several occasions. There is one more element of Olivier's research which is fitting to dwell on at this point. Olivier brings to the fore an idea which apparently originated with a French bishop and statesman called Pierre de Belleperche, who died in 1308. The idea is that 'the circumstances under which the fiction is to be applied must be possible'.[160] This means that a court may pretend that an Act of Parliament

158 Campbell put it somewhat differently: 'the falsity is not that of the fact which is relied upon, but of the inference by which it is arrived at': Campbell (n 61) 344.

159 Olivier (n 50).

160 Ibid. 15; see also Oliver R Mitchell, 'Fictions of the Law: Have They Proved Useful or Detrimental to Its Growth?' (1893) 7 Harvard LR 249, 252.

was passed on the first day of the session, but may not pretend a square circle. The former is wrong but possible; the latter is wrong and impossible.

We do not have to go far to find instances of this approach. In fact, we have already seen one in the previous chapter. Following the formal abolition of the fictions of ejectment and the implied promise in quasi-contract, English judges demanded that the fictitious fact (i.e., entry in ejectment and promise or contract in quasi-contract) be possible in theory. As Viscount Haldane LC said in *Sinclair v Brougham* (1914), 'The fiction can only be set up with effect if such a contract would be valid if it really existed.'[161] In that, the Lord Chancellor was a follower of Pierre de Belleperche.

Whatever the merits of limiting fictions to theoretically feasible suppositions, it is clear that English law has not generally respected any such limitation. As John Chipman Gray noted, English fictions were 'bolder, and if one may say so, more brutal'[162] than their Roman forerunners (which took the assumptive form). De Belleperche was of course interested in civilian fictions. In England, theoretically-impossible fictions like a finding that a woman was ordained (benefit of clergy) or a Mediterranean island enclosed within a London parish (geographical fictions) were sound law, if unsound logic. *Sinclair v Brougham* and its ilk were anomalous. Indeed, *Sinclair v Brougham* was held to have been wrongly decided, so we can discount it as an aberration.[163]

Actually, there is much to be said for the cavalier attitude of English lawyers in the face of logical impossibilities. The whole point of the fiction is that it is false.[164] What does it matter how false? If we approve of the use of fictions in general as a means to an end, as Roman lawyers certainly did, baulking at some fictions on pedantic grounds carries no clear benefit and may frustrate the end the fiction was devised to achieve. We saw this so clearly in *Sinclair v Brougham* itself, where the claimants could not recover monies lent pursuant to a void loan. The historical attitude of English law to fictions – 'anything goes' – underscores the perversity of the error which possessed the generation of Viscount Haldane, who, to be more Catholic than the pope, found an imaginary contract to be invalid.

161 [1914] AC 398 (HL) 415.

162 Gray (n 9) 32.

163 *Haugesund Kommune v Depfa ACS Bank* [2010] EWCA Civ 579, [2012] QB 549 [87]–[88] (Aikens LJ); as the cited paragraphs show, the Court of Appeal was able to depart from the House of Lords' decision in *Sinclair v Brougham* because it understood the House of Lords to have in effect already departed from *Sinclair v Brougham* in *Westdeutsche Landesbank Girozentrale v Islington LBC* [1996] AC 669 (HL).

164 See also Olivier (n 50) 77.

In conclusion, in English law, fictions have not been, and ought not to be, necessarily possible.

2.5.2.5 Pierluigi Chiassoni

Professor Chiassoni has recently published a wide-ranging treatise on interpretation, bearing the title *Interpretation without Truth*. A chapter of this jurisprudential study is dedicated to fictions. The author proposes an original definition of fiction:

> A *Judicial Fiction* is (a) a technique for overcoming axiological gaps, (b) to which the judges resort when the bad rule at hand cannot be directly defeated by means of ordinary interpretation techniques, (c) that consists in laying down an individual or a general fictional sentence, (d) on the basis of which the individual case at hand can be regulated by the good rule at hand, (e) which technique the judges assume to be authorized to employ, in virtue of a tacitly vested lawmaking power that is not preposterous from the standpoint of legal tradition, and is in tune with society's aversion to judicial activism.[165]

By 'axiologicial gap', Chiassoni means a situation where 'the law provides an answer to a case at hand, but, unfortunately, the answer is (considered to be) a "bad" answer, usually from the standpoint of justice and higher, fundamental, legal principles'.[166] This is to be distinguished from a 'normative gap proper': where the law provides no answer at all, whether good or bad.[167]

Chiassoni contends that legal fictions should be understood as filling axiological gaps, where such gaps cannot be filled by ordinary interpretive techniques. Put differently, if we have a bad rule, and we cannot interpret our way out of it, we resort to a legal fiction.

Chiassoni's account of fictions is persuasive. I agree that fictions tend to be invoked when there is a (perceived) 'bad rule' and no other way around it. This is borne out, as a matter of history, in the last chapter.

For my purposes, though, the 'axiological gap' does not seem to be a matter of definition. It describes the motive or context for using a fiction, not the fiction itself. I might use a gun in one context and not in another, but that is distinct from the definition of a gun. I will return to the motives for fictions, where Chiassoni's insights will be relevant, in Chapter 4.

165 Chiassoni (n 56) 194.
166 Ibid. 190.
167 Ibid. 189–90.

2.5.2.6 *Maksymilian Del Mar*

In 'Artefacts of Legal Inquiry', Maksymilian Del Mar takes an original approach to fictions. Del Mar's fascinating book was published in 2020, when the present monograph was already complete. I added this section (before going to print) not in the vain hope of doing justice to Del Mar's contribution to scholarship, but in order to explain how his approach sits with mine.

Del Mar defines legal fiction as the supposition that 'an operative fact of a rule has been proven, when it is known that it has not been, or it is uncertain whether it has been'.[168] This is alternatively stated as 'the temporary suspension of an operative fact, i.e., a proof requirement, of a rule, while retaining the normative consequences of that rule'.[169] What is particularly interesting, if not ground-breaking, is his broader model. Del Mar claims that a fiction does not change the law. In this he defies conventional wisdom, as he readily admits.[170]

For Del Mar, a fiction is a mere suspension of a legal requirement that signals that a change may be required. Future judges will have to choose between three responses to this signal:

(i) restoring the suspended requirement;
(ii) leaving it suspended for the time being, pending further elaboration;
(iii) declaring the law has been changed, making the suspension permanent.

In Del Mar's analysis, option (i) corresponds to rejecting the fiction; option (ii) to maintaining it; and option (iii) to de-fictionalising the fiction by surrendering to it (e.g., by recognising an exception).[171] In this way, Del Mar's model of fiction has a time dimension. Fictions should be viewed over time as part of the process of adjudication and legal development. This fits well with his broader argument that fictions (and other 'artefacts'; e.g., metaphors and scenarios) aid adjudication by facilitating 'inquiry'.[172] In sum, the fiction does not change the law, but sends a signal to the system that the law may need to change.

How does Del Mar's model affect my project? We begin with the definition of fiction, which is the subject of this chapter. To reiterate, Del Mar says that '[t]o employ a fiction . . . is to suppose that an operative fact of a rule has been

168 Maksymilian Del Mar, *Artefacts of Legal Inquiry* (Hart 2020) 240.
169 Ibid. 248.
170 Ibid. 237.
171 Ibid. 258, 263.
172 Ibid. 1, 258–9.

proven, when it is known that it has not been, or it is uncertain whether it has been'. His definition thus incorporates the element of falsity, including what I have called indifference to truth. Del Mar's definition also incorporates the element of consciousness ('when it is known that . . . ').

My definitions of Hard and Soft Fiction involve conditions or considerations that Del Mar does not go into (having an altogether different purpose). One such consideration is the degree of falsity. Another is the distinction between issues of fact and law that will appear shortly. Having said that, there is no necessary contradiction between my definitions and Del Mar's. I certainly do not dispute his, all of whose elements are contained in mine. Consistency between our definitions ultimately depends on what meaning one assigns to the words in them. I aim to make my meaning clear in these pages.

Where Del Mar and I diverge is his position that fictions do not change the law (at least initially). He says that fictions are not rules that can be relied upon in the future. They apply only to the instant case, temporarily suspending a requirement, indicating that something is awry with the law. Future courts pick up this signal and act in one of the three ways mentioned above. Of these, only (iii) (accepting the fiction as permanent by altering the rule) would mean a change in the law. So change may result from fictions, but not automatically. They are not the same thing. In point of fact, the change in the law is the death of the fiction.[173]

To my mind, fictions do represent a change in the law (even when used for the first time). To 'suspend' a requirement is to change the law. A temporary change is still a change. The requirement *is* the law. Without the suspension, the outcome of the case would have been different. Hence the law must have changed. Future litigants would seek to rely on this change – if it suited them. I accept that the change may be affirmed or rolled back in future cases: this is the way the common law develops with respect to any judicial innovation, fictitious or not. But I do not think the initial change can be denied.

It is possible that Del Mar has a more demanding definition of 'change in the law'. If so, our disagreement may be semantic and not substantive. At all events, nothing in my project turns on the notion of 'change in the law', so any disagreement on this point has no present relevance. Beyond this, I think our approaches are compatible (which is of course not to say that Del Mar agrees with me).

2.6 A PROPOSED DEFINITION OF HARD FICTION

Fuller believed that the ascertainment of fictions is a matter of degree: 'we reserve the term "fiction" for those distortions of reality which are outstanding

[173] Ibid. 253–5, 257–8.

and unusual'.[174] Professor John Miller agreed: 'The legal fiction shades into other forms of rules by degrees, but the concern . . . is to deal with it in its more distinctive variations.'[175]

I beg to differ. I contend it is possible to make a categorical distinction between legal fictions and other artificial constructs.

The reader will be pleased to know that in the preceding pages we have done almost all the work of constructing a definition. In dealing with the intellectual challenges and the existing definitions, we have incidentally constructed an almost complete definition. All that remains is to piece everything together and add some final touches.

2.6.1 *What Do We Know So Far?*

I started with two elements indispensable for a definition, namely consciousness and falsity. I then said, in respect of the Hard Fiction, that there are degrees of falsity and that I adopt the most stringent degree, which I have called a contradiction with the physical world. Turning to consciousness, I rejected calls to drop it altogether, but accepted that consciousness of falsity does not mean certain knowledge of falsity, but rather indifference to truth. Putting these ideas together in one sentence, I understand the Hard Fiction to be *something which is consciously decided irrespective of the facts*. But what is this 'something' on which the fiction is based?

2.6.2 *The Basis of Hard Fiction: Fact or Law?*

If falsity means contradiction with the physical world, it follows that the 'something' must be capable of contradicting the physical world. To contradict the physical world, that thing must be factual. Purely legal concepts, which have no parallel in the physical world to contradict (e.g., a company, a trust), cannot be fictitious.[176] It is clear then that the basis of all legal fictions must be some issue of fact. We have now identified a third element of the definition, namely that the statement has to be factual.

The following two examples illustrate the point. *Vi et armis* was a fiction because entry with force and arms is an event in the physical world and hence

174 Fuller, *Legal Fictions* (n 1) 47; see also 65–6.

175 John A Miller, 'Liars Should Have Good Memories: Legal Fictions and the Tax Code' (1993) 64 U Colorado LR 1, 8, 36.

176 See also Olivier (n 50) 56–7.

a fact. By contrast, the abolition by Parliament of the sealing requirement for deeds,[177] did not produce a fiction because a 'deed' (in the sense of document) is a purely legal creature. It has no meaning outside the law and thus cannot contradict the physical world.[178]

Unfortunately, it is not always so easy to distinguish between fact and law. It might even be argued that a deed, having for hundreds of years meant 'sealed document', had become a fact to laymen, such that a deed without a seal was like a table without legs. This is a philosophical quagmire,[179] which is beyond the scope of this work. To short-circuit this problem, it is proposed that an issue is to be considered factual or legal if it is so considered in the eyes of the law. For this last insight I am indebted to Kenneth Campbell, who argues that a statement is 'a legal fiction only if and insofar as it is an assertion of that which the law itself classifies as a question of fact'.[180]

And so, since the formal requirements of deeds are obviously a question of law (in the eyes of the law), the problem is avoided. By contrast, the law did not regard entry with force and arms as a matter of law, but as a factual allegation, leaving it to the jury. Hence unsealed deeds are not fictitious deeds, but entry *vi et armis* was fictitious.

In conclusion, we can now say that the basis of the fiction is some matter of fact which is up for determination.

2.6.3 *The Basis of Hard Fiction: Statement, Assumption or Issue?*

Most definitions describe a fiction as a 'statement', an 'assertion' or an 'assumption'.[181] Del Mar says that '[t]o call a fiction a "statement" seems artificial, especially in the adjudicatory context where it is surely more usefully

177 Law of Property (Miscellaneous Provisions) Act 1989, s 1(1)(b).

178 Miller broaches the interesting idea that the falsity of the statement must be assessed in a non-legal context: Miller (n 175) 6. Put differently, this means that only statements that have a non-legal meaning can be fictitious. In my view, it is easier to speak in terms of fact and law, a distinction familiar to lawyers.

179 In *Re St Stephen's, Walbrook* [1987] 3 WLR 726, the Court of Ecclesiastical Causes Reserved considered whether a Holy Table had to have legs, which in turn raised fine questions about altars in the reformed Church and indeed the theology of the Eucharist. The Bishop of Chichester, who gave the leading judgment, confessed he 'did not find it easy to follow the philosophical argument put forward by counsel for the archdeacon concerning the concept of "tableness"' (at 168). Sir Anthony Lloyd, concurring, said, 'the argument begins to remind one of Plato's Republic' (at 194). It was held that a table did not necessarily possess legs.

180 Campbell (n 61) 356.

181 See, e.g., Fuller, *Legal Fictions* (n 1) 9; Ogden and Bentham (n 104) cxvi; Maine (n 106) 32.

understood as a device of reasoning'.[182] Olivier argues that a fiction is an assumption and not a statement because it is 'a process of thought which may be subsequently expressed as a statement, but it is not in the first place a statement'.[183]

I believe that neither 'statement' nor 'assumption' is the proper basis for the Hard Fiction. 'Assumption' often implies justifiable or credible grounds. Thus the assumptions in, say, statistical studies or economic models are chosen because they are generally true or reliable enough, not because they are known to be false. Assumptions, like hypotheses, are mostly chosen for their probable truth. The word 'assumption' is therefore ill-suited to serve as the basis of the Hard Fiction, which is known to be false.

I have chosen the more general term 'issue' in preference to statement or assertion. This is because it is not always straightforward, or helpful, to reduce the fiction to a particular form of words. The constructive trust has been said to be a fiction, but the concept of the constructive trust in English law is not represented by any particular statement or assertion. We could come up with a statement to describe the trust, but it would be one of many possible formulations. We would be better advised to speak of the trust as a concept – which it really is – than as a statement. Then we would ask, without semantic distractions, whether the trust is a factual issue and consciously contradicts the physical world. The answer is of course no.

2.6.4 *A Definition of Hard Fiction*

We have established that a Hard Fiction is (i) an issue (ii) of fact (iii) which is false in the sense that it is decided irrespective of a contradiction with the physical world (iv) with the full knowledge of the legal community.

It may be tempting to suppose that element (iii) makes element (ii) otiose. If falsity can only arise out of a contradiction with the physical world, it is not necessary to require in addition an issue of fact. For how can a legal issue contradict the physical world? The argument is that element (iii) does all the work of element (ii).

Unfortunately, upon further consideration, we do need element (ii). This is because of the special category of legal terms which have lay or factual equivalents. The most obvious example is the contract. While a lawyer is

182 Maksymilian Del Mar, 'Legal Fictions and Legal Change in the Common Law Tradition' in LFTP, 229. Del Mar goes on to argue that a fiction is the 'suspension' of an operative fact, an idea redolent of Alf Ross's posed statement.

183 Olivier (n 50) 35.

likely to see the contract as a legal concept, a layman has a distinct conception of a contract, or agreement, as a fact in the physical world. Indeed, an agreement between people *is* a fact in the physical world (though whether the law recognises it is a separate question).

A contract, then, exists in both a legal and a factual sense. If we apply our definition without element (ii), which asks whether the law sees the contract as an issue of fact, we might reach strange conclusions. For example, the requirement of intention to create legal relations might mean that what is considered by laypeople to be an agreement is no binding agreement in law. Well, here we have a contradiction with the physical world, with the full knowledge of the legal community. Is the non-enforceability of such an agreement a legal fiction? Surely we are not prepared to say that it is.

This is why it is necessary to separately establish that the existence of a contract is an issue of law (in the eyes of the law) before we even come to the element of falsity. All four elements are necessary: a Hard Fiction is (i) an issue (ii) of fact (iii) which is false in the sense that it is decided irrespective of a contradiction with the physical world (iv) with the full knowledge of the legal community.

In short, a Hard Fiction is *a factual issue consciously decided irrespective of the facts*. Henceforth, this is the only formulation I will use for the Hard Fiction. The application of this definition entails consideration of three distinct questions, which will be taken in this order, whenever I apply the definition:

a. Is the issue of fact or law (the factual requirement)?
b. Is the issue decided irrespective of the facts (the falsity requirement)?
c. Is the issue *consciously* so decided (the consciousness requirement)?

2.7 A PROPOSED DEFINITION OF SOFT FICTION

We have said that the technical definition insisted upon by legal theorists is sound logically, but fails to capture all the shades of legal reasoning.

Hard Fiction is about an inconsistency with the physical world. True, an indifference to whether there is in fact an inconsistency is sufficient, but Hard Fiction still requires a potential inconsistency to which the judge is indifferent. An inconsistency with the physical world is therefore at the root of Hard Fiction. And this inconsistency is obvious. It is not a matter of opinion or argument. For if the judge believes there is no inconsistency, he is not conscious of an inconsistency.

Soft Fiction, by contrast, does not rest on an obvious inconsistency. It refers, instead, to what Fuller called 'partial consciousness' – that is to say, serious doubt but not the certainty of falsity (here used in the sense of contradiction with the physical world). We have used the example of a judge construing 'cats' to include 'jaguars' to exemplify this phenomenon. It is also possible, by way of another illustration, to discern a Soft Fiction in the Old Fiction of *vi et armis*. This factual allegation was made up of two separate elements: force and arms. There was no doubt that the defendant did not need to be armed. Therefore, the allegation *as a whole* was a Hard Fiction. However, if we look at the allegation of force on its own, Professor Ibbetson has shown that the violence implied in 'force and arms' was interpreted to mean 'very little more than an invasive interference with the plaintiff's land, goods, or person'.[184] In other words, the allegation of force had been watered down; so much so that a strained or unnatural meaning, though literally not false (since interference requires some exertion of force) had been imposed on the words of the writ. As Ibbetson found, '[i]f all that was needed was an unwanted tap on the shoulder or toe on the doorstep, then practically any physical interference could be brought within the scope of the action'.[185] And so, in our terms, '*armis*' was a Hard Fiction because the judge was indifferent to the absence of arms, but '*vi*' was only a Soft Fiction because the judge was not indifferent to the absence of force: some minimal force there had to be. The judge just strained the word 'force' beyond its natural meaning in context.

To conclude, what distinguishes Soft Fiction from Hard Fiction is that Hard Fiction involves falsity (in the sense of indifference to a contradiction with the physical world), whereas Soft Fiction involves a consciously strained interpretation. This consciousness is not normally revealed in the judgment, as indeed the consciousness of many Hard Fictions is not. But the artificiality is such that, if pressed, the judge would have to admit that the interpretation was not the intended one.[186] One such judge was Lord Evershed MR, who, dismissing a creative suggestion by counsel, said, 'I think myself that such a conclusion is startling. Indeed, I venture to doubt whether to anybody but a lawyer such a conclusion would even be comprehensible – at least without a considerable amount of explanation.'[187] This serves as an excellent description of what would have been a consciously unnatural interpretation – a Soft Fiction.

184 HILO, 41; Palmer held generally the same view: Robert C Palmer, *English Law in the Age of the Black Death, 1348–1381* (University of North Carolina Press 1993) 159.

185 HILO, 41.

186 I owe this last observation to Nicholas McBride, Fellow of Pembroke College, Cambridge.

187 *Re Rose* [1952] Ch 499 (CA) 507.

There are also cases where judges did not baulk at the consciously unnatural interpretation. The phenomenon of judges consciously straining the meaning of words for some higher purpose (which we have called a Soft Fiction), was laid bare by Lord Denning MR in *George Mitchell (Chesterhall) Ltd v Finney Lock Seeds Ltd* (1982).[188] The Master of the Rolls described the treatment of exclusion clauses before the Unfair Contract Terms Act 1977. Below are extracted several passages of the speech, not just for their moving eloquence, but because it is a real-life description of the most important idea in this chapter – the Soft Fiction:

> None of you nowadays will remember the trouble we had – when I was called to the Bar – with exemption clauses. They were printed in small print on the back of tickets and order forms and invoices. They were contained in catalogues or timetables. They were held to be binding on any person who took them without objection. No one ever did object. He never read them or knew what was in them. No matter how unreasonable they were, he was bound. All this was done in the name of 'freedom of contract'. But the freedom was all on the side of the big concern which had the use of the printing press. No freedom for the little man who took the ticket or order form or invoice. The big concern said, 'Take it or leave it.' The little man had no option but to take it. The big concern could and did exempt itself from liability in its own interest without regard to the little man. It got away with it time after time. When the courts said to the big concern, 'You must put it in clear words,' the big concern had no hesitation in doing so. It knew well that the little man would never read the exemption clauses or understand them.
>
> It was a bleak winter for our law of contract...
>
> Faced with this abuse of power – by the strong against the weak – by the use of the small print of the conditions – the judges did what they could to put a curb upon it. They still had before them the idol, 'freedom of contract'. They still knelt down and worshipped it, but they concealed under their cloaks a secret weapon. They used it to stab the idol in the back. This weapon was called 'the true construction of the contract'. They used it with great skill and ingenuity. They used it so as to depart from the natural meaning of the words of the exemption clause and to put upon them a strained and unnatural construction.[189]

And so, a Soft Fiction is *a factual issue decided by a consciously-unnatural interpretation*. Henceforth, this is the only formulation I will use for Soft

[188] [1983] QB 284 (CA).
[189] Ibid. 296–7.

Fiction. Like a Hard Fiction, it entails consideration of three distinct questions, which I will take in this order, whenever I apply the definition:

a. Is the issue of fact or law (the factual requirement – identical to the first requirement of the Hard Fiction)?
b. Is the issue decided by an unnatural interpretation (the unnatural interpretation requirement)?
c. Is the issue *consciously* so decided (the consciousness requirement – identical to the third requirement of the Hard Fiction)?

It will be observed that the only difference between Hard and Soft Fictions lies in the second requirement: falsity versus unnatural interpretation. Note also that while the third element of consciousness is identical in terms, the consciousness is of different things. In the case of the Hard Fiction, it is consciousness of deciding the issue irrespective of the facts. In the case of the Soft Fiction, it is consciousness of deciding the issue by an unnatural interpretation.

Finally, the Hard and Soft Fictions are mutually exclusive. The same device cannot be both. If a device is so false as to be a Hard Fiction, it cannot also be a mere unnatural interpretation. So if we are satisfied that a device is a Hard Fiction, there is no need to ask whether it is a Soft Fiction.

2.8 CASE STUDIES

In this part of the chapter, I will apply the definitions of Hard and Soft Fiction to two contemporary legal devices: the reasonable man and the tortious defence of *volenti non fit injuria*. By putting these two legal devices to the test, we will achieve the dual goal of seeing how the new definitions work in practice and finding whether each device is a Hard Fiction, Soft Fiction or no fiction at all (on my understanding of these terms).

It is concluded that the reasonable man is not a fiction at all and that *volenti non fit injuria* is a Soft Fiction.

2.8.1 *First Case Study: The Reasonable Man*

> The horse omnibus service which used to run between Knightsbridge and Clapham was discontinued in 1914. Lord Bowen, who is credited with the invention of its most famous passenger and lived, I think, near the Knightsbridge end of the route, died in 1894. And yet in courts of common law all over the world, the ghostly creak of the wheels and the crack of the driver's

> whip are still to be heard. Like the Flying Dutchman, it seems condemned to travel for all eternity. . . . Let us get on board . . . and see who is travelling today.[190]

In two recent decisions, *Healthcare at Home v Scottish Health Service* (2014) and *Helow v Secretary of State for the Home Department* (2008), two members of the highest court in the land described the reasonable man as a fiction.[191] No reason is given in their respective judgments; it is taken for granted. It is necessary therefore to speculate. Perhaps the reason is indeed obvious: the reasonable man does not exist. He does not exist on two levels. First, there is no 'reasonable man' who watches pre-contractual negotiations, or construes the terms of the contract, and is then asked what he understands the parties to mean. More vividly perhaps, to take the oft-invoked scene, first painted by Mackinnon LJ in *Shirlaw v Southern Foundries (1926) Ltd* (1939), there is no person who suggests an express term to the negotiating parties, only to be 'testily suppress[ed] . . . with a common "Oh, of course!"'[192]

On another level, the reasonable man has no existence at all since no particular person can ever be identified as the reasonable man – however reasonable such a person may be. The reasonable man has been described as 'the man on the Clapham omnibus',[193] and more recently as the 'man on the underground'.[194] However, as Lord Reed said in *Healthcare at Home*, 'it would be misconceived for a party to seek to lead evidence from actual passengers on the Clapham omnibus as to how they would have acted in a given situation'.[195] That is, none of the people on the bus is the reasonable man. He is any man and no man. If we keep referring to the judgement of someone who does not exist, do we not play with fiction?

Having seen that two justices of the Supreme Court believe the reasonable man to be fictitious, and having postulated a case for such a position, let us now put the reasonable man to the test by applying the definitions.

2.8.1.1 Is the Reasonable Man a Hard Fiction?

2.8.1.1.1 THE FACTUAL REQUIREMENT The first question is whether the reasonable man is an issue of fact. Since the distinction between fact and

190 Lord Hoffmann, 'Anthropomorphic Justice: The Reasonable Man and His Friends' (1995) 29 The Law Teacher 127, 127.

191 *Healthcare at Home* (n 25) [2] (Lord Reed); *Helow* (n 25) [1] (Lord Hope).

192 *Shirlaw v Southern Foundries (1926) Ltd* [1939] 2 KB 206 (CA) 227.

193 *Hall v Brooklands Auto Racing Club* [1933] 1 KB 205 (CA) 224 (Greer LJ).

194 *White v Jones* [1995] 2 AC 207 (CA) 236 (Steyn LJ).

195 *Healthcare at Home* (n 25) [3].

law is likely to be problematic in many contexts, it will be considered here at some length, though in the context of the reasonable man.

The modern statement of the principles of contractual interpretation, laid down by Lord Hoffmann in *Investors Compensation Scheme Ltd v West Bromwich Building Society* (1997), is probably the most-used bit of contract law these days. This statement defers repeatedly to the reasonable man and thus offers us a prime example of the test. Relevantly, it reads:

> (1) Interpretation is the ascertainment of the meaning which the document would convey to a *reasonable person* having all the background knowledge which would reasonably have been available to the parties . . .
> (2) The background . . . includes absolutely anything which would have affected the way in which the language of the document would have been understood by a *reasonable man* . . .
> (3) . . . The background may not merely enable the *reasonable man* to choose between the possible meanings of words which are ambiguous but even . . . to conclude that the parties must . . . have used the wrong words or syntax[196]

So, when the court asks itself what the reasonable man would understand, is it asking a question of law or fact? The starting point is that how a person understands a document is a matter of fact. We can only discover the answer by asking the person what he understood. Supposing the reasonable man to be just a type of man, it follows that the test is factual.

It may be objected, however, that this comparison is flawed. The reasonable man is objective: he embodies a legal standard, namely what a person *ought to have understood* rather than what he actually understood. In *Glasgow Corporation v Muir* (1943), Lord Macmillan said that '[t]he standard of foresight of the reasonable man is . . . an impersonal test. It eliminates the personal equation.'[197] In dispensing with the services of the reasonable man in frustration cases, Viscount Radcliffe stated, in *Davis Contractors Ltd v Fareham Urban UDC* (1956), that the reasonable man 'represents after all no more than the anthropomorphic conception of justice . . . and must be the court itself'.[198] This

[196] *Investors Compensation Scheme Ltd v West Bromwich Building Society* [1998] 1 WLR 896 (HL) 912–13.

[197] *Glasgow Corporation v Muir* [1943] AC 448 (HL) 457.

[198] [1956] AC 696 (HL) 728; see also *New England Coal & Coke Co v Northern Barge Corp (The TJ Hooper)* 60 F2d 737 (US Circuit Court of Appeals, 2nd Circuit 1932) 740 (Learned Hand J): 'Indeed in most cases reasonable prudence is in fact common prudence; but strictly it is never its measure . . . Courts must in the end say what is required; there are precautions so imperative that even their universal disregard will not excuse their omission.'

statement was quoted approvingly by Lord Reed in *Healthcare at Home* (2014).[199] Therefore, the argument runs, what the reasonable man 'understands' is a matter of law, not of actual, factual understanding. This is reflected in the law of evidence. A witness cannot give evidence as to what is reasonable in the circumstances.[200] That would be opinion, not fact.

Upon further inquiry, however, this argument founders. True it is that what the reasonable man would do is a question for the judge and not the witnesses, but that does not make it *ipso facto* a question of law. Judges decide factual questions as well. How then does the judge decide what a reasonable man would understand a particular document to mean? Would the judge find the answer in a textbook? Would she find the answer in a statute book? Can she deduce it from legal principles alone? Of course not: she will only find the answer in the facts of the case – or the facts of analogous previous cases. This is because the answer to the question of what a reasonable man would understand is factual. And if the answer is factual so is the question.

If we return to *ICS v West Bromwich* itself, we will see that what the reasonable man understands depends, heavily, on the facts. Everything turns on background knowledge and the words in context. Lord Hoffmann, in applying his own principles, took into account that the disputed text 'was obviously intended to be read by lawyers'[201] and that such lawyers would find one of the two constructions 'extremely odd'.[202] Evidently, we are dealing with a case-by-case factual decision, not a question of law, the answer to which automatically applies to all cases of a certain type. An analogy may be found in the distinction between terms implied in fact and in law. The latter means terms automatically inserted into all contracts of a certain type, whereas the former depends on the facts of each case.[203]

More broadly, the reasonable man in the cases is far from an impersonal or abstract legal concept – Viscount Radcliffe's 'anthropomorphic conception of justice'.[204] In fact, it is highly sensitive to the facts. As Lord Hoffmann wrote extra-judicially, 'a good deal of what Lord Macmillan [in *Glasgow Corporation*] calls the personal equation is by no means eliminated'.[205] The examples then invoked by His Lordship show that the reasonable man is not

199 *Healthcare at Home* (n 25).

200 Roderick Munday, *Evidence* (8th edn, OUP 2015) 320.

201 *ICS* (n 196) 913.

202 Ibid. 914.

203 *Lister v Romford Ice and Cold Storage Co Ltd* [1957] AC 555 (HL) 594 (Lord Tucker); *Liverpool City Council v Irwin and Another* [1977] AC 239 (HL) 257–8 (Lord Cross); *Scally v Southern Health and Social Services Board* [1992] 1 AC 294 (HL) 307 (Lord Bridge).

204 *Davis Contractors* (n 198) 728.

205 Lord Hoffmann (n 190) 129.

imposed on the facts but rather created by them. In *Daly v Liverpool Corporation* (1939), the Court refused to hold a hapless old lady liable for contributory negligence for failing to notice an approaching bus:

> Although her inability to see the bus and ... to take the necessary action would not have occurred in younger people, what she actually did was the best she could. I cannot believe that the law is quite so absurd as to say that if a pedestrian happens to be old and slow and a little stupid and does not possess the skill of the hypothetical pedestrian, he or she can only walk about his or her native country at his or her own risk.[206]

The House of Lords, in *Caswell v Powell Duffryn Associated Collieries Ltd* (1939), likewise treated the reasonable man as a creature of the facts, not as a legal concept descending from Justice Holmes's legendary 'brooding omnipresence in the sky':[207]

> What is all-important is to adapt the standard of what is negligence to the facts, and to give due regard to the actual conditions under which men work in a factory or mine, to the long hours and the fatigue, to the slackening of attention which naturally comes from constant repetition of the same operation, to the noise and confusion in which the man works, to his preoccupation in what he is actually doing at the cost perhaps of some inattention to his own safety.[208]

It follows that the standard of care expected of (in tort), or the understanding of terms by (in contract), the reasonable man is dictated by the facts of the case. The law has no position on what a document phrased in a particular way ought to mean to a reasonable man, or on how a reasonable man ought to act. It all depends on the facts of the case. It is therefore better to say that the reasonable man test is an issue of fact.

By way of pre-empting a criticism, let me clarify that this is not a legal categorisation of facts. One is not asking whether a fact falls within the scope of a rule. Rather, one is establishing *what the fact is*. What would the reasonable man understand? What would the reasonable man do? This is no different from asking what a patient would have done if she had been warned about a risk – an indisputably factual question.[209] All three questions have legal consequences, but in themselves they are factual. They do no more than

206 *Daly v Liverpool Corporation* [1939] 2 All ER 142 (Liverpool Assizes) 143 (Stable J).

207 *Southern Pacific Co v Jensen* 244 US 205 (1917) (SCOTUS) 222 (in dissent).

208 *Caswell v Powell Duffryn Associated Collieries Ltd* [1940] AC 152 (HL) 178–9 (Lord Wright); *Wilsher v Essex Area Health Authority* [1987] QB 730 (CA) 749 (Mustill LJ) (reversed on different grounds).

209 See, e.g., *Chester v Afshar* [2004] UKHL 41, [2005] 1 AC 134 [39] (Lord Hope).

inquire into what happened in the physical world, or what would have happened in the physical world.

But does not the application of any test depend on the facts of the case? What else can it depend on? If dependence on the facts proves that a question is factual and not legal, all questions are factual and the distinction is destroyed. Not so.

Let us take the definition of sufficient consideration in contract, which is undoubtedly a question of law. Now it is true that in order to find whether the alleged consideration in a given case is sufficient we need to know what the alleged consideration consists of (the facts). But that is not the question. The question of sufficiency of consideration is what constitutes sufficient consideration, not whether the facts in this or that case disclose sufficient consideration. There exists a body of cases, going back to the sixteenth century, classifying benefits and detriments as sufficient or insufficient consideration.[210] So, promising to do what the promisor is already bound to do by statute or public duty is not good consideration,[211] but promising to do what the promisor is already bound to do under a contract with a third party is good consideration.[212] This is entirely a matter of legal choice or policy; not of the facts of the case. That 'natural love and affection' is not good consideration does not depend on the facts of the case.[213] That the adequacy of consideration is immaterial does not depend on the facts of the case.[214] We do not need the facts of the case to answer the question of 'what constitutes sufficient consideration'. What constitutes sufficient consideration is a legal question, whereas whether a given consideration is sufficient is a factual question.

And so the strict distinction stands. A legal question is about the law and cannot be answered by factual examination. A factual question is about the physical world and cannot be answered by examining the law.

Returning to the reasonable man, if the question were 'Which standard is applied to the interpretation of contractual terms, objective or subjective?', then the question would be legal. We would answer that the standard is the reasonable man and not the parties' own beliefs or intentions. But when we come to apply the test of the reasonable man, we already know what the

[210] David Ibbetson, 'Assumpsit and Debt in the Early Sixteenth Century: The Origins of the Indebitatus Count' (1982) 41 CLJ 142, 152ff.

[211] *Collins v Godefroy* (1831) 1 B & Ad 950, 109 ER 1040 (KB) 1042 (Lord Tenterden CJ); *Glasbrook Brothers Limited v Glamorgan County Council and Others* [1925] AC 270 (HL) 281 (Viscount Cave LC).

[212] *New Zealand Shipping Co Ltd v A M Satterthwaite & Co Ltd (The Eurymedon)* [1975] AC 154 (PC) 168 (Lord Wilberforce).

[213] *Tweddle v Atkinson* (1861) 1 B & S 393, 121 ER 762 (QB) 764 (Crompton J).

[214] *Mountford v Scott* [1975] Ch 258 (CA) 265 (Cairns LJ).

standard is. The law is known. The only thing that remains is the question of what would happen in the physical world: what the reasonable man would actually understand. This is a question of fact.

The reasonable man test is an issue of fact. Therefore, the factual requirement is satisfied.

2.8.1.1.2 THE FALSITY REQUIREMENT Advancing now to the second requirement, we ask whether the reasonable man test is applied irrespective of the facts. This would be the case if, to continue with *ICS*, the House of Lords did not actually concern itself with how a reasonable man would read the document (like the King's Bench did not inquire into force and arms) or was satisfied with dubious evidence (such as the neck verse for the benefit of clergy). However, as we have seen, the House of Lords was greatly interested in how a reasonable man would understand the words. Lord Lloyd, in dissent, also asked himself what 'the ordinary investor to whom the claim form is addressed'[215] would understand. This is a representative example of the application of the test across all cases. Therefore, the test of the reasonable man is decided in accordance with the facts. It does not satisfy the falsity requirement.

2.8.1.1.3 THE CONSCIOUSNESS REQUIREMENT Since there is no falsity of which one can be conscious, it is unnecessary to consider the third requirement of consciousness. The reasonable man is not a Hard Fiction.

2.8.1.2 Is the Reasonable Man a Soft Fiction?

We already know the factual requirement, which is also the first requirement of the Soft Fiction, to be satisfied. We can therefore jump to the second requirement, namely unnatural interpretation. There is no hint in the cases or commentary that the reasonable man test is given a strained or far-fetched or contrived interpretation. The test is in any event so amorphous and pliable, so lacking in fixed content, that it is hard to strain. To apply the test unnaturally, courts would have to regard as reasonable what would be ordinarily considered unreasonable or at least scarcely reasonable. There is no evidence of such a practice. Having concluded that the second requirement is not satisfied, there is no need to visit the third requirement of consciousness. The reasonable man is not a Soft Fiction.

The view presented here is that, contrary to popular opinion, the reasonable man is not a legal fiction of any kind.

[215] *ICS* (n 196) 902.

2.8.1.3 Assessment

Having fed the reasonable man to the definition and received an answer at the other end, it is now appropriate to take a reality check. After all, the definition was always going to yield *an* answer. The question is whether the answer, apart from being technically correct according to our assumptions, stands to reason. Does it make sense that the reasonable man, who we know does not exist in the physical world, is not fictitious?

This conclusion, I argue, agrees with common sense. Asking what the reasonable man would understand is the same as asking what it is reasonable to understand. The 'man' is simply a way to illustrate that the question of reasonableness is not judged from the subjective point of view of the parties but from the objective point of view of a disinterested observer. There is no fiction because we never rely on the existence of an actual reasonable man. We do not posit anything that is untrue. The man is just an unnecessary vehicle for the question of what is objectively reasonable. This is why Lord Hoffmann, a champion of the objective approach, could advocate the retirement of the reasonable man without fear of contradiction.[216] To ask the reasonable man is to ask what is reasonable. To ask what is reasonable cannot be fictitious.

2.8.2 *Second Case Study:* Volenti non fit Injuria

2.8.2.1 Overview of the Defence

The maxim '*volenti non fit injuria*' literally means 'no injury is done to the willing'. It is a tort defence,[217] relevant mostly to negligence. Broadly, it stands for the principle that '[o]ne who has invited or assented to an act . . . cannot, when he suffers from it, complain of it as a wrong'.[218] Specifically, the defence can be said to have three elements. First, the claimant must be fully aware of the risk. Second, the claimant must agree (expressly or impliedly) to absolve the defendant from liability for his conduct. Third, this agreement must be truly voluntary in the sense that it is free of any pressure or necessity.[219]

216 Lord Hoffmann (n 190) 141.

217 James Goudkamp argues that while *volenti non fit injuria* is in principle a defence (in the sense that it does not contradict the elements of negligence), it is frequently applied – or misapplied – as a mere denial of the duty, breach or causation element: James Goudkamp, *Tort Law Defences* (Hart 2013) 55–8, 60, 70, 74.

218 *Smith v Baker* [1891] AC 325 (HL) 360 (Lord Herschell).

219 Respectively, *Wooldridge v Sumner* [1963] 2 QB 43 (CA) 69 (Diplock LJ); *Nettleship v Weston* [1971] 2 QB 691 (CA) 701 (Lord Denning MR); *Bowater v Rowley Regis Corporation* [1944] KB

It should be noted that while the *volenti* defence often overlaps with contributory negligence (in that the claimant takes a risk), the two defences are not co-extensive. Agreeing to run a risk is not necessarily negligent and acting negligently does not necessarily amount to a waiver of liability.[220] It is also noteworthy that contributory negligence can be a partial defence,[221] whereas *volenti* is a complete defence.[222]

Of the three elements of the *volenti* defence – knowledge, agreement, voluntariness – the second is the most crucial for our purposes. This is because it is the requirement of agreement to waive liability that might have generated a fiction. It is one thing to knowingly assume a risk. It is quite another thing to agree to absolve the defendant from liability. Whenever we get into a car we willingly and informedly take the risk of a car accident, but that is a far cry from releasing negligent drivers from liability in the event they injure us.[223] Considering also that people do not usually think in terms of discharging others from liability,[224] the requirement of agreement sets a high, almost insurmountable bar for defendants.

Nevertheless, the requirement to agree to waive a claim has been affirmed in a string of high-level judgments. In *Nettleship v Weston* (1971), Lord Denning MR stated:

> Knowledge of the risk of injury is not enough. Nor is a willingness to take the risk of injury. Nothing will suffice short of an agreement to waive any claim for negligence. The plaintiff must agree, expressly or impliedly, to waive any claim for any injury that may befall him due to the lack of reasonable care by the defendant.[225]

In *Morris v Murray* (1990), Stocker LJ stated:

> [I]n order to defeat an otherwise valid claim on the basis that the plaintiff was volens the defendant must establish that the plaintiff at the material time

476 (CA) 479 (Scott LJ). My summary closely mirrors Michael A Jones (ed), *Clerk & Lindsell on Torts* (22nd edn, Sweet & Maxwell 2018) para 3–107.

220 Christian Witting, *Street on Torts* (14th edn, OUP 2015) 197.

221 The court has power to apportion liability pursuant to s 1 of the Law Reform (Contributory Negligence) Act 1945.

222 *Imperial Chemical Industries Ltd v Shatwell* [1965] AC 656 (HL) 672 (Lord Reid), 686 (Lord Pearce); *Nettleship v Weston* (n 219) 701 (Lord Denning MR).

223 This is a contemporary adaption of an illustration by Lord Halsbury LC in *Smith v Baker* (n 218) 337; see also Stephen D Sugarman, 'Assumption of Risk' (1997) 31 Valparaiso U LR 833, 834.

224 See also Kenneth W Simons, 'Assumption of Risk and Consent in the Law of Torts' (1987) 67 Boston U LR 213, 224–5.

225 *Nettleship v Weston* (n 219) 701.

> knew the nature and extent of the risk and voluntarily agreed to absolve the defendant from the consequences of it.[226]

Endorsements of the agreement requirement abound.[227] At the time of writing it continues to be applied.[228] Let us see how it was applied in several hard cases.

2.8.2.2 The Problematic Cases

In *Titchener v British Railways Board* (1983),[229] a girl of fifteen was hit by a train in the suburbs of Glasgow. She had exploited a gap in the fence along the railway to cross the lines. The girl, who was seriously injured, sued the Railways for failing to maintain the fence.[230] The House of Lords found unanimously that there was no breach of duty and in any case that the *volenti* defence was available.

Discussion of the defence was cursory and left many questions unanswered. On what basis did the House find that a teenage girl 'had exempted [the Railways] from any obligation towards her'?[231] Was it the fact that she crossed the lines in full awareness of the danger? Did a fifteen-year-old impliedly agree to relieve the Railways of a statutory duty by committing a folly? Anthony Jaffey, who reviewed the defence in 1985, was unpersuaded by the Law Lords' reasoning:

> It is hard to see however how the plaintiffs entering on the defendant's land with full knowledge of the danger can amount to an agreement with, or promise to, the defendant. At what moment were the Railways relieved of their obligations in relation to the safety of the plaintiff? At the moment she passed through the gap in the fence, or perhaps a split second before that? We are clearly in the realm of fiction if a person's conduct in voluntarily taking a known risk is treated as an implied agreement with the person who created the danger.[232]

226 *Morris v Murray* [1991] 2 QB 6 (CA) 18.

227 See, e.g., *Smith v Baker* (n 218) 355 (Lord Watson); *Bowater* (n 219) 481 (Goddard LJ); *Shatwell* (n 222) 681 (Lord Hodson), 687–8 (Lord Pearce), 691 (Lord Donovan); *Wooldridge v Sumner* (n 219) 69 (Diplock LJ); *Letang v Ottawa Electric Railway Co* [1926] AC 725 (PC) 731 (Lord Shaw).

228 *The White Lion Hotel v James* [2021] EWCA Civ 31 [90], [97] (Nicole Davies LJ).

229 *Titchener* [1983] 1 WLR 1427 (HL).

230 The claim was brought under the Occupiers' Liability (Scotland) Act 1960, but the Court interpreted s 2(3) of the Act as importing the common law defence of *volenti non fit injuria*: Ibid. 1434 (Lord Fraser).

231 Ibid. 1434 (Lord Fraser).

232 AJE Jaffey, 'Volenti Non Fit Injuria' (1985) 44 CLJ 87, 91.

In *Imperial Chemical Industries Ltd v Shatwell* (1964),[233] two brothers were testing explosives in a quarry, in the service of the appellant. They had been instructed to do so from a faraway shelter but the cable was too short. A third employee was dispatched to get a longer cable. Several minutes passed. The brothers grew impatient and agreed to test the charges anyway, out in the open. This modus operandi placed the brothers in personal contravention of the regulations.[234] It was also proved that the employer had in the preceding months gone to great lengths to forbid precisely this conduct, educate the workers about its dangerousness and publicly discipline any employee who disobeyed the prohibition. Despite the risk of injury being low, both brothers were injured in the explosion. One brother then sued the employer for being vicariously liable for the other brother's contributory negligence.

The House of Lords held *per curiam* that *volenti* was a complete defence to the claim. As sensible as this outcome may seem, the questions which arose in *Titchener* as to the agreement requirement apply equally here. The claimant assumed a patent risk in full awareness that it was forbidden by his employer as well as illegal. But we know that is not enough. Did he also agree to waive the right to compensation? Many people would say that, to put it bluntly, he just took a stupid risk, heedless of the legal consequences.

Morris v Murray (1990)[235] involved probably the most reckless pastime imaginable. The claimant had a friend who could fly light aircraft. After an afternoon of heavy drinking with said friend, the claimant agreed to take a joy-ride on the friend's plane. The friend, who was by then very drunk, just managed to get the plane airborne before crashing, killing himself and severely injuring the claimant. The claimant sued the pilot's (i.e., friend's) estate in negligence.

All justices of the Court of Appeal agreed the claimant was *volens*. The colossal recklessness of the claimant dominated the reasoning. Sir George Weller said: 'It is difficult to conceive of anything more dangerous than to fly with a pilot who has consumed the equivalent of 17 whiskies.'[236]

That is a point one can hardly disagree with. But strictly speaking, the magnitude of the risk and the foolhardiness of the claimant do not of themselves mean he agreed to absolve the pilot from liability. The Court of Appeal

[233] *Shatwell* (n 222).

[234] Regulation 27(4) of the Quarries (Explosives) Regulations 1959 made under the Mines and Quarries Act 1954.

[235] *Morris v Murray* (n 226).

[236] Ibid. 31; see also 16–17 (Fox LJ), 29 (Stocker LJ).

did not directly confront this issue, though the agreement requirement had been recited in full.[237] The conduct, it seems, spoke for itself.

However, if the agreement requirement is automatically satisfied whenever the risk taken is very great, the requirement is not about agreement to waive liability at all, but simply about the magnitude of the risk.[238] Yet this is precisely what we have been told not to believe – indeed in *Morris v Murray* itself.[239] Has the agreement requirement become fictitious?

2.8.2.3 Is *Volenti non fit Injuria* a Hard Fiction?

2.8.2.3.1 FACTUAL REQUIREMENT Whether the claimant's conduct satisfies the three elements of the defence is quite clearly a matter of fact. Lord Esher MR, in his statement of the defence in *Yarmouth v France* (1887), removed all doubt:

> [M]ere knowledge of the danger will not do: there must be an assent on the part of the workman to accept the risk, with a full appreciation of its extent, to bring the workman within the maxim Volenti non fit injuria. If so, that is a question of fact.[240]

2.8.2.3.2 FALSITY REQUIREMENT For this requirement to be satisfied judges must decide one or more of the elements of the defence irrespective of the facts. I have focussed on the element of agreement. Given the ambiguity of implied agreement, it is not fair to say that judges just disregard the facts before them. It is arguable that by committing to an exceedingly dangerous course of action, the claimant has impliedly given up a right of action. In *Shatwell*, the case involving the brothers in the quarry, Lord Donovan said:

> When George invited James to join him in testing the electrical circuit without taking shelter George knew the risk he was running and accepted it voluntarily. He did not, of course, in express language, waive such rights as he might have against James if the risk matured and he was injured. But in my opinion that must be taken to be the tacit effect of the agreement between the two of them to test the circuit in the open. The situation lacks nothing of the elements necessary to support the plea of volenti non fit injuria.[241]

237 Ibid. 18 (Stocker LJ).

238 See also Richard Kidner, 'The Variable Standard of Care, Contributory Negligence and Volenti' (1991) 11 Legal Studies 1, 18.

239 *Yarmouth v France* (1887) LR 19 QBD 647 (QB) 657 (Lord Esher MR); *Nettleship v Weston* (n 204) 701 (Lord Denning MR); *Morris v Murray* (n 226) 18 (Stocker LJ).

240 *Yarmouth v France* (n 239) 657.

241 *Shatwell* (n 222) 693.

For all the queries I have raised, this wide interpretation of the agreement requirement cannot be dismissed as simply wrong. Lord Donovan did not *ignore* the facts.

Lord Pearce went even further in explaining why there was in fact an implied agreement:

> On the facts it was an implied term (to the benefit of which the employers are vicariously entitled) that George would not sue James for any injury that he might suffer, if an accident occurred. Had an officious bystander raised the possibility, can one doubt that George would have ridiculed it?[242]

This argument is open to some objections. For one thing, it is not clear into what contract this waiver of liability was to be implied. The brothers were not negotiating a contract of any kind. A contractual analysis would be artificial on these facts.[243] In addition, Lord Pearce's argument requires us to adopt an objective understanding of the agreement requirement such that a claimant could consent to a waiver he did not remotely consider, let alone intend.[244]

But whatever we think about the merits of the argument, we can be satisfied that the agreement requirement is not applied *irrespective* of the facts. If anything, Lord Pearce relied on the facts to argue the requirement was fulfilled. He may be right or he may be wrong. But a Hard Fiction, we remember, is not an argument we disagree with. It is a blatant indifference to the facts. As long as the proposition is arguable, even remotely, there cannot be a Hard Fiction. In the case of *volenti*, it is arguable that a claimant who embarks on a suicidal course thereby implicitly agrees to surrender a right of action. The falsity requirement is not made out.

2.8.2.3.3 CONSCIOUSNESS REQUIREMENT Since there is no inconsistency with the physical world, there cannot be consciousness of such an inconsistency. The consciousness requirement is also unsatisfied. Ergo, the defence *volenti non fit injuria* is not a Hard Fiction.

2.8.2.4 Is *Volenti Non Fit Injuria* a Soft Fiction?

2.8.2.4.1 FACTUAL REQUIREMENT As we have seen in the context of the Hard Fiction, the factual requirement is satisfied.

242 Ibid. 688.

243 See also Simons (n 224) 224–5.

244 The authors of *Clerk & Lindsell* argue the requirement is subjective: Jones (n 219) paras 3–118 to 3–119.

2.8.2.4.2 UNNATURAL INTERPRETATION REQUIREMENT Is the interpretation by successive courts of the agreement requirement as extending to situations where there is no actual agreement an unnaturally-strained interpretation? Is it like those forced interpretations of exclusion clauses recalled by Lord Denning in *George Mitchell* (quoted above)?[245]

It has been argued here that the courts' interpretation of *volenti* can be defended on the basis that the agreement may be implied and that the implication can be an objective one – having nothing to do with the claimant's state of mind or intentions. However, even an objective implication must have some basis in the facts. It is difficult to point to any act of the claimants in the cases we have discussed which indicates agreement – unless the very magnitude of the risk per se implies a waiver of liability. Such a proposition is arguable in the sense that it is not definitely wrong, but it does rob the agreement requirement of its substance and defeats the distinction the authorities draw between willing assumption of risk and agreement to waive a claim. If risk without more fulfils the agreement requirement, it is only a risk requirement.

The wide interpretation of the agreement requirement is not false in the same way that Minorca in London or imagined ouster or fake priests were false. We cannot say it is definitively wrong. But it is certainly a stretch. Moreover, it is a stretch that does not sit well with judicial orthodoxy on this very point. It is, in other words, an unnatural interpretation.

It must also be remembered that judges have a natural, and proper, desire to reach the 'right' result on the facts. To get to this result, the law, in some cases, is deployed by way of post-rationalisation, sometimes even manipulated. Reading the judgments in question, one can understand the judges' predicament. Take *Shatwell*, which involved the brothers in the quarry:

> My Lords, the employers had striven without compromise to prevent shot firers testing in the open. They had done everything that they could to enforce the safety rules. They had been influential in tightening up the regulations imposed on the shot firers personally, they had publicly punished and degraded a shot firer who tested in the open, and they had in consequence faced trouble with the union. They had arranged a system of work and pay designed to discourage the cutting of time and the taking of risks. The two shot firers, George and James, knew all this. In spite of it they deliberately broke the statutory regulations which were laid on them personally, and together tested in the open. As a result they blew themselves up. They were trained, trusted, certificated men and it would have been absurd to have someone to watch over them.

[245] *George Mitchell* (n 188) 296–7.

> Although in this action George alone is the plaintiff, each should be entitled, on the plaintiff's argument, to get damages from the employers on the ground that the other's negligence and breach of statutory duty renders the employers vicariously liable. And whatever precautions the employers had used to prevent the two men testing in the open, they would, if the men had managed to evade those precautions and blown themselves up, still be liable vicariously to the men for their negligence in doing so. That result offends against common sense.[246]

Plainly, to visit liability upon the exemplary employer by a technical trick of *respondeat superior* seemed unjust. The court needed a way out. The defence of *volenti* clearly suggested itself on the facts and fit almost perfectly. It seemed designed for this very situation. If avoiding an absurd outcome meant pushing the boundaries of the defence, so be it.

Similarly, in *Morris* (involving the drunk pilot), the judges could not bring themselves to award compensation for an act which they regarded as the height of irresponsibility. If it meant stretching the defence, so be it. After all, the common law has never been stagnant. It develops with each set of facts. Thus an unnatural interpretation, permissible but tenuous, was adopted in preference to an unsatisfactory result.

The unnatural interpretation requirement is met.

2.8.2.4.3 CONSCIOUSNESS REQUIREMENT It now falls to be decided whether the judges who heard the cases were conscious that they were stretching the agreement requirement beyond its natural meaning. If pressed, would Lord Donovan (for instance) admit, 'Yes, it was a bit of a stretch'? Would he admit that he stretched the requirement so far as effectively to neuter it? It seems clear that Lord Donovan understood the practical effect of the extension, that he knew what he was doing, that he really meant to say that when the risk was so great the agreement requirement was constructively fulfilled – or, put differently, dispensed with.

That is not to say that Lord Donovan would have admitted he was wrong. Indeed, I do not say he *was* wrong. The point is that he must have known, and any jurist who cared to examine the subject would have known, that the agreement requirement was downgraded by a strained, far-fetched or contrived interpretation. There was consciousness of an unnatural interpretation.

Volenti non fit injuria is a Soft Fiction.

246 *Shatwell* (n 222) 683 (Lord Pearce).

2.8.2.5 Final Note

Nicholas McBride and Roderick Bagshaw take the view that agreement is not a necessary ingredient of the defence.[247] This is because the facts of recent cases cannot be reconciled with such a stringent requirement. I do not dispute this last point. Indeed, this conclusion is a corollary of the argument that the agreement requirement has been fictionalised. To say that a requirement has been fictionalised is to say that it does not exist in practice – at least in its original form.

In my view, however, it is better to say that the requirement is a Soft Fiction than to deny its existence altogether. My reason for this is that the cases – even those cases where the fiction is in operation – still insist on the presence of an agreement to absolve the defendant from liability.[248] The practical effect of this Soft Fiction is that the agreement requirement is replaced with a high-threshold assumption of risk requirement.

It is arguable that the requirement of agreement has been even further diminished. In *Blake v Galloway* (2004),[249] adolescents played a game of throwing twigs at each other. One sustained an eye injury and sued his assailant in negligence and battery. The *volenti* defence succeeded. It is suggested that such play, though it involved some risk, was not reckless or even unusual. It is certainly not in the same league as boarding a plane with an inebriated pilot or detonating explosives unshielded. Has the agreement requirement been emasculated to the point where any risk will do?

In my view, we should approach *Blake v Galloway* with caution. The Court of Appeal found there was no breach of duty so *volenti* was not discussed in relation to negligence.[250] *Volenti* did, however, negate battery on the facts; but then battery is defeated by consent *simpliciter*.[251] There is no need for an agreement to exclude liability. So *Blake v Galloway* was not a case of the full-blown defence being applied. As such, the case had nothing to do with the agreement requirement.

It appears that the best view is that the defence of *volenti non fit injuria* will apply only in cases of exceptional recklessness.[252] In these cases, it will apply

247 Nicholas J McBride and Roderick Bagshaw, *Tort Law* (6th edn, Pearson 2018) 705, esp fn 36.

248 *Titchener* (n 229) 1434 (Lord Fraser); *Shatwell* (n 224) 681 (Lord Hodson), 686–7 (Lord Pearce), 691–2 (Lord Donovan); *Morris v Murray* (n 226) 18 (Stocker LJ).

249 *Blake v Galloway* [2004] EWCA Civ 814, [2004] 1 WLR 2844.

250 Ibid. [19] (Dyson LJ).

251 *Collins v Wilcock* [1984] 1 WLR 1172 (QB) 1177 (Goff LJ); *Re F (Mental Patient: Sterilisation)* [1990] 2 AC 1 (HL) 72 (Lord Goff); *Blake v Galloway* (n 249) [20] (Dyson LJ).

252 It did not apply, for example, in *Marshall v Osmond* [1983] QB 1034 (CA) 1038 (Sir John Donaldson MR), where the claimant was injured evading arrest.

with the help of a Soft Fiction, whereby the exceptional recklessness manufactures an implied agreement to waive liability.

2.9 CONCLUSION

In the previous chapter, I discussed fictions under the Old System. This chapter began with the observation that the abolition of the Old System created a new paradigm where fictions were conceptual rather than procedural. This paradigm shift presented a challenge: how to isolate conceptual fictions from the rest of the law. What was the fiction when it ceased to be a non-traversable pleading (or equivalent)? I met this challenge by proposing two definitions of legal fiction: a Hard Fiction, built upon manifest falsehood, and a Soft Fiction for unnatural interpretations. In reaching this outcome, I defended the fiction from various theoretical assaults and examined existing definitions.

This duality of Hard and Soft Fictions is offered as a more nuanced alternative to the seemingly endless debate in search of the fictional holy grail, the one-and-only, make-or-break formula for legal fiction. The twin definitions recommended here will, it is hoped, bring clarity and consistency to the identification of fictions, an exercise hitherto dogged by obscurity and disagreement. Legal fiction would then become a term of art, understood by all in the same way, capable of being deployed with the exactitude so beloved of lawyers and so necessary for the coherent development of the law.

In applying the new definitions of Hard and Soft Fictions, we learned that the reasonable man was neither and that *volenti non fit injuria* was the latter.

* * *

It was said in the General Introduction that the aim of this book was to develop an Acceptance Test for fictions. This Acceptance Test would tell us which fictions to accept and which to reject.

The Hard and Soft definitions of legal fiction are an important element of the Acceptance Test and bring us a step closer to it.

In the next chapter, I will continue to develop the Acceptance Test by applying the new definitions to a range of modern-day fictions. For the first time in this book, fictions will be *normatively* judged: are they good or bad? Should we keep them? The answer to this last question will bring us even closer to the Acceptance Test.

3

New Fictions Explored

In writing of the legal fiction it is easy to slip into the past tense. We have . . . a feeling that the fiction belongs to a stage in the development of the law which is now safely passed . . . Yet a moment's reflection is sufficient to show that there is little basis for this feeling.

Lon Fuller[1]

3.1 INTRODUCTION

The first chapter was an account of fictions under the Old System. The second chapter was an attempt to clarify the nature of fictions under the New System, our system. I concluded that fictions existed in two forms: Hard and Soft. This third chapter is devoted to the study of contemporary fictions. I will go through a list of present-day devices thought to be fictions. One by one, I will describe the operation of each device; then check whether it is really a fiction (on my definitions); if so, consider alternatives; and, finally, evaluate the fiction. This last step is a normative judgement: is it good for the law to have this fiction in view of the alternatives?

The following (alleged) fictions will come under the microscope: (i) the equitable maxim that equity treats as done that which ought to be done; (ii) estoppel; (iii) *volenti non fit injuria* (revisited for evaluation); (iv) the single meaning rule in defamation; (v) the common intention constructive trust; (vi) remoteness in negligence; and (vii) reading down exclusion clauses. The list is by no means exhaustive but space is limited. These (alleged) fictions have been chosen for their variety and their importance to private law.

[1] Lon L Fuller, *Legal Fictions* (Stanford University Press 1967) 93.

3.2 A COMMON MISUNDERSTANDING CONCERNING THE EVALUATION OF FICTIONS

Unlike justice or art, fictions are not pursued for their own sake. None of the fictions we have encountered so far, Old or New, was created because lawyers liked fictions and wanted to have more fictions in the law. Fictions were *tolerated* because they accomplished something external to themselves. For example, in the case of geographical fictions, judges prevented the defendant from traversing the misstatement of place, not because they thought the misstatement good in itself, but as a means to an end – namely the extension of English law to places outside England. The distinction between means and ends is crucial to the evaluation of fictions.

In evaluating fictions, it is important to beware of the following pitfall. Evaluating a fiction (a means) is not the same as evaluating its aim (an end). For example, suppose we are evaluating the geographical fictions. We should not fall into the trap of evaluating the aim of the geographical fictions (i.e., whether it is good for the law that an overseas action should be triable in the common law courts). That may be a good or bad thing. But if it is a good thing, it does not follow that the fiction is a good way of achieving it. Conversely, if it is a bad thing, it does not follow that it is a bad thing *because it is a fiction*. A non-fictitious rule with the same effect would be just as bad. There are two separate questions here. One is the question of aim: is it good for the law that a foreign action should be triable in the common law courts? The other is the question of means: is the fiction a good way of achieving a *given* aim?

If we are evaluating geographical fictions and not the aim thereof, the arguments we use must relate to the merits of the fiction itself. A legitimate argument against the geographical fiction would be that it is unprincipled, inelegant and brings the law into dispute. A legitimate argument in favour of the fiction would be that it is efficient in the sense that it gets the job done with minimal disturbance to existing law. Another legitimate argument for the fiction would be that there was no other way, as the system then stood, to achieve the desired aim. These would be arguments about the merits of the fiction. An *illegitimate* argument against the fiction would be that English courts should not usurp the jurisdiction of foreign courts. An *illegitimate* argument for the fiction would be that English subjects deserve English justice wherever they may be. These last two arguments are about the desired aim, which can be achieved with or without the fiction. Such aim-based arguments only obscure the debate about the use of the fiction.

Because it is natural to view the fiction and its aim as one subject of assessment, and indeed to judge things by their results, this conflation of the merits of the fiction with the merits of its desired product is tempting. We must guard against this temptation. When it comes to fictions, the proof of the pudding is *not* in the eating.

To be sure, the separation of fiction and aim should not be carried too far. I should not be taken to mean that if we decide the aim is bad (e.g., we decide it is wrong to try foreign actions in common law courts), we should still not abolish the geographical fiction (because fiction and aim are separate). Of course, in such a case, we would support the abolition of the fiction along with the extra-territorial jurisdiction we have decided against. After all, the fiction *directly results* in the extension of jurisdiction (the misstatement of place avoids the issue). The point is that we would support the abolition of the fiction not because it is a fiction, and because we believe fictions are bad; but simply because we do not think English courts should be intervening in foreign actions. Indeed, we would abolish this extra-territorial jurisdiction just the same if it were not founded on a fiction.

To summarise, in evaluating a fiction, we should not take into account the merits of the aim of the fiction.

3.3 CLASSIFICATIONS OF FICTIONS

In the previous two chapters, I introduced three different classifications of fictions. It would not be amiss to pause to review these classifications and the relations between them. First, I distinguished between Old Fictions and New Fictions. This is simply a matter of date. All fictions prior to the Common Law Procedure Act 1852 are Old, and all later fictions are New. As we have seen, the Old Fictions that outlived the Old System changed in character, becoming New Fictions (they were no longer non-traversable pleadings or the like).[2] I shall call this classification the 'Age Classification'.

The second classification was between Jurisdictional, Auxiliary and Essential Fictions. The Jurisdictional Fiction does not affect the substance of any action, but simply which court the action may be brought in. An example of a Jurisdictional Fiction is the writ of *quominus*, which did not change the nature of debt claims. It simply permitted them to be brought in the Court of Exchequer, where the claimant could take advantage of the superior enforcement process of that Court. The Auxiliary Fiction affects the substance of the law, but without disturbing its conceptual basis. As we recall, it is a mere incantation or text for form's sake, legal lip service, which no lawyer takes seriously as the reason for the result of a case. An example of an

[2] Estoppel is an exception; see Section 3.5.

Auxiliary Fiction is the benefit of clergy. No one thought that a sham reading test was the real reason criminals were spared the gallows. But it did change criminal law by exempting a large class of people from the death penalty. The Essential Fiction affects the substance of the law through doctrine. Unlike Auxiliary Fictions, Essential Fictions are seen as a conceptual basis for the result of a case. An example of an Essential Fiction is quasi-contract. Lawyers believed that certain situations should be treated as analogous to contract. The law was changed and the reason for the change and the fiction were one. I will call this classification the 'Effect Classification'.

The third classification was the recognition of two definitions of fiction, Hard and Soft. This is the 'Nature Classification'. A Hard Fiction, we remember, is a factual issue consciously decided irrespective of the facts. A Soft Fiction is a factual issue decided by a consciously unnatural interpretation.

As for the relations between these three classifications, there is no necessary link between them. They are independent of each other. In practice, however, there are some correlations. For example, Old Fictions tend, overwhelmingly, to be Hard Fictions. Still, it does not mean that a fiction must be Hard to be Old.[3] The classifications are discrete. I will revisit the correlations between the classifications in the next chapter.

We are now ready to meet the New Fictions.

3.4 EQUITY TREATS AS DONE THAT WHICH OUGHT TO BE DONE

3.4.1 *Description*

This is one of the maxims of equity. As with all maxims, it is too broad to be read literally – as Lord Esher MR pointed out, somewhat crossly, in 1887: 'I detest the attempt to fetter the law by maxims. They are almost invariably misleading: they are for the most part so large and general in their language that they always include something which really is not intended to be included in them.'[4] Lord Wright echoed these sentiments in 1940: 'Indeed these general formulæ are found in experience often to distract the court's mind from the actual exigencies of the case, and to induce the court to quote them as offering a ready made solution.'[5]

3 As noted above, the '*vi*' element of '*vi et armis*' was a Soft Fiction despite being an Old Fiction.

4 *Yarmouth v France* (1887) LR 19 QBD 647 (QB) 653.

5 *Lissenden v CAV Bosch Ltd* [1940] AC 412 (HL) 435; see also *Patel v Mirza* [2016] UKSC 42, [2016] 3 WLR 399 [95] (Lord Toulson).

We will be well-advised to heed these warnings in the present discussion. As Professor Graham Virgo wrote, a maxim is 'a way of summarizing some complex principles or rules in a pithy statement'.[6] What then is the rule summarised in the maxim? The rule is that equity will deem a specifically enforceable obligation, yet to be performed, to have been performed. Lindley LJ stated the principle in *Re Anstis* (1886):

> Equity, no doubt, looks on that as done which ought to be done; but this rule, although usually expressed in general terms, is by no means universally true. Where the obligation to do what ought to be done is not an absolute duty, but only an obligation arising from contract, that which ought to be done is only treated as done in favour of some person entitled to enforce the contract as against the person liable to perform it.[7]

But what is the practical meaning of something being treated as done, an obligation treated as performed? In practice, the maxim is invoked in cases involving a duty to transfer property.[8] In such cases, the maxim results in a constructive trust over the property in favour of the party ultimately entitled to receive the property.[9] Indeed, the obligation will be deemed performed as soon as it is undertaken. For example, if Alice is under an obligation to transfer property to Ben, and Ben is entitled to specific performance of this obligation (say under a contract for the sale of land), then Alice will hold the property on trust for Ben immediately Alice assumes the obligation.[10] This is so even if the time for performance under the contract has not arrived and even if Alice has not done anything wrong (e.g., breached the contract).[11]

It is as if equity is impatient and cannot wait for Alice to actually transfer the property so it deems the property to have been transferred instantly. A split in ownership results: Ben is now the owner in equity but Alice remains legal owner. Ergo Alice holds the property on trust for Ben. As AJ Oakley noted, the effect of the maxim is 'to separate the legal and equitable ownership of the property'.[12]

6 Graham Virgo, *The Principles of Equity & Trusts* (2nd edn, OUP 2016) 28.

7 *Re Anstis* (1886) 31 Ch D 596 (CA) 605–6.

8 Ben McFarlane, Nicholas Hopkins and Sarah Nield, *Land Law* (3rd edn, OUP 2015) 297.

9 *Shaw v Foster* (1871–72) LR 5 HL 321 (HL) 333 (Lord Chelmsford), 338 (Lord Cairns); *Attorney-General for Hong Kong v Reid* [1994] 1 AC 324 331–2, 334, 336 (Lord Templeman); *FHR European Ventures LLP v Cedar Capital Partners LLC* [2014] UKSC 45, [2015] AC 250 [49], [50] (Lord Neuberger P).

10 A helpful summary of the authorities is found in *Englewood Properties Ltd v Patel* [2005] EWHC 188 (Ch), [2005] 1 WLR 1961 [40]–[42] (Lawrence Collins J).

11 Virgo (n 6) 38.

12 AJ Oakley, *Constructive Trusts* (3rd edn, Sweet & Maxwell 1997) 275.

While the rule as stated is of general application, these days it has two main applications.

3.4.1.1 First Application: Disposition of an Interest in Land

It is no coincidence that the maxim should pertain to land transactions. Unlike most contracts, contracts relating to an interest in land are by default (though not invariably) specifically enforceable.[13] As already noted, specific enforceability is a precondition for the operation of the maxim (where there is a contract).[14]

This brings the maxim into the sphere of day-to-day conveyancing. Dispositions of an interest in land, especially the sale of land, normally take place in two stages. At first, the parties enter into a contract. Sometime later, at 'completion', the agreement is performed with the vendor conferring the interest and the purchaser paying the price. At common law, the interest does not pass until completion (and, in many cases, registration). In equity, however, by dint of the maxim, the purchaser is deemed to receive the equitable title, automatically so to speak, upon the formation of a valid contract.[15] This is because as soon as the contract is made, the vendor has a specifically enforceable obligation to confer title on the purchaser. Equity then 'treats as done that which ought to be done': the vendor is deemed to have conferred title and the purchaser is deemed to have paid the price. The result is a constructive trust of the land with the vendor as trustee and purchaser as beneficiary.

This particular constructive trust that subsists between vendor and purchaser is one of the oldest in English law. It was already known in 1651.[16] The application of the maxim to conveyancing has many aliases, including 'the equitable doctrine of conversion',[17] 'the doctrine of anticipation'[18] and 'the rule in *Walsh v Lonsdale*' (1882).[19]

It should be noted that the maxim works its magic also in the absence of a contract. In *Mountney v Treharne* (2002),[20] a district judge ordered

13 This is because land is unique. Damages are therefore an inadequate remedy.

14 *Central Trust & Safe Deposit Co v Snider* [1916] 1 AC 266 (PC) 272 (Lord Parker).

15 Validity includes the requirement of writing in s 2 of the Law of Property (Miscellaneous Provisions) Act 1989. On some views, it also includes the requirement that the vendor has made, or the purchaser accepted, title. This latter requirement is discussed later.

16 Oakley (n 12) 275, citing *Lady Foliamb's Case* (1651), unreported, which is in turn cited in *Davie v Beversham* (1661) Rep Ch 4, 21 ER 711 (Ch).

17 Simon Gardner and Emily MacKenzie, *An Introduction to Land Law* (Hart 2015) 116; Oakley (n 12) 275ff.

18 McFarlane, Hopkins and Nield (n 8) ch 9.

19 (1882) 21 Ch D 9 (Ch).

20 [2002] EWCA Civ 1174, [2003] Ch 135.

a husband to convey a matrimonial home to his wife. The husband was then declared bankrupt – before the transfer was effected. The Court of Appeal held that the trustee-in-bankruptcy took the property subject to the wife's equitable estate – since equity deemed the transfer from husband to wife to have been effected instantly, that is before the bankruptcy.[21]

3.4.1.2 Second Application: Bribes and Secret Commissions

The maxim has also been found useful where an agent takes a bribe or secret commission. The difference between the two, incidentally, is that a bribe is given dishonestly to secure a favour. A secret commission is simply a benefit received by an agent without the knowledge of the principal, even if the purpose is not corrupt.[22]

This second application of the maxim is nicely illustrated by *Attorney-General for Hong Kong v Reid* (1993).[23] Mr Reid was an unscrupulous Acting Director of Public Prosecutions for Hong Kong. In breach of his fiduciary duty to the Crown, he obstructed the prosecution of several suspects in exchange for money bribes. The ill-gotten gains were then invested in real estate in his native New Zealand. Reid was convicted and sentenced to eight years' imprisonment. In civil proceedings, the Crown claimed ownership of the properties in New Zealand. The Privy Council agreed:

> As soon as the bribe was received [by Reid] it should have been paid or transferred instanter to the person who suffered from the breach of duty [i.e., the Crown]. Equity considers as done that which ought to have been done. As soon as the bribe was received, whether in cash or in kind, the false fiduciary held the bribe on a constructive trust for the person injured.[24]

The specifically performable obligation was to pay the bribe to the government (because the breach of fiduciary duty created an obligation to account for the value of the bribe).[25] Equity deemed it done, whereupon Reid held the bribe on trust for the government. Whatever he then did with the monies, he did as trustee for the government. When he bought land in New Zealand with the trust monies, the government was the equitable owner of the land.

21 Ibid. [76] (Jonathan Parker LJ).
22 Peter Millett, 'Bribes and Secret Commissions' (1993) 1 Restitution LR 7, 7 fn 2.
23 *Reid* (n 9).
24 Ibid. 331 (Lord Templeman).
25 *Regal (Hastings) Ltd v Gulliver* [1967] 2 AC 134, 144–5 (Lord Russell); *FHR* (n 9) [6] (Lord Neuberger P).

This advice of the Privy Council was not followed by the Court of Appeal in *Sinclair Investments (UK) Ltd v Versailles Trade Finance Ltd* (2011).[26] However, in *FHR European Ventures LLP v Cedar Capital Partners LLC* (2014), the Supreme Court approved *Reid* and overruled *Sinclair*.[27] The *Reid* conclusion, that a 'false fiduciary' holds bribes (and indeed traceable assets) on constructive trust for his principal, is good law.[28] This is because equity treats as done that which ought to be done.[29]

3.4.1.3 Cautionary Note

As potent as the maxim is, its power is not without limit. It cannot be used to create property *ex nihilo*. If Alice assigns to Ben property that does not yet exist, the maxim does not operate to complete the transaction by creating the property and transferring it to Ben. Instead, nothing happens until the property is actually created (if at all), at which point the maxim springs into action and gives Ben an equitable right in the newly-created property.[30] This is because, as we have seen, the maxim splits ownership into legal and equitable interests. It does not create property where none exists.

This language of magic, deeming and 'treating as if' certainly has the whiff of fiction about it, bringing to mind the peevish observation of AP Herbert's Lord Mildew: 'There is too much of this damned deeming.'[31] But before we can be sure that the maxim is a legal fiction, we need to consult the definitions of Hard and Soft Fictions, formulated in the last chapter.

3.4.2 *Is the Maxim a Hard Fiction?*

In *Wall v Bright* (1820), Sir Thomas Plumer MR called the vendor-purchaser constructive trust a 'fiction of equity'.[32] In *Shaw v Foster* (1872), Lord Hatherley LC used the same words to describe the same device: a 'fiction of Equity which supposes the money to be paid away with one hand and the

[26] [2011] EWCA Civ 347, [2012] Ch 453 [76]–[87] (Lord Neuberger MR).

[27] *FHR* (n 9) [50] (Lord Neuberger P). Interestingly, Lord Neuberger, as President of the Supreme Court, overturned his own decision as Master of the Rolls in *Sinclair*, ibid.

[28] Swadling argues the case was a misapplication of the maxim: William Swadling, 'The Vendor-Purchaser Constructive Trust' in Simone Degeling and James Edeman (eds), *Equity in Commercial Law* (Lawbook Co 2005) 473–4.

[29] While the Supreme Court did not explicitly rely on the maxim, the maxim was, I submit, implicit in, and consistent with, the Court's reasoning: *FHR* (n 9) [6]–[7] (Lord Neuberger P).

[30] Virgo (n 6) 39.

[31] AP Herbert, *More Uncommon Law* (Methuen 1982) 80.

[32] (1820) 1 Jac & Walk 494, 37 ER 456 (Ch) 459.

estate to be conveyed away with the other'.[33] But judicial opinion is not in itself determinative. As the last chapter demonstrated, the word 'fiction' means different things to different people. Nor is there a judicial consensus as to the meaning of the term. Here I will analyse fictions according to the model developed in the previous chapter. And so, I address myself to the familiar questions.

3.4.2.1 Factual Requirement

The maxim deems as done specifically what has *not* been done. The husband did not transfer the house to his wife, but was held to have done so. The agent did not transfer the bribe money to his principal, but was held to have done so. Here the word 'transfer' is used in its everyday practical sense: a willed human act of handing over. Whether or not a person transfers something in this sense is a fact in the physical world. It may be that the law, in some situations, implies a transfer; but, if so, the transfer is 'implied' because there was no actual transfer; because there was no fact in the physical world. This suggests the maxim falsifies a *fact* in the physical world and thus fulfils the factual requirement.

Sceptics may argue that ownership is a matter of law and so the passing of ownership is also a matter of law. According to this view, a transfer occurs whenever the law says it does. If the law says that the house changes hands without the husband's lifting a finger, it is otiose to look for some human act. Inasmuch as the maxim governs the passing of property, the argument goes, the operation of the maxim is a point of law and has nothing to do with fact.

In my opinion, this sceptical argument is only specious. It looks at the *result* of the maxim, which is the unwilled passing of property or the creation of an equitable interest. It ignores the fact that the result is reached through the fiction. The maxim is triggered in the first place only because something *has not been done*. Whether something has been done is indubitably a question of fact. The maxim then deems the undone to be done. It is all about the failure *to do*, which is factual.

Even more damning to the sceptical view is the reverse proposition: if there were no question of fact – to wit, nothing *to do* – there would be no need for the maxim. There would be nothing to treat as done. The maxim only exists because there is a factual question. So much is conceded in the words of the maxim itself. I conclude that the issue is factual.

33 *Shaw v Foster* (n 9) 357.

3.4.2.2 Falsity Requirement

To satisfy the falsity requirement, the factual issue must be decided irrespective of the facts. There is no doubt that the question whether property is transferred is decided irrespective of the facts. The maxim, like a deeming provision, tells us to treat A as B. In fact, it goes further in terms of falsity than the ordinary deeming provision. It tells us to treat A as the opposite of A. This element of the definition is clearly present.

Unlike other fictions, the maxim is a counterfactual on its face: the name of the fiction is a counterfactual. I discussed the relationship between fictions and counterfactuals in the last chapter. Since the maxim is a simple counterfactual ('A is deemed to be B'), rather than a hypothetical counterfactual ('What would have happened if A had been Z'), the maxim is capable of being a fiction.

3.4.2.3 Consciousness Requirement

As for consciousness, too, it cannot be doubted that the judges who apply the maxim know they are falsifying the facts by treating the undone as done. This conscious treatment is apparent in the maxim itself.

All the elements of the Hard Fiction are present. The maxim 'Equity treats as done that which ought to be done' is a Hard Fiction. It is unnecessary to ask whether it is a Soft Fiction. As I established in the previous chapter, if a device is a Hard Fiction, then it cannot also be a Soft Fiction.

3.4.3 *Effect Classification of the Maxim*

The maxim is not a Jurisdictional or an Auxiliary Fiction. It has nothing to do with any court's jurisdiction and it is not meaningless text for form's sake. It is an Essential Fiction because it expresses the justification for the result of the case. As we have seen in *Mountney v Treharne*, the true reason the wife was held to have received the house though the husband had not transferred it was that he *ought* to have transferred it. The fiction is the consummation of that obligation and therefore closely tied to the reason for the result of the case. The maxim is an Essential Hard Fiction.

3.4.4 *Difficulties in Application*

We now know how the maxim generally works and that it is a New Essential Hard Fiction. I now turn to its practical consequences. What happens when we apply this Hard Fiction to a variety of cases? The answer is clear: the maxim has brought about serious complications. So far, in the interest of explication, I have spared the reader the various uncertainties and peculiarities surrounding the maxim. Now is the time to discuss these. For reasons of space, I will deal with only three of the complications relating to the vendor-purchaser constructive trust. These are by no means the only complications arising from the maxim.[34]

3.4.4.1 First Complication: Nature of the Trust

We have seen that the effect of the maxim is to separate legal and equitable ownership and create a constructive trust in favour of the person ultimately entitled to receive property. Let us again consider the first application of the maxim, namely the vendor-purchaser situation. Let us also suppose that there is a written contract signed by both parties, whereby the vendor agrees to sell, and the purchaser to buy, an estate in fee simple. On close reflection, the scenario reveals a few oddities.

First, it is odd that the purchaser should get an equitable estate before she has paid the price. But this follows if the trust is created immediately upon the making of a valid contract. It seems as though the maxim only completes the vendor's obligation under the contract (to confer title) but not the purchaser's obligation (to pay). This imbalance is easily put right. The authorities tell us that the vendor-trustee is automatically given a lien on the property for the price.[35]

But the oddness does not stop there. The reality of the conveyancing process is that the vendor normally continues to reside in the property (or collect rent if he is a lessor) until completion. This means that the purchaser, though a beneficiary under the trust of the property before completion, is not a beneficial owner (at least in the usual sense of the term). This is not only anomalous but also at variance with the principle of equity that the trustee,

[34] Even the requirement of specific performance has been doubted: Simon Gardner, 'Equity, Estate Contracts and the Judicature Acts: Walsh v Lonsdale Revisited' (1987) 7 OJLS 60. For other complications, see DWM Waters, *The Constructive Trust* (Athlone Press 1964) 125–41. For complications arising from the second application (to bribes), see Millett (n 22); Peter Watts, 'Bribes and Constructive Trusts' [1994] LQR 178; Peter Watts, 'Tyrrell v Bank of London – An Inside Look at an Inside Job' [2013] LQR 527; Graham Virgo, 'Profits Obtained in Breach of Fiduciary Duty: Personal or Proprietary Claim?' [2011] CLJ 502; Terence Etherton, 'The Legitimacy of Proprietary Relief' (2014) 2 Birkbeck LR 59.

[35] *Lysaght v Edwards* (1875–76) LR 2 Ch D 499 (Ch) 506 (Sir George Jessel MR); *London and Cheshire Insurance Co Ltd v Laplagrene Property Co Ltd* [1971] Ch 499 (Ch) 514 (Brightman J).

being a fiduciary, cannot benefit from the trust.[36] McFarlane, Hopkins and Nield summarised the position of the parties under the trust as follows:

> Until full payment of the purchase money on completion, the trustee (the vendor) remains in possession, has a significant interest in the land, is entitled to income generated from the land, and is responsible for outgoings. The purchaser (the beneficiary under the trust) becomes entitled to capital benefits, such as any increase in the value of the land. In principle, risks pass to the purchaser, although these may be passed back to the vendor by the terms of the contract.[37]

Dr Peter Turner, in a meticulous study of the vendor-purchaser constructive trust, described it as a composite of equities that arise at different points, and upon different conditions, between the formation and performance of the contract. According to Turner's illuminating account, 'The equities that arise between vendor and purchaser aggregate together as equitable property that is distributed between vendor and purchaser.'[38] He identified four main equities that made up the purchaser's interest:

> (1) an interest in land, enforceable against third parties, that the purchaser may:
> a) use to claim priority over holders of rival interests in enforcing the vendor's promise to convey the land to the purchaser; and
> b) assign, charge, devise, and pass (as land) on intestacy;
> (2) an equitable right that the vendor exercise due care to preserve and maintain the land pending completion;
> (3) an equity to rents and profits received by the vendor between the agreed time for completion and the actual date of conveyance; and
> (4) a lien for repayment of the purchase price in the event of non-performance.[39]

The judicial views of the position of the *vendor* were catalogued by Lord Collins in *Southern Pacific Mortgages Ltd v Scott* (2014):

> The position of the vendor as trustee has been variously described as: (1) 'something between what has been called a naked or bare trustee, or a mere trustee (that is, a person without beneficial interest), and a mortgagee who is not, in equity (any more than a vendor), the owner of the estate, but is, in

[36] *Bray v Ford* [1896] AC 44 (HL) 51 (Lord Herschell); *FHR* (n 9) [5] (Lord Neuberger P).
[37] McFarlane, Hopkins and Nield (n 8) 304.
[38] PG Turner, 'Understanding the Constructive Trust between Vendor and Purchaser' [2012] LQR 582, 584.
[39] Ibid. 585–6 (footnotes omitted).

> certain events, entitled to what the unpaid vendor is, viz, possession of the estate' and 'a constructive trustee': *Lysaght v Edwards* ... [per] Sir George Jessel MR; or (2) 'constructively a trustee': *Shaw v Foster* ... per Lord O'Hagan; (3) 'a trustee ... with peculiar duties and liabilities': *Earl of Egmont v Smith* ... per Sir George Jessel MR; (4) 'a trustee in a qualified sense only': *Rayner v Preston* ... per Cotton LJ; and (5) 'a quasi-trustee': *Cumberland Consolidated Holdings Ltd v Ireland* ... per Lord Greene MR.[40]

It is plain that the operation of the maxim, at least in the case of the vendor-purchaser situation, has created a complex legal relationship. While it is classified generally as a constructive trust, it is in fact a *sui generis* constructive trust of an exotic nature. Commentators have described or decried it as 'curious',[41] 'an equitable riddle',[42] 'extremely unusual',[43] even 'fundamentally implausible'.[44]

3.4.4.2 Second Complication: Timing

Adding to the complexity of this many-headed trust is the question of when exactly each head of this equitable Hydra comes into existence. It is stated in the general description above that the constructive trust materialises as soon as a valid contract is constituted. This statement implicitly adopts Turner's view that, despite there being several equities which may or may not arise at different times, a trust of some kind exists 'at every stage' from formation of contract to final performance.[45] The view that a trust arises at the moment of contract is shared by Graham Virgo,[46] Simon Gardner and Emily MacKenzie.[47] However, AJ Oakley,[48] Ben McFarlane, Nicholas Hopkins, Sarah Nield[49] and, it appears, DWM Waters[50] believe that a trust only arises once the vendor has made, or the purchaser accepted, title; but then the trust is backdated to the time of contract.

40 [2014] UKSC 52, [2015] AC 385 [61].
41 Charles Harpum, Stuart Bridge and Martin Dixon, *The Law of Real Property* (8th edn, Sweet & Maxwell 2012) [15-053].
42 Turner (n 38) 605.
43 Oakley (n 12) 277.
44 Gardner (n 34) 64.
45 Turner (n 38) 597.
46 Virgo (n 6) 38.
47 Gardner and MacKenzie (n 17) 116.
48 Oakley (n 12) 282–5.
49 McFarlane, Hopkins and Nield (n 8) 298.
50 Waters (n 34) 84.

Charles Harpum, Stuart Bridge and Martin Dixon have points of agreement with the aforementioned authors but seem to regard the equitable interests that arise at different times (e.g., upon contract, establishment of title, part-payment of the price, completion date) as different trusteeships, themselves quite uncertain in scope.[51] James LJ thought that the trust arose 'when the contract is performed by actual conveyance, or performed in everything but the mere formal act of sealing the engrossed deeds', but then applied retroactively from the time of contract.[52] Dr Waters traced the shifting judicial positions on the timing issue from Lord Keeper Wright to Lord Chancellor Hardwicke, from Master of the Rolls Plumer to Vice-Chancellor Kindersley to Lord Chancellor Hatherley, culminating in Sir George Jessel's influential judgment in *Lysaght v Edwards*[53] as Master of the Rolls.

The question of timing is not merely academic. In the *Jerome v Kelly* (2001–4) litigation, the timing of the trust affected the date of 'disposal' of an asset for the purposes of capital gains tax.[54] The Special Commissioners held there was a disposal, which was reversed by the High Court, which was in turn reversed by the Court of Appeal, only to be reversed by the House of Lords (holding there was no disposal).[55]

Of course, the question of when the trust arises may be less important than the timing of the various equities that, per Turner, make up the irregular relationship between vendor and purchaser. The point of highlighting these difficulties is not to improve on Turner's analysis, which seems to me the most precise. Indeed, I lack the space to plumb the depths of these interesting questions. The point is to show the complexities that this seemingly simple fiction – that 'equity treats as done that which ought to be done' – has spawned. DWM Waters has gone so far as to call the attempt to resolve the timing issue futile: 'a linguistic merry-go-round. For the problem is insoluble and insoluble it remains.'[56]

3.4.4.3 Third Complication: Effect on Third Parties

So far I have considered the relationship between vendor and purchaser. Now I ask: to what extent do the various equities that arise in favour of the purchaser

51 Harpum, Bridge and Dixon (n 41) [15-052]–[15-056].

52 *Rayner v Preston* (1880–81) LR 18 Ch D 1 (CA) 13.

53 *Lysaght v Edwards* (n 35).

54 Specifically, under s 27(1) of the Capital Gains Tax Act 1979.

55 [2001] STC (SCD) 170 (Special Commissioners); [2002] EWHC 604 (Ch), [2002] STC 609; [2002] EWCA Civ 1879, [2003] STC 206; [2004] UKHL 25, [2004] 1 WLR 1409.

56 Waters (n 34) 75; cf Turner (n 38) 599.

bind third parties? After all, the distinguishing feature of property rights is that they are capable of binding strangers. Say Alice has a specifically performable contract to transfer land to Ben. We know that, before legal title is transferred, Alice holds the land on constructive trust for Ben. If, during this time, Alice transfers the land to Charlie, can Ben claim the land from Charlie? Can Ben, during the subsistence of the trust, transfer his equitable interest, whatever it is, to David or bequeath it to Ed? Can Ben, during the life of the trust, lease his interest to Fred? Traditionally, the answer to these questions was thought to be positive[57] (though the usual formalities applied[58]).

Recently, however, in *Southern Pacific Mortgages Ltd v Scott* (2014), the Supreme Court unanimously held that Ben could not grant an (equitable) lease to Fred. That is, the purchaser-beneficiary under the constructive trust could not grant a lease to a third party. Lord Collins, with whom Lord Sumption agreed, stated: '[I]n my judgment, the appeal should be dismissed on the principal ground that the [purchaser] acquired *no more than personal rights* against the [vendor]. . . . *Those rights would only become proprietary* and capable of taking priority over a mortgage when they were fed by the . . . acquisition of the legal estate on completion.'[59]

While the decision involved statutory interpretation, Lady Hale DP concluded that the Land Registration Act 2002 merely reflected the position under the general law.[60] It would appear therefore that the interest held by the purchaser is not a right *in rem* after all. His rights are purely contractual. If he has no property, can he properly be called a trust beneficiary? Is there a trust at all? This decision casts doubt on the very essence of the vendor-purchaser constructive trust.[61]

Professor Richard Nolan has counselled against classifying the beneficiary's interest as either exclusively *in rem* or *in personam*: some aspects of the interest are proprietary, others personal.[62] Even so, one may query whether the beneficiary under the vendor-purchaser constructive trust has *any* proprietary interest. Nolan argues the 'key feature' of a proprietary interest is 'the ability to exclude others from some defined enjoyment of an asset'.[63] It does not appear that the purchaser-beneficiary can exclude others from the enjoyment of the property. He does not even enjoy it himself. The vendor retains the beneficial

57 Gardner and MacKenzie (n 17) 119. See e.g., *Shaw v Foster* (n 9) 333 (Lord Chelmsford).

58 Thus, for example, for Ben's interest to bind Charlie (Alice's disponee), Ben has to register the interest or be in apparent occupation.

59 *Southern Pacific* (n 40) [79].

60 Ibid. [111]–[114], [122].

61 Gardner and MacKenzie (n 17) 118 fn 15.

62 RC Nolan, 'Equitable Property' [2006] LQR 232, 253–4, 258.

63 Ibid. 234–5, 251, 264.

interest until the trust dissolves by the performance of the contract. On Nolan's persuasive definition, then, this relationship is not proprietary.[64] This is consistent with *Southern Pacific*. The maxim has undeniably led to complications. The very name of vendor-purchaser constructive *trust* may be a mistake.

3.4.5 *Evaluation*

In the preceding pages, I explained the operation of the maxim 'Equity treats as done that which ought to be done', established that it is a Hard Fiction and discussed some uncertainties concerning its application. In the light of this discussion, I now wish to evaluate this fiction. To recap, we have seen that the fiction addresses situations where an obligation relating to property is pending. In every case where the fiction applies, we have a transferor and an intended transferee. As we have seen, the fiction creates a constructive trust in favour of the intended transferee. It is assumed below that the transfer is specifically enforceable.

3.4.5.1 The Aim of the Fiction

In Section 3.2, I was at pains to show that the merits of a fiction were not to be confused with the merits of the aim of the fiction. The value of a fiction can only be judged as a means of achieving a *given* aim. Therefore, in order to assess a fiction, we must first identify the aim of the fiction. Then we can ask whether the fiction is the best way of achieving this aim.

It is submitted that the aim of the maxim is to protect the 'performance interest', so called by Professor Daniel Friedmann. The learned author was concerned with contractual obligations, but his comments are valid *a fortiori* for absolute duties as well:

> The essence of contract is performance. Contracts are made in order to be performed. This is usually the one and only ground for their formation. Ordinarily, a person enters into a contract because he is interested in getting that which the other party has to offer and because he places a higher value on the other party's performance than on the cost and trouble he will incur to obtain it. This interest in getting the promised performance (hereafter the 'performance interest') is the only pure contractual interest.[65]

64 Though Nolan accepts that the word 'property' may bear other meanings; 'to assert otherwise is to defy the English language': Ibid. 236, 252–3.

65 Daniel Friedmann, 'The Performance Interest in Contract Damages' [1995] LQR 628, 629 (footnote omitted); see also Nicholas J McBride, 'Duties of Care – Do They Really Exist?' (2004) 24 OJLS 417, 417 fns 3–4 and the citations therein.

Turner borrows the terminology from Friedmann to argue that the vendor-purchaser constructive trust protects the performance interest in the underlying property transaction.[66] Actually, the protection of the performance interest is the aim of the maxim in general (not just in the vendor-purchaser context). This is apparent in Lord Diplock's speech in *Harvela Investments Ltd v Royal Trust Co of Canada (CI) Ltd* (1985):

> Just as damages at common law for breach of contractual obligations are intended to put the party not in breach in the same position, so far as money can do so, as if the contractual obligations had been performed by the other party, so too the equitable remedy of specific performance is intended to put both parties in the same position as if their respective contractual obligations had been timeously performed by both of them. This finds expression in the maxim 'equity treats as done that which ought to have been done'.[67]

In practice, the protection of the performance interest in property transactions normally means the protection of the fragile interest of the intended transferee. We do not want the transferor's conduct to destroy or diminish this interest. An example of this concern was *Mountney v Treharne*, discussed above, where the result of the maxim was to protect the wife's interest in the yet-to-be-transferred matrimonial home from falling into the husband's bankrupt estate. That would, in all likelihood, have resulted in a serious diminution of the interest.

Likewise, we do not want the transferor to benefit from conduct which destroys or diminishes the transferee's interest. An example of this concern is *Reid*. There the result of the maxim was to ensure that the corrupt official could not, by failing to account to the Crown for the bribe, deny the Crown a traceable proprietary interest.

Underneath these concerns lies the belief, well-founded or not, that an obligation to transfer property is worthier of protection than other obligations; for the maxim does not operate where there is no property. The extent of this protection may be unclear, but there can be no doubt that protecting the performance interest is the general aim of the fiction.

There is admittedly a legitimate argument as to whether it is right to protect the intended transferee's interest (e.g., vis-à-vis the transferor's creditors or subsequent actual transferees) or indeed whether it is proper to undermine the formalities of land registration. But we know now that such arguments are irrelevant. We are assessing the fiction as a means to a given end and not the

66 Turner (n 38) 601–2.

67 [1986] AC 207 (HL) 227; see also *Burton v Todd* (1818) 1 Swans 255, 36 ER 380 (Ch) 382 (Sir Thomas Plumer MR).

end itself. So the question, properly framed, is whether the maxim is the best way to protect the performance interest.

3.4.5.2 The Case for the Fiction

The solution the fiction represents is to put the parties, to the extent possible, in the positions they would have been in had they performed their respective obligations. It is to give the transferor and transferee the intended interests in substance, while relegating the legal transfer to a mere technicality that should not affect the outcome. This is accomplished by the unimaginative trick of pretending that the obligations have been performed. That the trick is so obvious is, I say, an argument *for* the fiction. It recommends a solution that it is clear, simple and convenient.

More importantly, we know that the maxim is an Essential Fiction. This means that it is the real reason for the result of the case. The pretence that the intended transferee has the interest is not meaningless text, lip service or verbal flourish. When we say that we treat the intended transferee as if he has the interest, we really mean that and believe that this *should* be the case. For this reason, this fiction should not share in the opprobrium that some have heaped on certain Old Fictions which were ridiculous in appearance and whose substance had nothing to do with the true reasons for the determination of cases. Thus, at the risk of an oxymoron, this fiction is a 'genuine' one. It genuinely represents our view of what should be and seems an epigrammatic way of expressing this view. It is the opposite of a superficial fix. While the fiction is superficially untrue, it emanates from, or reflects, a *deeper* truth.

Given its simplicity and genuine content, the maxim is prima facie a sensible way to achieve the stated aim of protecting the performance interest.

3.4.5.3 The Case against the Fiction

It is hard to deny that the fiction, as a standalone rule, is vague. The maxim that 'Equity treats as done that which ought to be done' is broadly phrased and lacks the specificity of most rules. It reveals little about its application and raises more questions than it provides answers. The courts have had to imbue it with content in different contexts – and not without difficulty.

Of course, few areas of the law are free of uncertainty, whether they are fictitious or not. But in general, it should be accepted that a fictitious solution is more likely to bring about complications in application than a non-fictitious solution. This is because of the contradiction with reality inherent in the fiction.

The maxim has *indeed* sown complications in the law. These complications show no sign of being uprooted. They include the nature of the trust, its timing and the effect it has on third parties. It seems, at least in the case of the vendor-purchaser constructive trust, that a trust does not quite fit the reality of the situation and has to be forced upon it. In the result, we find ourselves with a strange, bespoke trust, where the trustee holds the beneficial interest.

Be that as it may, the complications should not be overstated. In many instances, the fiction achieves its aim quite smoothly. In the case of the husband and wife (*Mountney v Treharne*), it was convenient to assume that she had the interest and no complications arose therefrom. In the case of the corrupt official (*Reid*), it was also convenient to assume that the Crown had beneficial ownership. We run into problems in more complex situations, such as the sale of land, where, in the period between contract and intended completion, the intended transferee has the interest for some purposes but not for others. The intended transferee has the interest for the purpose of devising the land and asserting ownership against subsequent transferees of the vendor, but not for the purpose of occupation or rent. On balance, the fiction creates complications in some cases but not others.

Ultimately, the gravamen of the case against the fiction is that it obfuscates the law. We start from a false premise so it is no surprise that we end up with a muddled result. The fiction, at least in the vendor-purchaser context, has bequeathed generations of lawyers a legal Gordian knot that we are still struggling to untie.

3.4.5.4 Weighing the Fiction against the Alternatives

How do we reach the same result of protecting the performance interest without a fiction? At the simplest level, we could make a rule that, as soon as there is a specifically enforceable obligation to transfer property, the intended transferee obtains an equitable interest in the property. This would achieve the same result as the fiction without a fiction. It is not clear, though, why such a rule would be intellectually superior to the maxim. It also lacks the explanatory power of the maxim.

Furthermore, it is hard to see how a non-fictitious rule that imposes a constructive trust will avoid *any* of the complications. Exactly the same consequences will ensue. It follows then that the complications I discussed do not stem from the fiction, but from the underlying situation or the broad type of solution (i.e., the trust).

It would be possible to avoid these complications by codifying the vendor-purchaser constructive trust and clearly answering all the questions about its nature, timing and effect on third parties. But even with codification, it is not clear why the change from a fictitious to a non-fictitious rule as such answers any of the questions, or advances us so far as an inch in answering them. In this case, at least, it is difficult to impute to the fiction any negative effects, except perhaps general vagueness. It is not even embarrassing as other fictions are. On the contrary, it has persuasive force and elegance.

But there is another alternative. We could be more daring and make a rule that cuts out equity – and the problematic constructive trust – altogether. We can do so by granting the intended transferee certain rights *at common law*. This approach, which implies a fusion of law and equity, will need to reconcile these new legal rights with the absence of any transfer at common law and the non-compliance with legal formalities. This can in turn be addressed by reforming the law of property and the formalities. Clearly, this more daring approach to eliminating the fiction will require a root-and-branch rethinking of proprietary transfers, if not property law as a whole. That may be more than we bargained for when we set out to protect the performance interest.

To conclude our discussion of alternatives, the first (minimalist) alternative to the fiction (a rule creating the trust without a fiction) has no clear advantage over the fiction and the same disadvantages. The second alternative to the fiction (which entails a re-conceptualisation of legal transfers) will create more complications for the law than the fiction has. It is a Pandora's Box that nobody wants to open. It appears that the fiction has the virtue of efficiency: it is the least disruptive and effortful solution to the problem at hand – the shortest route to the destination. At worst, it is just as good, or just as problematic, as either of the alternatives. At best, it is a more efficient and self-explanatory solution.

A final point is that the vagueness of the fiction is not all bad: it allows courts to fit the maxim to different situations. A more rigid rule might cause greater friction since it is harder to adapt.

3.4.5.5 Conclusion

The maxim 'Equity treats as done that which ought to be done' is a New Essential Hard Fiction. While it has its drawbacks, it is suggested here that it is better than the alternatives and should be retained.

3.5 ESTOPPEL

3.5.1 *Description*

Estoppel means that a party cannot deny a point of fact or law which that party, or the court, has affirmed. In the words of Sir Edward Coke, 'a man's own act ... closes his mouth to allege or plead the contrary'.[68] Estoppel is of ancient origin and manifold. Lord Denning MR charted the rise and divergence of estoppel:

> It was brought over by the Normans. They used the old French 'estoupail'. That meant a bung or cork by which you stopped something from coming out. It was in common use in our courts when they carried on all their proceedings in Norman-French ...
>
> From that simple origin there has been built up over the centuries in our law a big house with many rooms. It is the house called Estoppel. In Coke's time it was a small house with only three rooms, namely, estoppel by matter of record, by matter in writing, and by matter in pais.[69] But by our time we have so many rooms that we are apt to get confused between them. Estoppel per rem judicatam, issue estoppel, estoppel by deed, estoppel by representation, estoppel by conduct, estoppel by acquiescence, estoppel by election or waiver, estoppel by negligence, promissory estoppel, proprietary estoppel, and goodness knows what else.[70]

Estoppel by contract, lately discovered, may be added to the list.[71] Returning now to Lord Denning:

> These several rooms have this much in common: They are all under one roof. Someone is stopped from saying something or other, or doing something or other, or contesting something or other. But each room is used differently from the others. If you go into one room, you will find a notice saying, 'Estoppel is only a rule of evidence.' If you go into another room you will find a different notice, 'Estoppel can give rise to a cause of action.' Each room has its own separate notices. It is a mistake to suppose that what you find in one room, you will also find in the others.[72]

Nevertheless, eighteen months later, Lord Denning attempted to extrapolate a common principle (at least for estoppels based on mutual assumption):

68 Co Litt 352a.

69 The reference is to Co Litt 352a. 'Record' meant the court records and certain certified documents; 'writing' meant different types of deeds; 'pais' meant different types of conduct; see also *Legione v Hateley* (1983) 152 CLR 406 (HCA) 430 (Mason and Deane JJ).

70 *McIlkenny v Chief Constable of the West Midlands* [1980] QB 283 (CA) 317. This case was part of the infamous Birmingham Six saga. Here, estoppel *per rem judicatam* was used to dismiss the appellants' claim that their confessions had been procured by police violence.

71 *Springwell Navigation Corp v JP Morgan Chase Bank* [2010] EWCA Civ 1221, [2010] 2 CLC 705 177 (Aikens LJ); see also Jo Braithwaite, 'The Origins and Implications of Contractual Estoppel' [2016] LQR 120.

72 *McIlkenny* (n 70) 317.

> All these can now be seen to merge into one general principle shorn of limitations. When the parties to a transaction proceed on the basis of an underlying assumption … on which they have conducted the dealings between them – neither of them will be allowed to go back on that assumption when it would be unfair or unjust to allow him to do so.[73]

It will profit us nothing, in our present endeavour, to describe in detail each species of estoppel. The main differences between the estoppels lie in the conditions under which they arise. For example, promissory estoppel requires detrimental reliance and does not require a contract, whereas contractual estoppel requires a contract but not detrimental reliance.[74] But the bottom line is always the same: estoppel prevents a party from proving the true state of affairs. It is a gag.

3.5.2 *Applications*

The power of estoppel is perhaps best illustrated by the startling facts of *Ashpitel v Bryan* (1863).[75] This case concerned a bill of exchange drawn by a dead man. It was in truth a conspiracy by two of his kin. John Peto, a businessman, died intestate, leaving stock-in-trade. A relative, John Bryan, wanted these goods and conspired with the late Peto's son, James Peto, to make it look as if the father had sold the stock-in-trade to Bryan in his lifetime. That would prevent the goods from falling into the deceased's estate. So the conspirators prepared a bill of exchange, ostensibly drawn by the late John Peto, for goods sold, indorsed to Peto junior and accepted by John Bryan. The result was a simple debt owed by John Bryan to James Peto – but the point was that the goods were saved from intestacy. Bryan took possession of the goods but refused to pay. He opportunistically claimed the bill was improperly indorsed, indeed impossibly indorsed, by a deceased John Peto. But Bryan was estopped (by an estoppel *in pais*) from relying on the death and was ordered to pay.[76] The Court of King's Bench did not let Bryan have it both ways.

A more mundane, yet more questionable,[77] application of estoppel is the advice of the Privy Council in *Prime Sight Ltd v Lavarello* (2013). This Gibraltarian appeal related to the oft-used contractual acknowledgement

73 *Amalgamated Investment & Property Co Ltd (In Liquidation) v Texas Commerce International Bank Ltd* [1982] QB 84 (CA) 122.

74 *JP Morgan Bank v Springwell Navigation Corp* [2008] EWHC 1186 (Comm) [556] (Gloster J).

75 (1863) 3 B & S 474, 122 ER 179 (QB).

76 Ibid. 184–5 (Wightman J).

77 See e.g., KR Handley, 'Reinventing Estoppel in the Privy Council' [2014] LQR 370.

that money consideration has been received. Here the acknowledgement was in the form 'In … consideration of the sum of £499,950 … (receipt and payment of which the assignor hereby acknowledges).'[78] In fact, the consideration was never paid, the transaction being part of some complex restructuring. When the payee went into bankruptcy, the official trustee demanded the consideration from the payor. The trustee failed before the Privy Council.[79] This time it was estoppel by deed.[80] Standing in the shoes of the payee, the official trustee was estopped from denying the above-quoted words of the deed.

In the same vein, the Court of Appeal has held that 'no reliance' clauses raise a contractual estoppel (provided the clause itself is valid under consumer legislation).[81] This recent line of authority is controversial[82] because it has abandoned the requirements of reliance and unconscionability, which limit estoppel by representation or convention. It has thereby created a contractual estoppel, which is supported by a contract alone (like estoppel by deed, but subject to consideration[83]). The full impact of contractual estoppel on consumer law is yet to be discovered.[84] What is clear is that estoppel is thriving in the twenty-first century.

3.5.3 *Is Estoppel a Hard Fiction?*

3.5.3.1 Factual Requirement

If estoppel is a gag, is it an issue of fact or law? The answer lies, I believe, in our understanding of 'legal issue', as discussed in the previous chapter. To restate, the distinguishing characteristic of legal questions is that they can be answered without specific reference to the facts of the case. Factual questions, by contrast, can only be determined by examination of the facts. A legal question, like what standard of proof applies, or what kind of thing constitutes sufficient consideration, is not about what the parties say. It is a question internal to the law and independent of any parties and any dispute. If a legal issue is

78 [2013] UKPC 22, [2014] AC 436 [8] (Lord Toulson).
79 Ibid. [59] (Lord Toulson).
80 Ibid. [24], [46] (Lord Toulson).
81 *Springwell* (n 71) [171] (Aikens LJ); *Peekay Intermark Ltd v Australia & New Zealand Banking Group Ltd* [2006] EWCA Civ 386, [2006] 2 Lloyd's Rep 511 [57] (Moore-Bick LJ).
82 Nelson Goh, 'Non-reliance Clauses and Contractual Estoppel: Commercially Sensible or Anomalous?' [2015] JBL 511; Braithwaite (n 71).
83 Though in *Prime Sight v Lavarello* (n 78) there was no actual consideration, it being the subject of the estoppel. In other words, a constitutive requirement of contractual estoppel was fulfilled only through reliance on the estoppel.
84 Braithwaite (n 71) 147.

independent of the parties and what they say, it follows that preventing a party from saying something cannot be a matter of law.

True it is that the party is gagged by operation of law, but this cannot be the criterion because all fictions are in that sense operations of law. The distinction made here is between, say, the trust as an institution on one hand and estopping a party from denying a trust on the other hand. The former is an issue of law, internal to the law and independent of any specific parties or disputes. The latter is dependent on the parties and the dispute and has no bearing on the trust as an institution.

To those who say that estoppel is merely an exclusionary rule of evidence, I would answer that that is neither here nor there. It was argued in the last chapter that rules could be fictitious – so to say that something is a rule is not an objection. The rule of estoppel is that the court ignores the truth. I am not interested in the mechanics, but in the substance. The rule of estoppel ignores the truth just as much as the rule that 'Cats are deemed to be dogs.'

Those who wish to be pedantic may say that estoppel, rather than being a fiction, necessarily creates a fiction. I would regard this as a distinction without a difference. The rule contains the fiction within it. It *forces* the fiction. The factual requirement is made out.

3.5.3.2 Falsity Requirement

In my understanding, falsity means that the issue is decided irrespective of a contradiction with the physical world. It will be readily seen that the whole point of estoppel, wherein lies its force and utility, is to prevent the truth of the physical world from being proved, relied upon, given effect. The court comes very close to the figurative shutting of the ears. Indeed, if it were not the truth we were shutting out, there would rarely be a need for estoppel. If the father in *Ashpitel v Bryan* had been alive at the time of the bill, there would have been nothing to estop. If the consideration had been paid in *Prime Sight v Lavarello*, estoppel would never have been raised. It is the truth that hurts and must be suppressed. This is why John Rastell's definition of estoppel in his lexicon, *Les Termes de la Ley*, nails estoppel, whereas modern definitions only describe it: 'Estoppel is, when one is . . . forbidden in law to speak against his own act or deed, yea, *though it be to say the truth.*'[85]

Estoppel has the purpose and effect of suppressing the truth. The court proceeds on a factual basis which is false in the sense that it contradicts the physical world. Estoppel satisfies the falsity requirement.

[85] John Rastell, *Les Termes de La Ley* (first published 1527, J Johnson 1812) 206 (emphasis added).

3.5.3.3 Consciousness Requirement

Do the judges who proceed irrespective of the facts as a result of estoppel do so knowingly? They most assuredly do. In most cases, they know the basis to be positively false, as in *Ashpitel v Bryan* and *Prime Sight v Lavarello*. There are many more cases, but I will not multiply examples. The consciousness requirement is fulfilled.

In conclusion, estoppel is a Hard Fiction. It is not necessary to inquire whether it is a Soft Fiction as the definitions are mutually exclusive.

It is worthy of note that estoppel closely resembles those Old Fictions that functioned as non-traversable pleadings. A non-traversable allegation was a statement that the defendant was not allowed to deny. This is precisely what an estoppel is. It is still a New Fiction,[86] in its present incarnation, but it may be seen as an echo of the Old System in our ever-changing world.

3.5.4 *Reality Check*

Estoppel fits very smoothly into my definition of Hard Fiction. The parallel with the non-traversable pleading vindicates this conclusion. And, yet, estoppel is not usually regarded as a fiction by the legal community, despite the liberality with which the term fiction is used. Fuller expressly distinguished between fiction and estoppel.[87] So did Lord Millett, extra-judicially.[88] All this while legal devices such as companies, trusts and the reasonable man are routinely called fictions (unhelpfully in my view). Estoppel, a supposedly clearer fiction, is overlooked. JW Carter and John Baker are notable exceptions in this regard.[89] William Swadling comes very close to saying estoppel is a fiction.[90] Generally, however, estoppel does not make the list.[91] My conclusion that estoppel is a Hard Fiction seems out of kilter with conventional wisdom. This should give us pause. At the very least, it calls for an explanation.

This is a necessarily speculative exercise, but I would venture the following explanation. Estoppel *does* differ from the usual fictions in that it is not an institution like a trust, nor a concept like consideration, nor a test like the

86 By my classification, a fiction is New if it exists under the New System.

87 Fuller (n 1) 73–5.

88 Millett (n 22) 21 fn 71.

89 JW Carter, 'Discharge as the Basis for Termination for Breach of Contract' [2012] LQR 283, 301; LTB, 38.

90 William Swadling, 'Constructive Trusts and Breach of Fiduciary Duty' [2012] Trust & Trustees 985, 999.

91 It is hard to prove a negative, but it is indicative that a recent book dedicated to fictions does not mention estoppel as a fiction once: LFTP.

reasonable man; nor an allegation like *vi et armis*. Instead, it is an inability to say something. It may be that people do not call estoppel a fiction because it is not a *thing* that can exist or not exist and therefore be real or unreal. The question of its reality does not even arise.

My definition does not have this limitation. It looks at the substance of the legal decision. If a factual issue is decided consciously irrespective of the facts, a Hard Fiction is at play and that is all. I see no reason to abandon this definition (of the Hard Fiction) in light of the peculiarity of estoppel just observed. *Au contraire*: suddenly treating non-traversable allegations as *not* fictitious – after centuries of treating them as fictions – would call for an explanation.

Further to the hypothesis urged above, there is, I believe, another reason why estoppel is rarely called a fiction. This reason is probably more important than the first. It is simply that, in current usage, lawyers reserve the term 'fiction' for things they dislike.[92] It has become a legal term of abuse or, at least, a catchphrase for disapproval.[93] Since estoppel is generally regarded as a good and sensible thing, there is no motive to call it a fiction. My definition, however, does not bend to one's opinion of the device. It aims at objectivity.

I said at the outset that my definition may not always agree with common usage. This is one of these instances of disagreement. For the reasons above, and mainly because I cannot conceive why we should suddenly stop calling non-traversable allegations fictions, I suggest that estoppel is indeed a Hard Fiction.

3.5.5 *Effect Classification of Estoppel*

Estoppel is not a Jurisdictional Fiction because it does not affect the choice of court. It is not an Auxiliary Fiction either because it does not consist of pure lip service, meaningless text, that has nothing to do with the reason for the result of the case. In fact, estoppel has no text at all and there is nothing random about it. It is grounded in principle.

In respect of estoppel *per rem judicatam*, the principle is the finality of litigation. In *Thrasyvoulou v Secretary of State for the Environment* (1989), Lord Bridge opined, 'The doctrine of res judicata rests on the twin principles which cannot be better expressed than in terms of the two Latin maxims

92 This phenomenon is not new: Fuller (n 1) 3–4; Douglas Lind, 'The Pragmatic Value of Legal Fictions' in Ibid. 87.

93 Anonymous, 'Lessons from Abroad: Mathematical, Poetic, and Literary Fictions in the Law' (2002) 115 Harvard LR 2228, 2249.

"interest reipublicae ut sit finis litium" and "nemo debet bis vexari pro una et eadem causa". These principles are of . . . fundamental importance.'[94] These maxims may be freely rendered as 'it is in the public interest that litigation should have an end' and 'nobody should be vexed twice for the same cause'. It is only right then that 'when a litigant has obtained a judgment in a Court of justice . . . he is by law entitled not to be deprived of that judgment without very solid grounds'.[95]

In respect of other estoppels, the principle is fairness in the form of consistency. A party cannot play fast and loose with the ground rules. To paraphrase Dr Jo Braithwaite, a party cannot contract on one basis and litigate on another.[96] I return to Lord Denning MR for an authoritative statement:

> I go back to the general principles governing estoppel. . . . It is a principle of justice and of equity. It comes to this: when a man, by his words or conduct, has led another to believe in a particular state of affairs, he will not be allowed to go back on it when it would be unjust or inequitable for him to do so.[97]

Estoppel is founded on principle. It is the reason, or *a* reason, for the result of the case. In *Prime Sight v Lavarello*, the Board held that the consideration should be treated as paid even though it had not been paid *because* the parties themselves had so treated it and expressed this agreement in a deed. As the true reason for the result of a case, estoppel is an Essential Fiction.

To conclude the descriptive part of our discussion of this fiction, estoppel is a New Essential Hard Fiction.

3.5.6 *Evaluation*

In evaluating the fiction of estoppel, we ask whether it is a good means of accomplishing its twin aims of finality in litigation and fairness as consistency. Actually, both aims are about consistency: consistency of legal determinations and consistency of dealings. The fundamental aim of estoppel may therefore be said to be consistency.

Estoppel achieves its aim of consistency rather simply. Once the relevant estoppel is triggered, it imposes consistency by refusing even to entertain inconsistencies. If a fact is inconsistent with the accepted state of affairs, it

94 [1990] 2 AC 273 (HL) 289.

95 *Brown v Dean* [1910] AC 373 (HL) 374 (Lord Loreburn LC).

96 Braithwaite (n 71) 146.

97 *Moorgate Mercantile Co Ltd v Twitchings* [1976] QB 225 (CA) 241 (reversed on different grounds); see also *Grundt v Great Boulder Proprietary Gold Mines Ltd* (1937) 59 CLR 641 (HCA) 674 (Dixon J); *Prime Sight Ltd v Lavarello* (n 78) [29] (Lord Toulson).

cannot be heard. It is a blunt instrument, but it is effective in achieving the goal.

I will not make the mistake of confusing the evaluation of the fiction with the evaluation of its aim. I will not ask, to name one example, whether the enforcement of 'no reliance' clauses against vulnerable consumers is good or bad. This line of argument is illegitimate because it questions the aim of the fiction. We *assume* the result, which upholds the aim of fairness as consistency, and look for the best way to achieve it.

Of course, we *can* argue about the requirements of the various estoppels and whether they uphold the aim of consistency. One can also ask if we really need so many estoppels or should unite them in a single coherent doctrine.[98] These questions are legitimate because they concern the way in which we achieve the aim. But let us suppose that we conclude that this or that requirement should be changed, or that the estoppels should be merged. The solution will be to change the requirements or harmonise them. It will not be that estoppel will cease to be what it is now, namely a gag. At most, these changes will determine *when* the gag is applied. Inasmuch as the fiction is in the gag, none of these interesting arguments about the requirements of different estoppels bears on the fiction; let alone on whether it is a good means of achieving the aim of consistency.

Estoppel *as such* does not come under attack. It is widely recognised as a valuable tool.[99] It is based on sound principle and public policy. It gives effect to these considerations efficiently and straightforwardly: efficiently, because gagging avoids changing the content of the law; straightforwardly, because the application is so simple, like the non-traversable pleading. It has not led to significant complications. For Lord Denning, the estoppel doctrine was 'one of the most flexible and useful in the armoury of the law'.[100] Lord Wright agreed with Sir Frederick Pollock that it was 'beneficial' and 'perhaps the most powerful and flexible instrument to be found in any system of court jurisprudence'.[101]

Those who follow in the footsteps of Jeremy Bentham[102] and oppose fictions categorically should take note of estoppel. Here we have a perfectly defensible fiction. It is actually difficult to find fault with it. The neo-Benthamites may reply that estoppel is not a fiction, but then they would have to explain why *vi et armis* is a fiction and estoppel is not when both are non-traversable allegations.

98 Elizabeth Cooke, *The Modern Law of Estoppel* (OUP 2000) 170.

99 Baker (n 89) 36–8; Ibid. 170.

100 *Amalgamated Investment* (n 73) 122.

101 *Canada and Dominion Sugar Co Ltd v Canadian National (West Indies) Steamship Co Ltd* [1947] AC 46 (PC) 55.

102 See below: Chapter 4, Section 4.3.1.

Of course, estoppel does not prove the opposite – that all fictions are good. It only shows that we should not take an extreme position, that fictions are either all bad or all good. We need to judge each fiction on its merits. As we will discuss in the next chapter, it may be that we should have a preference or a default position. For example, the default position may be that fictions should be avoided unless they are indispensable. For the moment, all that I have established is that fictions should not be automatically rejected for being fictions.

Harvard law professor Jeremiah Smith, a neo-Benthamite, personified the automatic-rejection school. A century ago, he called for a bonfire of the fictions:

> We believe that, at the present day, the use of fiction in law should be entirely abandoned . . . if a fiction does not, in any degree or to any extent, represent a legal truth, then its continued use can result only in evil. If, on the other hand, it represents . . . some clumsily concealed legal truth, then it is capable of being translated into the language of truth, and we should adopt Mr. Bentham's remedy – 'Burn the original, and employ the translation in its stead.'[103]

I reject this school of thought represented by Jeremy Bentham and Jeremiah Smith. In fact, there is good reason to believe that following it to the letter will damage the law. The obliteration of all fictions will doubtless include beneficial fictions (like estoppel) and, in any event, cause much unnecessary disruption.

To conclude our evaluation of estoppel, it is a New Essential Hard Fiction, which should definitely be retained.

3.6 *VOLENTI NON FIT INJURIA*

This tort defence was a case study in the last chapter. It was found to be a Soft Fiction. I revisit it now to decide whether it should be retained. I therefore skip the description and the application of the definitions and go straight to classification and evaluation.

3.6.1 *Effect Classification*

The *volenti* defence is an Essential Fiction because it is the conceptual reason for the result of the case. As we have seen, the judges specifically relied on it to

103 Jeremiah Smith, 'Surviving Fictions' (1917) 27 Yale LJ 147, 154.

argue that the claimants could not and should not recover. The conceptual reason the claims in *Titchener*, *Shatwell* and *Morris* failed was the extreme recklessness on the part of the claimants. That reason is the *volenti* principle in its strained, Soft Fiction form.

Bringing the three classifications together, *volenti non fit injuria* is a New Essential Soft Fiction.

3.6.2 *Evaluation*

To assess the success or failure of the fiction we need to know what it is supposed to do. An understanding of the aim of the fiction will also protect us from the error of evaluating the aim instead of the means to achieve it.

It is evident from the detailed discussion in the previous chapter that the reason for straining the *volenti* principle was to prevent extremely reckless claimants from recovering compensation for their own recklessness. It seemed ridiculous and unjust. The aim of the fiction, then, is to bar recovery by extremely reckless claimants.

If the aim and effect of the fiction are to create an exception to one of the elements of the defence (agreement not required where the negligence is extreme), why not officially recognise the exception? Instead of acknowledging the exception, judges continue to state the law without the exception. At the same time, they strain the facts in order to satisfy the agreement requirement, thereby creating a Soft Fiction. The choice is between openly introducing an exception and straining the facts.

It cannot be argued that the recognition of the exception will introduce uncertainty or have unintended consequences because we already live with the consequences. In practice, the rule has already been changed: extremely reckless claimants cannot recover. There are, however, negative consequences in refusing to officially recognise the change in the law. It means that in order to know the law, we need to discount the judicial statements of the law and to read between the lines. It requires a close analysis of the case law and a scepticism towards stated orthodoxy. Knowing where the law now stands means disbelieving it. This creates uncertainty and ambiguity, even among judges.

In the nature of things, straining a fact is more uncertain than falsifying it. In terms of certainty, it is better to know that the answer to a question is the opposite of the truth than that it is a strained truth. The rule that 'Cats are deemed to be dogs for the purposes of pet tax' is far more certain than the rule that 'The definitions of some pets can be strained for the purposes of pet tax.' Note that the former is more certain than the latter even though – or perhaps because – it is more clearly fictitious. This is a crucial difference between the Hard Fiction and the Soft Fiction. The Soft Fiction is more elusive, more amorphous, more susceptible to manipulation than its older sister. As we will see in the next chapter, this insight will be a central plank of this monograph's conclusion – the Acceptance Test.

In the meantime, let us concentrate on the *volenti* defence. The choice is between the recognition of an exception and the Soft Fiction, whereby facts are made to fit the unmodified defence. The fiction does not serve us in any way, but it does us a disservice in obfuscating the reasoning in the cases. It creates a need for judicial acrobatics and unconvincing arguments. Of course, there is no deceit. Consciousness (on the part of judges and lawyers) is an element of the Soft Fiction. The judges know they are straining the facts and we know they are straining the facts. But it is a consciousness of the 'wink-wink' kind, not the open kind of the Hard Fiction. We need to disbelieve the judges' own statements of the law to obey the law, which is not the case with the Hard Fiction. That is a not a process of reasoning that becomes our legal system. *Volenti non fit injuria* should be abolished to the extent that it is fictitious and replaced with an exception.

3.7 THE SINGLE MEANING RULE

3.7.1 *Description*

The single meaning rule applies in the tort of defamation. Briefly, the tort has three core elements: (i) publication by the defendant (ii) of a statement referring to the claimant (iii) which is defamatory of the claimant.[104] 'Defamatory' means 'substantially affects in an adverse manner the attitude of other people towards [the claimant], or has a tendency so to do'.[105] Several defences are available.[106]

There is a cognate tort known as malicious falsehood. Its elements are (i) a falsehood (ii) maliciously published by the defendant (iii) which actually damaged the claimant.[107] The relevance of this similar but distinct tort will shortly become apparent.

The single meaning rule concerns the meaning of the impugned words in defamation. The rule says that the impugned words can only have one

104 Nicholas J McBride and Roderick Bagshaw, *Tort Law* (6th edn, Pearson 2018) 503.

105 *Thornton v Telegraph Media Group Ltd* [2010] EWHC 1414 (QB), [2011] 1 WLR 1985 [96] (Tugendhat J) (parentheses omitted).

106 Principally Defamation Act 2013, ss 2–7 and privilege.

107 *Ratcliffe v Evans* [1892] 2 QB 524 (CA) 527 (Bowen LJ).

reasonable meaning.[108] Conversely, this means that a statement cannot be understood in different ways by different people acting reasonably. As far as English law is concerned, one statement has one objective meaning.

This may be seen as the necessary consequence of the objective approach to interpretation. For if the reasonable man (or 'right-thinking man', as he is known in defamation[109]) understands the statement to mean X, then X is the objective meaning. The objective meaning is singular just as the man is singular. We do not have several right-thinking men, each forming his own 'right' understanding.

The *locus classicus* of the single meaning rule is the judgment of Diplock LJ in *Slim v Daily Telegraph* (1968):

> Libel is concerned with the meaning of words. Everyone outside a court of law recognises that words are imprecise instruments for communicating the thoughts of one man to another. The same words may be understood by one man in a different meaning from that in which they are understood by another and both meanings may be different from that which the author of the words intended to convey. But the notion that the same words should bear different meanings ... conflicts with the whole training of a lawyer. Words are the tools of his trade. He uses them to define legal rights and duties. They do not achieve that purpose unless there can be attributed to them a single meaning as the 'right' meaning. And so the argument between lawyers as to the meaning of words starts with the unexpressed major premise that any particular combination of words has one meaning which ... is capable of ascertainment as being the 'right' meaning by the adjudicator.[110]

The House of Lords endorsed this view in *Charleston v News Group Newspapers Ltd* (1995):

> [A]lthough a combination of words may in fact convey different meanings to the minds of different readers, the jury ... is required to determine the single meaning which the publication conveyed to the notional reasonable reader and to base its verdict and any award of damages on the assumption that this was the one sense in which all readers would have understood it.[111]

The problem with the single meaning rule, as conceded in the passages just quoted, is that many statements are inherently ambiguous. They are capable

108 *Ajinomoto Sweeteners Europe SAS v Asda Stores Ltd* [2010] EWCA Civ 609, [2011] QB 497 [1], [3] (Sedley LJ); *Curistan v Times Newspapers Ltd* [2008] EWCA Civ 432, [2009] QB 231 [14] (Arden LJ).

109 *Sim v Stretch* [1936] 2 All ER 1237 (HL) 1240 (Lord Atkin).

110 [1968] 2 QB 157 (CA) 171–2.

111 [1995] 2 AC 65 (HL) 71 (Lord Bridge).

of being *reasonably* understood in more than one way. *Ajinomoto Sweeteners Europe SAS v Asda Stores Ltd* (2009) is a case in point.[112] In 2007, Asda launched a new line of food products under the name 'Good for you'. What was special about these products was that they contained no artificial colours or flavours and were conspicuously marketed as such. The packaging included such text as 'No artificial colours or flavours, no aspartame & no hydrogenated fat'; 'No hidden nasties'; and 'Zero sugar, zero aspartame'. (Aspartame is an artificial sweetener used as a sugar substitute.)

The claimant was a distributor of aspartame. It sued Asda for malicious falsehood. The claimant argued that the reasonable meaning of 'No hidden nasties', combined with 'no aspartame' and juxtaposed with 'Good for you', was that aspartame was dangerous to health. Asda contended that the reasonable meaning was that the products were for consumers who found aspartame objectionable.

So what was the single meaning of 'nasty' or of being contrasted with 'good for you'? Is there a single meaning? Can reasonable minds differ on this point? The judgment of Tugendhat J in the case is a candid exposition of the single meaning rule in action:

> I would accept that a substantial number of consumers would understand the words on the food packaging to mean that aspartame is potentially harmful or unhealthy. ...
>
> However, I also find that a substantial number of consumers would understand that these words ... are not seriously meant to convey information, but rather ... to attract as customers those who are already inclined to hold the view (reasonably or otherwise) that there is something objectionable about aspartame. ...
>
> *Both views would, in my view, be open to a reasonable person to hold.* So I have to decide which is to be the single meaning.[113]

The judge chose the latter, innocuous meaning.[114] The case was decided on the basis that that was the only meaning. The decision was reversed on appeal, but on the presently irrelevant ground that the single meaning rule did not apply to malicious falsehood.[115] This remains the case. In defamation, the single meaning rule is alive and well. At any rate, *Ajinomoto* shows us that the single meaning rule can be the difference between winning and losing.

112 [2009] EWHC 1717 (QB), [2010] QB 204.

113 Ibid. [77]–[79] (emphasis added).

114 Ibid. [84]–[85].

115 *Ajinomoto* (CA) (n 108) [35] (Sedley LJ), [42] (Rimer LJ), [45] (Sir Scott Baker). For a critique, see Mihir Naniwadekar, 'The Application of the Single Meaning Rule to Cases Other than Defamation' [2010] International Company and Commercial LR 408.

3.7.2 *Is the Rule a Hard Fiction?*

In *Ajinomoto*, Sedley LJ and Rimer LJ both referred to the single meaning rule as a 'fiction'.[116] Other judges have also explicitly described the rule as fictitious.[117] It was a 'legal fiction' for Professor John Murphy as well.[118] Nicholas McBride and Roderick Bagshaw seemed to concur in this conclusion,[119] as did Andrew Scott.[120] The authors of *Hepple and Matthews' Tort Law* described the rule as 'an extraordinarily unrealistic assumption both as a matter of linguistic and philosophical theory and as a matter of everyday experience'.[121] These opinions deserve great respect and point to a wide acceptance that the rule is fictitious. But they are not dispositive of the question. I will now apply the definition of Hard Fiction.

3.7.2.1 Factual Requirement

In the previous chapter, when looking at the reasonable man, I concluded that the question 'What is the standard of contractual interpretation?' was a legal question because the answer to it ('The reasonable man') was independent of the facts of any case. I also concluded that the question 'What would the reasonable man understand?' was a factual question because the answer depended on the facts of the case.

Similarly here, the question 'What is the standard of statement interpretation?' is a legal question, independent of the facts of any case, the answer to which is 'an objective single meaning' (which, actually, is equivalent to the reasonable man standard). Continuing the analogy, the question 'What is the single meaning?', like the question 'What would the reasonable man understand?', is a factual question, dependent on the facts of the case, to which the answer is such or such specific meaning.

At the risk of repetition, the law's decision to adopt the single meaning rule, or the reasonable man, as a standard of interpretation is legal. But the decision *on* the single meaning – what it is – is factual in every case. Otherwise, judges would not have recourse to the words in context. Tugendhat J's painstaking factual examination of the packaging of Asda's products in *Ajinomoto* confirms

116 *Ajinomoto* (CA) (n 108) [3] (Sedley LJ), [40]–[41] (Rimer LJ).

117 *Lait v Evening Standard Ltd* [2011] EWCA Civ 859, [2011] 1 WLR 2973 [19] (Laws LJ); *Galloway v Telegraph Group* [2004] EWHC 2786 (QB), [2005] EMLR 7 [34] (Eady J).

118 John Murphy, 'A Legal Fiction? Pt 1' (2015) 165 New LJ 13.

119 McBride and Bagshaw (n 104) 508–9.

120 Andrew Scott, 'Ceci n'est pas une Pipe: The Autopoietic Inanity of the Single Meaning Rule' in Andrew T Kenyon (ed), *Comparative Defamation and Privacy Law* (CUP 2016) 45–6.

121 David Howarth et al., *Hepple and Matthews' Tort Law* (7th edn, Hart 2015) 995.

that the meaning of the offending words, decided under the single meaning rule, is an issue of fact.[122]

Moreover, it is instructive that the question of meaning can be decided by a jury. In fact, from Fox's Libel Act 1792[123] until the Defamation Act 2013, meaning lay with the jury. Under the new regime, a jury will only be convoked in exceptional circumstances.[124] Still, that the meaning of the statement has long been, and still can be, tried by jury is consistent with the conclusion that the meaning is a question of fact.[125] The factual requirement is satisfied.

3.7.2.2 Falsity Requirement

The single meaning rule is false in my terms if it is decided irrespective of a contradiction with the physical world. The rule contradicts the physical world if it can be shown that statements can have more than one reasonable meaning.

In a historical study of defamation, Professor Paul Mitchell describes the single meaning rule as 'an apparently unrealistic attitude to interpreting defamatory words' and notes that it is at odds with academic linguistic analysis.[126] Andrew Scott, in a book chapter on the single meaning rule, draws attention to the inherent ambiguity of meaning: '[T]he same form of words is semantically capable of bearing a number of slightly differing, and progressively more serious, interpretations. The words may elicit a number of "shades of meaning".'[127] He then gives an example of the inferences readers may draw from a purely factual statement:

> [T]he statement 'X is helping police with their inquiries into a murder' could be taken to mean any or all of the following: that X murdered someone else, that he or she was complicit in the murder, that he or she knew about the murder, that the police believe that he or she might know something about the murder or about its surrounding circumstances, or that he or she was a forensic psychologist involved in suspect profiling.[128]

The list can be expanded. The statement can likewise mean that X is a suspect. It is easy to forget that the statement can also mean no more than what it says:

122 *Ajinomoto* (HC) (n 112) [42]–[48].
123 32 Geo III c 60.
124 Defamation Act, s 11.
125 But note that the judge can determine whether the words have a defamatory meaning at all: *Rubber Improvement Ltd v Daily Telegraph Ltd* [1964] AC 234 (HL) 258 (Lord Reid), 268 (Lord Morris).
126 Paul Mitchell, *A History of Tort Law 1900–1950* (CUP 2015) 39.
127 Scott (n 120) 44.
128 Ibid. fn 18.

X is helping police with their inquiries. One may say that some of these meanings are less reasonable than others; even discount some completely. But it would be hard to say that only one of the meanings is reasonable.

The cases tell a similar story. *Bonnick v Morris* (2002) was a Jamaican appeal to the Privy Council regarding a newspaper report written by Morris about Bonnick.[129] Bonnick had just been fired as the managing director of a company. The report contained a direct quotation from an unnamed 'authoritative source', criticising Bonnick's decision to sign certain contracts. The quotation was: 'nobody . . . could be so mad as to agree to that'. The report went on to say, 'Bonnick's services as managing director were terminated shortly after the second contract was agreed.'[130]

Bonnick sued in defamation, alleging that the last-quoted statement meant that he had been sacked for impropriety or incompetence. Morris, the journalist, argued that it was a simple statement of fact without implication – he signed the contract and then he was fired. The 'reasonable' meaning in this case turned on how much one read into the statement, what voluntary connections one made with the surrounding statements, and what gaps one decided to fill.

The trial judge found for Bonnick.[131] The Jamaican Court of Appeal reversed on meaning and also accepted the defences of justification, honest comment and qualified privilege (which had been rejected at first instance). Forte P dissented on meaning.[132] The Privy Council restored Langrin J's finding on meaning but dismissed the claim on the ground of qualified privilege. Lord Nicholls commented on the disagreement between the judges as to meaning:

> This divergence of view is neither surprising nor unusual. Language is inherently imprecise. Words and phrases and sentences take their colour from their context. The context often permits a range of meanings, varying from the obvious to the implausible. Different readers may well form different views on the meaning to be given to the language under consideration.[133]

If we return to the celebrated judgment in *Slim*, Diplock LJ was even more explicit:

> [O]ne man might be *reasonable* in drawing one defamatory inference from the words and another man might be *reasonable* in drawing another

129 [2002] UKPC 31, [2003] 1 AC 300.
130 Ibid. [2] (Lord Nicholls).
131 Ibid. [6] (Lord Nicholls).
132 Ibid. [7]–[8] (Lord Nicholls).
133 Ibid. [20].

> defamatory inference. Where, as in the present case, words are published to the millions of readers of a popular newspaper, the chances are that if the words are *reasonably capable of being understood as bearing more than one meaning*, some readers will have understood them as bearing one of those meanings and some will have understood them as bearing others of those meanings.[134]

Taking a broader perspective, the language chosen in many instances is *deliberately* ambiguous. Satirical or subversive literature is more likely to be subtle than direct in its criticism. Visual art is famously ambivalent. Humour feeds on innuendo and *double-entendre*. Journalists may use oblique references precisely to avoid liability. Understatement is common in spoken and written English. The idea that statements are, as a rule, capable of only one reasonable meaning is too simplistic.

To conclude, the single meaning rule is that a statement can have only one reasonable meaning. In fact, many statements bear more than one reasonable meaning. The rule therefore contradicts the physical world. The falsity requirement is satisfied.

3.7.2.3 Consciousness Requirement

It is relatively easy to establish the judges' awareness of the falsity of the single meaning rule. This is because they are so open about it. In *Slim*, as we have seen, Diplock LJ accepted that 'one man might be reasonable in drawing one defamatory inference from the words and another man might be reasonable in drawing another defamatory inference'[135] and described 'the meaning ascribed to words for the purposes of the tort of libel' as 'so artificial'.[136] In *Bonnick*, Lord Nicholls called the same 'highly artificial'.[137] In *Charleston*, the highest court in the land emphatically approved of Diplock LJ's candid statement of the fiction, noting that 'readers of mass circulation newspapers vary enormously in the way they . . . interpret what they read'.[138] In *Ajinomoto*, Sedley LJ said that '[t]he *fiction* that there is a single reasonable reader, so that words, duly taken in context, have only one meaning, has remained embedded in the law of defamation'.[139] In the same case, Rimer LJ acknowledged that '[t]he court . . . satisfies itself with the *fiction*, contrary to its own finding, that

134 *Slim* (n 110) 173 (emphasis added).
135 Ibid. 173.
136 Ibid. 172.
137 *Bonnick v Morris* (n 129) [21].
138 *Charleston* (n 111) 71–2 (Lord Bridge), 73–4 (Lord Nicholls).
139 *Ajinomoto* (CA) (n 108) [3] (emphasis added).

the entire consuming public will interpret the defendant's packaging as bearing a single ... meaning'.[140] There is no doubt that judges know that the single meaning rule is inconsistent with reality. The consciousness requirement is satisfied.

We conclude therefore that the single meaning rule is a Hard Fiction. It is therefore unnecessary to check whether it is a Soft Fiction. The conclusion that the rule is a legal fiction accords with the prevailing judicial and academic view.

3.7.3 *Effect Classification of the Single Meaning Rule*

The single meaning rule is not a Jurisdictional Fiction because it has nothing to do with the choice of court. Nor is it an Auxiliary Fiction, as it is not meaningless text. The parties do not allege that there is a single meaning simply to pay lip service. The single meaning is indeed the meaning which the court proceeds upon as the only meaning.[141] The whole point of the fiction, for better or for worse, is to isolate one meaning as the true meaning. The single meaning rule is the true reason for the result of the case. It is therefore an Essential Fiction.

Bringing together our three classifications of fiction, the single meaning rule is a New Essential Hard Fiction.

3.7.4 *Evaluation*

3.7.4.1 Judicial Opinion

Judges have been vocal in their criticism of the single meaning rule. In fact, some judges denounce the rule even as they apply it. The very statement of the fiction by Diplock LJ in *Slim* ended with a cry for help: 'I venture to recommend once more the law of defamation as a fit topic for the attention of the Law Commission. It has passed beyond redemption by the courts.'[142] That was in 1968. In 2010, Sedley LJ found himself in no better position: 'The choice we are presented with is constrained by an immovable object, the single meaning rule ... as Diplock LJ said in the *Slim* case ... it has passed beyond redemption by the courts ... the rule itself is anomalous, frequently otiose and, where not otiose, unjust.'[143]

140 Ibid. [41] (emphasis added).
141 *Ajinomoto* (CA) (n 108) [41] (Rimer LJ).
142 *Slim* (n 110) 179.
143 *Ajinomoto* (CA) (n 108) [27], [31].

In *Vodafone Group plc v Orange Personal Communications Services Ltd* (1996), Jacob J, with characteristic honesty, said, 'As a comparative stranger to this branch of the law I find the "one meaning rule" strange.'[144] In *Interflora Inc v Marks & Spencer plc* (2013), Arnold J observed that 'the single meaning rule which exists in English defamation law is widely regarded as anomalous'.[145] The prevailing view of the fiction within the judiciary appears to be negative.

At the same time, one judge, a voice in the wilderness, rallied to the defence of the fiction. Sitting as a Non-Permanent Justice of the Final Court of Appeal of Hong Kong in *Oriental Daily Publisher Ltd v Ming Pao Holdings Ltd* (2012), Lord Neuberger mounted a spirited defence of the single meaning rule.[146] Fainter endorsements of the fiction were offered by Lord Nicholls[147] and Laws LJ in other cases.[148]

Before I consider the arguments for and against the single meaning rule, I must first identify its aim. We know that we cannot question the aim of a fiction in the process of evaluating it. Without knowing the aim, we cannot evaluate the utility of the fiction in achieving the aim.

3.7.4.2 The Aim of the Fiction

The tort of defamation is about harmful words. The mechanism by which the meaning of words is decided is of the highest importance. In evidence to the Joint Committee on the Draft Defamation Bill (which became the Defamation Act 2013), Tugendhat J said that in libel actions 'very often if not always the most important issue is meaning'.[149] In *Merivale v Carson* (1887), Bowen LJ considered the question of meaning to be uppermost: 'We must begin with asking ourselves, what is the true meaning of the words used in the alleged libel?'[150] His brother, Lord Esher MR, was of the same mind.[151] Andrew Scott agrees.[152]

I noted earlier that even a matter-of-fact statement ('X is helping police with their inquiries') can breed a host of interpretations. I also noted the challenge of hermeneutics. How is the sacred meaning, on which the tort is based, to be

144 [1997] EMLR 84 (Ch) 88.
145 [2013] EWHC 1291 (Ch), [2013] ETMR 35 [224].
146 [2012] HKCFA 59, (2012) 15 HKCFAR 299.
147 *Charleston* (n 111); *Bonnick v Morris* (n 129) [21].
148 *Lait* (n 117) [19]; *Curistan* (n 108) [83].
149 Joint Committee on the Draft Defamation Bill (Oral and associated written evidence), vol 2 (2010–12, HL 203, HC 930-II) 466.
150 (1887) 20 QBD 275 (CA) 282.
151 Ibid. 279.
152 Scott (n 120) 42.

extracted from this quagmire? The law needs a mechanism to cut through the mire. This mechanism is the single meaning rule. It presents a simple, perhaps simplistic, solution to the problem of meaning: choose the most reasonable meaning and ignore all other meanings. The cases testify that the single meaning rule is seen by judges as a solution to the problem of meaning. By way of introducing the rule, Lord Neuberger said, 'The first question to be considered must, of course, be: what did the statement mean?'[153] The classic judgment in *Slim* and the advice in *Bonnick* also present the rule as the lawyer's answer to the problem of meaning.[154] The aim of the fiction is thus to solve the problem of meaning – that is, to determine the meaning of the impugned statement.

The single meaning rule is not the only solution to the problem of meaning that the law could have settled upon. There is nothing inevitable about it. Other solutions include:

- Treating all meanings that are judged 'reasonable' in the way the single meaning is treated now
- Recognising only meanings that pass some quasi-quantifiable measure like 'understood by a substantial number of people'
- Assigning probability values to each reasonable meaning and awarding damages accordingly
- Making the determination of meaning an empirical, subjective exercise by dropping reasonableness altogether and admitting evidence as to what recipients actually understood[155] (which might again lead to multiple meanings)

The question before us, in evaluating the fiction, is whether the fictitious solution of the single meaning is the best solution to the problem of meaning, in view of the alternatives. I will now set out the arguments.

3.7.4.3 The Case for the Fiction

The first argument in favour of the single meaning rule is that (far from being 'anomalous') it is standard and unremarkable in other areas of the law. This is the basis of Lord Neuberger's defence of the fiction in *Oriental Daily*. When we interpret a contract, or a statute, or a notice, it is taken for granted that in

[153] *Oriental Daily* (n 146) [139].

[154] *Slim* (n 110) 171–2 (Diplock LJ); *Bonnick v Morris* (n 129) [21] (Lord Nicholls).

[155] For the current unempirical position, see *Hough v London Express Newspaper Ltd* [1940] 2 KB 507 (CA) 515 (Goddard LJ); Mitchell (n 126) 38.

the end the law will only enforce one meaning – the meaning that is deemed reasonable. This is so even if as a matter of 'linguistic philosophy', the words admit of more than one meaning.[156] There is thus nothing exceptional in ascribing a single meaning to words.

The second argument, which flows from the first, is that the alternative to a single meaning is chaos. Lord Neuberger explained the danger at some length:

> While the consequences of applying the rule may sometimes seem a little harsh, if a court could hold that a provision in a statute, a contract or a notice could, as a matter of law, have more than one meaning, it would self-evidently lead to chaos and uncertainty in many cases, both in outcome and in procedure.
>
> ... If the single meaning rule did not apply in defamation, it would similarly lead to greater uncertainty in outcome and increased legal expenses. Instead of a statement with two possible meanings giving rise to a problem requiring a binary resolution, it would give rise to a problem which had a multiplicity of potential answers, along what might be seen as a continuous spectrum. Abolition of the single meaning rule would also lead to the dispiriting, expensive, and time-consuming prospect of many witnesses being called by each party, to explain how they understood the statement in question.[157]

Lord Nicholls captured the chaos argument when he said that 'readers ... vary enormously in the way they read articles. ... It is, indeed, in this very consideration that the law finds justification for its single standard.'[158] It is *because* there are so many possible meanings that we need a single meaning.

Another argument in favour of the single meaning fiction comes from the submissions of counsel for the defendant in *Ajinomoto*.[159] It is an argument of public policy. Defamation law is a delicate balance between freedom of expression and good name. If the single meaning fiction is abolished, there will be meanings galore and the claimant's hand will be strengthened. The more meanings there are, the more likely it is that one of them is defamatory. All claimants would have to do (so it is feared) would be to articulate one possible defamatory meaning that passes some low threshold of reasonability. Sedley LJ paraphrased counsel's argument (which he ultimately rejected):

156 *Oriental Daily* (n 146) [140]–[141] (Lord Neuberger NPJ).
157 Ibid. [141]–[142].
158 *Charleston* (n 111) 173–4.
159 *Ajinomoto* (CA) (n 108) 500–1 (Andrew Caldecott QC).

> [The single meaning rule] moves the law into the middle ground between the author's intent, a test highly favourable to defendants, and multiple meanings, a test which puts all the cards in the claimant's hand. Having ruled out untenable meanings, the court proceeds by fixing on the most tenable one and trying out the question whether it is libellous. This is practical and fair.[160]

According to this third argument, the single meaning fiction is a pragmatic compromise between values. Put less kindly, it represents a kind of rough justice.

Finally, in *Curistan v Times Newspapers Ltd* (2008), Laws LJ opined: 'The single meaning rule is, I think, not so much a rule of policy as a function of the need to understand and interpret expressions in the context in which they appear; and this is a matter of common sense and fairness.'[161] This is the last argument for the fiction that will be considered here.

3.7.4.4 The Case against the Fiction

The basic argument against the single meaning rule is that it turns a blind eye to the facts. In other words, the primary argument against the fiction is that it is a fiction. Obviously, this is a circular objection to fictions. Nevertheless, if we face a choice between truth and fiction, all other things being equal, we should – of course – choose truth. Valuing truth is an axiom of reason. I will pursue this line of thought in the next chapter. For now, it suffices to say that the mere fact that a device is fictitious is an argument against it – by no means a conclusive or compelling argument, maybe not even a strong one – but it is a *negative*. If all other arguments cancel each other out, I will always prefer to avoid fiction than to indulge it.

The deeper argument against the single meaning rule is that it produces unjust outcomes. This is apparent in *Ajinomoto*. The trial judge found two reasonable meanings: one damaging (aspartame is unhealthy), one innocuous (the product is for people who wish to avoid aspartame). The judge chose the latter as the single meaning. On appeal, Sedley LJ condemned the rule:

> On the judge's unchallenged findings, the meanings which reasonable consumers might put on the claimant's health-food packaging include both the damaging and the innocuous. Why should the law not move on to ... the consequential damage without artificially pruning the facts so as to presume the very thing – a single meaning – that the judge has found not to be the case?[162]

160 Ibid. [19].
161 n 108 [83].
162 *Ajinomoto* (CA) (n 108) [33]; see also [41] (Rimer LJ).

If the purpose of the action is to protect people's reputation from unjustified harm, why should publishers not be liable for the reasonable interpretations of their publications? Olsson J, in the Supreme Court of South Australia, agreed with earlier Australian authority that 'to insist upon an innocent interpretation where any reasonable person could, and many reasonable people would, understand a sinister meaning is to refuse reparation for a wrong that has in fact been committed'.[163] And so, to return to Sedley LJ, the injustice of the single meaning rule lies in 'denying any remedy to a claimant whose business has been injured in the eyes of some consumers on the illogical ground that it has not been injured in the eyes of others'.[164] None of the aforementioned alternative solutions to the problem of meaning produces this injustice. The unfairness can only be imputed to the fiction of single meaning.

There is a third argument against the single meaning rule. Courts seem to accept that, historically speaking, the use of civil juries in defamation is at least partly responsible for the existence of the rule.[165] Now that juries have been all but eliminated from defamation litigation by the Defamation Act 2013,[166] the historical basis for the rule has been removed.[167] The rule, it is argued, should go the same way.

3.7.4.5 Consideration

We begin with the jury argument because it can be summarily disposed of, clearing the way for the real issues. Nowadays the jury is not normally a factor in defamation trials. If it has ever been a justification for the fiction,[168] it is no longer. If the fiction seeks to justify itself, it will have to look elsewhere.

We turn now to the argument made in passing by Laws LJ in *Curistan* that the fiction is justified 'as a function of the need to understand and interpret expressions in the context in which they appear'.[169] With respect, it is not true that the single meaning rule is about understanding words in context. The rule is not that the interpretation must be contextual. The rule is that there is only one reasonable meaning. It is submitted that this justification is factually incorrect.

163 *Entienne Pty Ltd and Cosenza v Festival City Broadcasters Pty Ltd* [2001] SASC 60, (2001) 79 SASR 19 [41]. His Honour went on to hold, at [42], that the single meaning rule did not apply in South Australia.

164 *Ajinomoto* (CA) (n 108) [34].

165 *Slim* (n 110) 174 (Diplock LJ); *Vodafone* (n 159) 89 (Jacob J).

166 s 11.

167 Scott (n 120) 48.

168 Andrew Scott argues that the jury was never a good justification: Ibid. 48–9.

169 *Curistan* (n 111) [83].

Next, I deal with the argument that the single meaning rule is necessary to strike a fair balance between freedom of expression and protection of reputation. This argument can also be dealt with relatively quickly. It is premised on the assumption that, in a world of multiple meanings, claimants would have an unfair advantage. In my view, claimants *would* have an advantage, compared with the status quo, but it would not be unfair. As Sedley and Rimer LJJ and Olsson J said, I should not be allowed to publish material which is defamatory in the eyes of the reasonable man. That there is another reasonable interpretation is beside the point. I should be liable for the defamatory meaning. The idea that I should be able to persist in the defamation, libelling the defendant with impunity in the eyes of reasonable men and women, is not a 'fair balance'. Damages can be reduced to reflect the fact that some recipients are deemed to have formed the non-defamatory reasonable meaning. It is difficult to see how the present all-or-nothing system is a 'balance' of any kind. I would dismiss the fair balance argument.

But the fiction is not yet beaten. Lord Neuberger's argument that single meaning is an accepted theory of common law interpretation is a formidable proposition. The burden of this argument is that words in the defamation context should be interpreted in the same way that words are interpreted in the contractual and statutory contexts: the court considers the words from the perspective of the reasonable man and identifies a single meaning.

Andrew Scott says that this argument is 'for the most part ... manifestly misdirected'.[170] Scott's rebuttal is that there is no analogy between the interpretation of words in defamation and the interpretation of words in contracts and statutes. This is because the meaning of a contract or a statute is a matter of law, whereas the meaning of words in defamation is a matter of fact.[171] If Scott is right about this distinction, Lord Neuberger's argument by analogy falls to the ground.

I seriously doubt that Scott *is* right. In the last chapter, I took great pains to argue that the test of the reasonable man (holding up contractual interpretation as an example) is a factual test. The standard of interpretation is a question of law, but what the words of a particular provision mean is a question of fact. On this conception of law versus fact, interpretation of contracts and statutes is just as factual as interpretation in defamation.

170 Scott (n 120) 47.
171 Ibid.

Even if this conception is open to question, what is not open to question is that both tests of interpretation (defamation and contract/statute) involve asking what the reasonable man would understand. I do not see why the same question should be factual in one context but legal in another. It is true that contracts and statutes are inherently legal documents, whereas the impugned words in defamation are rarely found in legal documents. But the question is still the same: what the reasonable man would understand by the words. It is the same exercise and the same assessment. Either both tests are legal or they are both factual. Scott's differentiation between interpretation in defamation and interpretation in other areas is difficult to sustain.

If this is true, Lord Neuberger's argument by analogy remains formidable. If we impose a single meaning on words in a contract, why should we not follow our own example in defamation? After all, the imposition of a single meaning on contracts and statutes is uncontroversial.

I would submit that there is at least one reason for having one rule for contracts and statutes and another for defamation. In contracts and statutes, we *must* have one meaning. In defamation, we do not. If a contract or statute has two or more inconsistent meanings, it is unenforceable. Rights and obligations either exist or they do not. Provisions either cover certain events or they do not. There is no room for pluralism. In defamation, the impugned words are not *enforced*. There is no hindrance, practical or logical, to the recognition of multiple meanings.

I would offer another, less definite, reason for treating defamation differently from contracts and statutes. The problem of meaning arises in large part because of the subtleties of language. A satirical poem like Alexander Pope's *Rape of the Lock* or John Dryden's *Absalom and Achitophel* is rife with innuendo, caricature and allusive references to people and events. It is precisely the *reticence* of the language wherein lies its genius. But what is clever in a Pope or a Dryden is negligent in a draftsman. Contracts and statutes are not written to be allusive or equivocal, but to be clear and precise. To be sure, contracts and statutes have been known to be ambiguous.[172] But the problem of meaning arises in defamation more acutely than in contracts and statutes. This is because legal drafting is not artistic, or even journalistic.[173] It makes sense then for the law of defamation to adopt a more liberal standard of interpretation than the law of contract or statutory interpretation.

172 For a recent example, see *Wood v Sureterm Direct Ltd* [2017] UKSC 24, [2017] 2 WLR 1095 [24] (Lord Hodge).

173 Justice Scalia of the US Supreme Court once remarked that '[t]he main business of a lawyer is to take the romance, the mystery, the irony, the ambiguity out of everything he touches': speech at the Juilliard School (22 September 2005).

What remains of Lord Neuberger's argument by analogy? It seems that the analogy with contract and statute is quite limited. Yes, the reduction of words to a single meaning is normal in English law. But the reason such a reduction is necessary in other areas (i.e., words have to be enforced) is absent in defamation. Conversely, the reason the reduction is largely unproblematic in contract and statute (i.e., the language tends to be bland and exact) is absent in defamation. What is more, there is no positive reason *to* import the single meaning rule from contract into defamation. Why not import the non-singular standard of interpretation from the law of trademarks or passing-off,[174] which, incidentally, is more relevant? In the final analysis, the argument by analogy fails.

The last pro-fiction argument I have to consider is the threat of chaos: will the proliferation of meanings in defamation complicate and increase the costs of litigation? Andrew Scott contends, quite persuasively, that the abolition of the rule will not have the dreaded effect.[175] Most importantly, the abolition of the single meaning rule does not compel us to abandon the objective approach to interpretation. The various alternatives to the rule enumerated above include other objective approaches, such as deeming any meaning which is reasonable and defamatory to have harmed the reputation of the claimant. Damages can be adjusted down if there are other reasonable meanings that are not defamatory. This approach is not empirical and will not result in the calling of witness after witness on the question of meaning (as Lord Neuberger prophesied).

Furthermore, under current practice, the court already canvasses a range of meanings, put forward by the parties. In *Ajinomoto*, for example, the High Court and the Court of Appeal both grappled with four possible meanings of the impugned labels, three put forward by the claimant and one by the defendant.[176] The point is that abolishing the fiction will not introduce more meanings into the discussion and thereby complicate everything. The multiple meanings are already part of the discussion.

On the other hand, it is possible that the abolition of the rule, which will tilt the balance in favour of claimants (arguably rightly), will embolden unworthy claimants and open the floodgates. Observers are already concerned about the chilling effect of the tort of defamation and what some see as its abuse by the

174 'Substantial proportion of the public': *Reed Executive plc v Reed Business Information Ltd* [2004] EWCA Civ 159, [2004] ETMR 56 [82] (Jacob LJ); *Interflora* (n 145) [224] (Arnold J) (reversed on other grounds).

175 Scott (n 120) 49–50.

176 *Ajinomoto* (CA) (n 108) [7] (Sedley LJ).

wealthy.[177] In this respect, the abolition of the fiction might make a bad situation worse.

The truth is that we do not know what the effects of abolition will be. Necessarily, the answer I give must be hypothetical. The only way to discover the effects of abolition is to abolish the rule and see what happens. Prophecies of doom often fail to materialise, but there is a risk that an ill-advised change in the law will solve one problem at the cost of creating others. That is the strength of the status quo; it is the evil we know.

If the only argument marshalled against the fiction were that it is a fiction, the spectre raised by Lord Neuberger would be reason enough, in my mind, to act conservatively; that is to say, to retain the fiction and avoid unnecessary upheavals. Indeed, in ordinary circumstances, I would not counsel change for pure intellectual satisfaction. The common law, like nature's organisms, has evolved in a particular way for certain reasons. In the famous words of Oliver Wendell Holmes, 'The life of the law has not been logic; it has been experience.'[178] It is the sum of innumerable cases, decided by different judges on different facts in different eras, and in jurisdictions from British Columbia to New Zealand. We must accept a degree of incongruity in such an edifice. It is a wonder that it works at all. I believe the common law deserves our respect. We should correct its harmful aberrations, but be slow to 'rationalise' it from above for purely theoretical reasons.[179]

That said, the reasons in this case are not purely theoretical. I do not seek to abolish the fiction simply because it is a fiction or because I have found another way to try defamation, which I think is superior. The problem with the single meaning rule is that it is capable of real injustice which (partially) frustrates the tort. People can get away with publishing statements which defame others in the eyes of right-thinking members of society. This should not be tolerated.

The question I posed at the start of this evaluation was whether the fictitious solution of the single meaning is the best solution to the problem of meaning, in light of the alternatives. The answer is no. It would be better to abolish the single meaning rule and replace it with one of the other objective solutions.

177 McBride and Bagshaw (n 104) 500–1.

178 Oliver Wendell Holmes, *The Common Law* (Belknap Press 2009) 3.

179 This argument seems to run counter to the position expressed earlier in this chapter that 'the mere fact that a device is fictitious is an argument against it'. This tension will be resolved in the next chapter.

3.8 COMMON INTENTION CONSTRUCTIVE TRUST

3.8.1 *Description*

This much-discussed device lies at the intersection of equity and land law. It is a special type of constructive trust, whereby a registered owner of land holds part of it for another, usually a cohabitant. It arises where the cohabitants, normally partners, had a 'common intention' that, in return for contributions by both, beneficial ownership would be shared.[180] If this beneficial ownership is not already reflected in the registered ownership, equity intervenes to impose a constructive trust to give effect to the beneficial ownership.[181] Like all constructive trusts, it is imposed because the conscience of the trustee is bound. The registered owner is conscience-bound to give effect to the common intention. In light of the contributions made by the cohabitant, it would be unconscionable for the registered owner to deny the cohabitant the intended beneficial interest.[182]

The common intention constructive trust typically becomes relevant following the breakdown of a domestic relationship, where one partner seeks ownership of part of the family home. Even so, the breakdown is irrelevant in terms of property rights: the trust exists regardless of the breakdown.[183] These days, this kind of trust is most relevant for cohabiting couples who are neither married nor in a civil partnership because they have no recourse to the redistributive powers in the Matrimonial Causes Act 1973[184] and must fall back on the general law.[185]

This niche of trust law is concerned with two key questions: (i) is there a trust at all; and, if so, (ii) in what proportions is beneficial ownership held? The cases speak of this duality as a two-stage test and reiterate that the two stages are very different.[186] At the first stage, for there to be a trust at all, we must find an actual understanding between the cohabitants. This is the eponymous common intention. It may be express or implied, but it must be actual. It is not what the judge thinks would have been fair or what reasonable parties would have agreed.[187]

180 *Gissing v Gissing* [1971] AC 886 (HL) 900 (Viscount Dilhorne), 904–5 (Lord Diplock); *Jones v Kernott* [2011] UKSC 53, [2012] 1 AC [51] (Lord Walker and Lady Hale).

181 *Stack v Dowden* [2007] UKHL 17, [2007] 2 AC 432 [58] (Lady Hale).

182 *Grant v Edwards* [1986] Ch 638 (CA) 656 (Sir Nicolas Browne-Wilkinson V-C). Recent decisions have arguably downgraded the contributions, seeing them as evidence of the common intention: *Stack v Dowden* (n 181) [69]–[70] (Lady Hale); *Jones v Kernott* (n 180) [51], esp [51F].

183 *Pettitt v Pettitt* [1970] AC 777 (HL) 803 (Lord Morris).

184 s 24.

185 See also *Stack v Dowden* (n 181) [2] (Lord Hope), [43]–[44] (Lady Hale).

186 *Capehorn v Harris* [2015] EWCA Civ 955, [2016] HLR 1 [16]–[17] (Sales LJ).

187 *Jones v Kernott* (n 180) [51] (Lord Walker and Lady Hale).

By contrast, at the second stage, to determine the size of the beneficial shares, we seek the answer in the intentions of the parties as manifested in their conduct; but if no allocation can be deduced therefrom, the court is permitted to decide for itself what is fair and reasonable.[188] In the words of Lord Walker and Lady Hale in *Jones v Kernott* (2011), 'where it is clear that the beneficial interests are to be shared, but it is impossible to divine a common intention as to the proportions . . . the court is driven to impute an intention to the parties which they may never have had'.[189] The difference between the two stages is stark: the first stage is an inference or nothing; the second stage is an inference or, failing that, an imputation.

Judges have gone out of their way to stress the difference between an inference and an imputation.[190] For Lord Walker, 'of all the questions to be asked about "common intention" trusts . . . the most crucial is whether the court must find a real bargain between the parties, or . . . impute a bargain'.[191] This difference is also crucial for our purposes. Lord Neuberger's articulation of the difference, below, in his dissent in *Stack v Dowden* (2007), won the strong approval of Lord Kerr in *Jones v Kernott*:[192]

> The distinction between inference and imputation may appear a fine one . . . but it is important. . . . An inferred intention is one which is objectively deduced to be the subjective actual intention of the parties. . . . An imputed intention is one which is attributed to the parties, even though no such actual intention can be deduced from their actions and statements, and even though they had no such intention. Imputation involves concluding what the parties would have intended, whereas inference involves concluding what they did intend.[193]

To conclude, the common intention constructive trust will only arise if the common intention actually existed. If no common intention can be found, there is no trust – no matter how unfair such an outcome would be to the party who has made contributions but is not on the register. However, as soon as we conclude that there was *a* common intention, there will be a constructive trust even if we cannot know what the shares were intended to be. In such a case, the court will make its own judgement in allocating the shares.

188 Ibid.

189 Ibid. [31].

190 In addition to the authorities that follow in the main text, see *Pettitt v Pettitt* (n 183) 804–85 (Lord Morris), 823–5 (Lord Diplock); *Gissing v Gissing* (n 180) 897 (Lord Reid), 898 (Lord Morris), 900 (Viscount Dilhorne); *Grant v Edwards* (n 182) 652 (Mustill LJ); cf *Gissing v Gissing* (n 180) 902 (Lord Pearson).

191 *Stack v Dowden* (n 181) [17].

192 *Jones v Kernott* (n 180) [73].

193 *Stack v Dowden* (n 181) [125]–[126].

A note on terminology is in order. Given the current emphasis on finding an actual intention in the parties' dealings (the first stage), commentators like Graham Virgo doubt that the common intention constructive trust is still a *constructive* trust. They prefer to view it as an express trust. There is much to be said for this viewpoint. However, this taxonomical dispute has no bearing on our discussion. This is not the place to resolve it. Since the most senior judges continue to refer to the common intention trust as a constructive trust, I will do so too.[194]

3.8.2 *Is the Common Intention Constructive Trust a Fiction?*

Having by now applied the definitions step-by-step five times, I will dispense with the formal structure from now on and focus on the contentious points.

The prime suspect for fiction in the context of the common intention constructive trust is the imputation in the second stage. We invent intentions rather than find them. Some commentators have certainly taken the view that the second stage is 'entirely fictional'.[195] The problem with this view is that there is no falsity. The issue would be falsely decided if the court 'found' an intention that never was. But the court does no such thing. The judge simply says, 'I don't know what the intention was, so I'll tell you what I think is right.' It cannot be that a judge transparently deciding what is fair is a legal fiction. In the absence of falsity, there can be no Hard Fiction.

Could it be that the common intention constructive trust is a Soft Fiction? Well, it is possible that the evidential basis for the inference in the first stage (finding an actual common intention) is in practice so tenuous that it is not an inference but an imputation. If true, this strained inference might be a Soft Fiction. To say that the inference is a Soft Fiction, we need a trend in the case law of judges 'inferring' a common intention on flimsy grounds.

In *Pettitt v Pettitt* (1969), Lord Diplock noted the 'numerous cases decided in the last 20 years ... in which in the absence of evidence that spouses formed any actual intention ... the courts have imputed an intention to them'.[196] This trend continued into the seventies and eighties.[197] It is

194 *Jones v Kernott* (n 180) [17], [24] (Lord Walker and Lady Hale), [78], [82] (Lord Wilson).

195 James Lee, '"And the Waters Began to Subside": Imputing Intention under Jones v Kernott' (2012) 5 Conveyancer and Property Lawyer 421, 427; Mark Pawlowski, 'Imputing a Common Intention in Single Ownership Cases' (2015) 29 Trust Law International 3, 13.

196 *Pettitt v Pettitt* (n 183) 824.

197 *Stack v Dowden* (n 181) [21] (Lord Walker).

exemplified by two cases. In *Eves v Eves* (1975), the man told the woman she was getting no share in the house on the (false) pretext that, being under twenty-one, she could not own property.[198] The Court of Appeal inferred a common intention (that she *would* have a share) because the man's excuse was invalid and insincere. 'It seems to me', said Brightman J, 'that this [excuse] raises a *clear* inference that there was an understanding between them that she was intended to have some sort of proprietary interest in the house: otherwise no excuse would have been needed'.[199] Lord Denning MR and Browne LJ concurred.[200] The quality of this reasoning is much to be doubted. If I reject a bargain for a bad reason, surely I cannot be taken to have accepted it. Yet Brightman J found a 'clear' inference of an agreement in the very refusal thereof.

In *Grant v Edwards* (1986), the man again expressly refused to give the woman a share; this time because it would prejudice the woman's divorce proceedings with her then-husband.[201] And again the Court of Appeal inferred a common intention despite, or indeed from, the refusal.[202] Mustill LJ thought that 'the nature of the excuse . . . must have led the [woman] to believe that she would in the future have her name on the title'.[203]

Simon Gardner, writing in 1993, found the reasoning in these cases 'fallacious': 'It is hard to think that the judges concerned really believed in it. One can only conclude that they too were engaged in the business of inventing agreements on women's behalf.'[204] John Mee, writing in 2007, likewise believed the courts made it 'very difficult for a defendant to resist a claim'.[205]

It seems arguable that the inference requirement, at least in the pre-*Kernott* days, was a Soft Fiction because it was a factual question, which the courts consciously answered in a strained, unnatural way. This Soft Fiction should be classified as Essential because it went to the core of the action. The inference was not meaningless text. In the difficult cases, judges went to great lengths to argue that there was in fact an inference.

Be that as it may, there seems to have been an about-face in English law following the elucidation of the inference/imputation distinction in *Stack*

198 [1975] 1 WLR 1338 (CA) 1340 (Lord Denning MR).
199 Ibid. 1344 (emphasis added).
200 Ibid. 1342, 1343.
201 *Grant v Edwards* (n 182) 643 (Nourse LJ).
202 Ibid. 649 (Nourse LJ), 656 (Sir Nicolas Browne-Wilkinson V-C).
203 Ibid. 653.
204 Simon Gardner, 'Rethinking Family Property' [1993] LQR 263, 265.
205 John Mee, 'Joint Ownership, Subjective Intention and the Common Intention Constructive Trust' [2007] Conveyancer and Property Lawyer 14, 14.

v Dowden and *Jones v Kernott*. In two recent cases,[206] the Court of Appeal rebuked the trial judge for conflating imputation with inference. In *Capehorn v Harris* (2015), Sales LJ said:

> As regards [the property], the judge made clear findings that . . . there was no agreement that Mr Harris would have any beneficial interest in it. . . . Yet despite all this . . . the judge asked herself the question: ' . . . whether the extent of Mr Harris's contribution to the business . . . should be sufficient to impute an intention to the parties . . . '.
>
> She concluded that . . . she 'should impute to the parties . . . an acceptance of the fact that Mr Harris, by reason of his contribution of the business . . . has acquired a beneficial interest in [the property]' of 25 per cent.
>
> In my judgement, the judge erred. . . . She imputed an intention to the parties for the first stage of the two-stage analysis rather than identifying an actual agreement made by them. . . . No actual agreement . . . was ever made . . . as the judge's findings elsewhere in the judgment made clear.[207]

A few months later, the Court of Appeal met with the same issue in *Barnes v Phillips* (2015).[208] Here Lloyd Jones LJ was unsure *what* the trial judge had decided:

> [T]he judge has moved directly from . . . concluding that there was 'no specific agreement' to considering what intention must be imputed as to the shares. . . . As we have seen, the judge was well aware of the structure laid down in *Jones v Kernott* within which the issues should be addressed. . . . He cannot be taken to have departed from it in the radical manner submitted by the appellant. Moreover, he must have appreciated that there would be no point in discussing the shares in which the property is held following variation if no common intention to vary had been established. In these circumstances, it is at the very least strongly arguable that the judge must be taken to have concluded that there was such a common intention. Nevertheless, this stage of the reasoning is totally absent from his judgment.[209]

Faced with this lacuna, and a possible elision of the two steps, His Lordship examined the facts himself and concluded that a common intention should be inferred.[210]

206 Cases identified in Andrew Dymond, 'Inference and Imputation: Cases after Jones v Kernott' (2016) 19 Journal of Housing Law 57, 58ff.

207 n 186 [19]–[21].

208 [2015] EWCA Civ 1056, [2016] HLR 3.

209 Ibid. [29].

210 Ibid. [30]–[34].

The latest case law makes it impossible to continue to regard the inference as a Soft Fiction. At most, the current case law can be said to show that there is a temptation to impute instead of infer, but appellate courts resist any slippage. Even if there is slippage in the eyes of some,[211] it is not conscious on the part of the judiciary. The unnatural interpretation and consciousness requirements are not satisfied. Today, the inference is not a Soft Fiction.

It may be added, by way of postscript, that Nick Piska maintains that the inference/imputation distinction is itself illusory.[212] This is because the parties' actual (i.e., subjective) intentions are regardless determined objectively by their conduct. So even in inferring actual intentions, we are imputing objective intentions. To this I would respond that even if Piska is right, there is a chasm of difference between finding intentions on the basis of conduct and finding intentions on the basis of fairness, which is not 'finding' at all.

As a second postscript, it should be recorded that further scepticism towards the inference/imputation dichotomy may be found in Lord Collins's speech in *Jones v Kernott*: 'what is one person's inference will be another person's imputation'.[213] Even the leading joint judgment of Lord Walker and Lady Hale in that case makes this concession: 'While the conceptual difference between inferring and imputing is clear, the difference in practice may not be so great.'[214] Given the breadth of the judicial discretion to infer a common intention, these observations are probably true. Still, for a Soft Fiction, we need not a tricky or grey area but an unnatural interpretation (which is not the same as a borderline case) *consciously* imposed on the facts. The recent cases point decidedly in the other direction.

In conclusion, the common intention constructive trust is neither a Hard nor a Soft Fiction.

3.8.3 *Evaluation*

The heresy of imputation in the first stage was stamped out by the Supreme Court in *Jones v Kernott*. The abolition of the Soft Fiction by the judiciary notwithstanding, we can learn important lessons from evaluating it. In hindsight, was it a good idea to remove that laxity in drawing inferences?

211 See e.g., Andy Hayward, 'Common Intention Constructive Trusts and the Role of Imputation in Theory and Practice' (2016) 3 The Conveyancer and Property Lawyer 233, 237.

212 Nick Piska, 'Intention, Fairness and the Presumption of Resulting Trust after Stack v Dowden' [2008] MLR 120, 127–8.

213 *Jones v Kernott* (n 180) [65].

214 Ibid. [34].

Emphatically, it was. One may believe that a constructive trust should be based on a factual inference, or one may believe that it should be based on the court's assessment of deservedness. But whatever one decides, one should do what one has decided to do. If the courts, in their wisdom, have decided that the first stage is an inference, an inference it should be. When lower courts trump up inferences or indeed, as we have seen, deduce agreements from the refusal to agree, they betray the doctrine of precedent. When any court imposes an unnatural interpretation on a rule of law (i.e., develops a Soft Fiction), legal certainty is compromised. The courts say one thing but do the opposite. This system of adjudication is hard to defend.

It may be retorted that this objection could be levelled against the fictions I voted to keep. Not so: estoppel, for example, does not undermine the certainty of transactions. The opposite is true: estoppel *per rem judicatam* ensures certainty. 'Equity treats as done that which ought to be done'; likewise, is not a case where the courts say one thing and do the opposite. This argument will be further expounded in the next chapter. The conclusion of this evaluation is that it was right to abolish the fiction of inference in the first stage of the common intention constructive trust.

3.9 REMOTENESS IN NEGLIGENCE

3.9.1 *Description*

Remoteness of damage is a vexed issue. The problem is this: to what extent are negligent people liable for the consequences of their negligence? It is easy to say that they should be liable for all the damage they have caused. But a chain of factual causation – cause and effect – is potentially infinite.[215] It may involve intervening acts, unforeseeable occurrences and unusually vulnerable victims. As a matter of factual or 'but for' causation, all the events in the chain would not have occurred but for the seminal negligent act. So at what point along the causal chain of increasingly remote consequences do we refuse to visit liability on the tortfeasor?

The modern test was laid down by Viscount Simonds, delivering the advice of the Privy Council in *The Wagon Mound (No 1)* (1961): 'whether the damage is of such a kind as the reasonable man should have foreseen'.[216] In other

[215] See *Spencer v Wincanton Holdings Ltd (Wincanton Logistics Ltd)* [2009] EWCA Civ 1404, [2010] PIQR P8 [15] (Sedley LJ).

[216] *Overseas Tankship (UK) Ltd v Morts Dock & Engineering Co (The Wagon Mound)* [1961] AC 388 (PC) 426.

words, the kind of damage has to be reasonably foreseeable. If it is not, the damage is too remote and irrecoverable.

Dr Janet O'Sullivan has advanced the argument that the courts have so watered down the foreseeability requirement that virtually any damage, no matter how *un*foreseeable, can satisfy the test.[217] The primary example cited by O'Sullivan is the replay of *The Wagon Mound (No 1)*, namely *The Wagon Mound (No 2)* (1966).[218] The Wagon Mound was docked in Sydney Harbour. Furnace oil leaked from the ship into the harbour. The oil ignited and two nearby ships were damaged by fire. The owners of the damaged ships sued for negligence. In the Privy Council, the question was whether the risk of fire was too remote. Walsh J, in the Supreme Court of New South Wales, had made these findings:

> (1) Reasonable people in the position of the officers of the Wagon Mound [who were responsible for the spillage] would regard the furnace oil as very difficult to ignite upon water. (2) Their personal experience would probably have been that this had very rarely happened. (3) If they had given attention to the risk of fire from the spillage, they would have regarded it as a possibility, but one which could become an actuality only in *very exceptional circumstances*. (4) They would have considered the chances of the required exceptional circumstances happening whilst the oil remained spread on the harbour waters as being *remote*. (5) I find that the occurrence of damage ... was not reasonably foreseeable.[219]

The Privy Council accepted, as points of fact, findings (1) to (4), but overturned finding (5), which was the crucial legal conclusion. Lord Reid, speaking for the Board, held that the ignition of the oil was a possibility, 'a real risk', albeit an exceptional one. Therefore the risk of fire could be 'realised or foreseen'.[220] This raises serious questions. If a 'very exceptional' risk is a foreseeable risk, what risk is not foreseeable?

Is an unforeseeable risk one that has no possibility of occurring even in 'very exceptional circumstances'? It seems that nothing short of the scientific impossibility of oil catching fire on water would have sufficed.[221] But an impossible risk is not a risk. If so, the deconstructed *ratio* of *The Wagon Mound (No 2)* is that, despite the lip service to the

217 Janet O'Sullivan, *O'Sullivan & Hilliard's The Law of Contract* (9th edn, OUP 2020) 349, para 14.46.

218 *Overseas Tankship (UK) Ltd v The Miller Steamship Co Pty and Another (The Wagon Mound No 2)* [1967] 1 AC 617 (PC).

219 Ibid. 633 (Lord Reid quoting Walsh J) (emphasis added).

220 Ibid. 643–4.

221 Ibid. 633, 641 (Lord Reid).

irrelevance of 'far-fetched' risks,[222] any risk, however remote, may be foreseeable.

Where Lord Reid led, others followed. In *H Parsons (Livestock) Ltd v Uttley Ingham & Co Ltd* (1977),[223] the claimant pig farmers bought a hopper from the defendants. The ventilators on the hopper were negligently installed and the nuts stored inside turned mouldy. Alas, the contaminated food, when eaten by the pigs, triggered an outbreak of *E coli*, which decimated the herd. Though ostensibly a case in contract, all three judges of the Court of Appeal agreed that foreseeability should be treated the same in contract and tort.[224] On foreseeability, Lord Denning MR said: 'They ought reasonably to have foreseen that, if the mouldy pignuts were fed to the pigs, there was a possibility that they might become ill. *Not a serious possibility*. Nor a real danger. But still a slight possibility. On that basis the makers were liable for the illness suffered by the pigs.'[225]

Scarman LJ concurred: 'It does not matter, in my judgment, if they thought that the chance of physical injury ... was slight, or that the odds were against it, provided they contemplated as a serious possibility the type of consequence, not necessarily the specific consequence, that ensued upon breach.'[226] Again, the question from *The Wagon Mound (No 2)* demands our attention: if a risk that is 'slight', 'not a serious possibility', 'nor a real danger' is a foreseeable risk, what risk is *not* foreseeable? Only an impossible one it seems: a non-risk.

In *Jolley v Sutton LBC* (2000),[227] two boys decided to repair an abandoned boat on council land. They used a car-jack and some wood to prop up the dilapidated vessel. This support gave way, crushing the claimant and resulting in catastrophic spinal injuries. He sued the council. The House of Lords held the damage was foreseeable.[228] In the Court of Appeal, Lord Woolf MR noted that 'there is no case of which counsel on either side were aware where want of care on the part of a defendant was established but a plaintiff, who was a child, has failed to succeed because the circumstances of the accident were not foreseeable'.[229]

In his historical study of tort law, Professor Paul Mitchell reviewed cases like *Jolley v Sutton*, where children were injured as a result of their own carelessness

222 Ibid. 643 (Lord Reid).
223 [1978] QB 791 (CA).
224 Ibid. 804 (Lord Denning MR), 805 (Orr LJ), 806 (Scarman LJ).
225 Ibid. 804 (emphasis added).
226 Ibid. 813.
227 [2000] 1 WLR 1082 (HL).
228 Ibid. 1093 (Lord Hoffmann).
229 *Jolley v Sutton London Borough Council* [1998] 1 WLR 1546 (CA) 1553.

and sued some responsible authority or corporation in negligence.[230] These cases, too, confirm the trend (pre-*Wagon Mound*): once want of care was proved, foreseeability was no hurdle. Any mischief, however ingenious, by children, was deemed reasonably foreseeable.[231] Having discussed attempts to 'tighten the foreseeability test', Mitchell concluded: 'judges keen to limit liability were going to need sharper doctrinal tools than a foreseeability test'.[232] The case of *Jolley v Sutton*, and those collected by Mitchell,[233] strengthen the impression that foreseeability is sometimes a fig leaf for other policy reasons. In practice, foreseeability is not a limit on liability.

One final instance of the dilution of foreseeability is worthy of mention. *Spencer v Wincanton Holdings Ltd* (2009)[234] concerned a series of increasingly unfortunate events. In 2000, the claimant injured his knee in a minor workplace accident. The defendant employer admitted liability. The knee was still painful in 2003, so the claimant made an informed decision to undergo an above-knee amputation and be fitted with a prosthesis. The employer accepted liability for this follow-on damage as well. To his credit, the claimant was a hardy man. Undaunted by his injury, he found a new job that accommodated his handicap and did his best to live without reliance on others. Later in 2003, the claimant was refuelling at a petrol station. Rather than call for assistance, he operated the pump himself, without his prosthetic leg, which was in the backseat, steadying himself against the car. He had done this many times before. This time he tripped over a raised manhole and fell, rupturing his quadriceps tendon. It left him paraplegic for life. For this last injury, the employer denied liability on the ground that it was not a foreseeable consequence of the initial workplace accident.

In the Sheffield County Court, Judge Bullimore held the employer liable for the second accident (at the petrol station) but reduced the damages due to contributory negligence. His Honour explained his conclusion as follows:

> [The employer] submits that it was unforeseeable . . . that the claimant would fall while hopping round his car. . . . That in my view places too much emphasis on what exactly is to be foreseen. The direct result of the first accident was the loss of the leg. A one-legged man is less stable: it is foreseeable that in going about his daily business a one legged man is more vulnerable to trips and slips than a two legged man. It is quite unnecessary to ask if

230 Mitchell (n 126) 109ff.
231 Ibid. 109.
232 Ibid. 110–11.
233 Ibid. 109–10.
234 n 215.

> the Defendant . . . could or should have also foreseen the trip occurred when the Claimant was filling his car with fuel.[235]

The Court of Appeal unanimously upheld the trial judge's decision, with Sedley LJ holding that '[l]ike the amputation, the fall was . . . an *unexpected* but real consequence of the original accident'.[236]

The question again calls for an answer: if an 'unexpected' risk is foreseeable, what risk is unforeseeable? Here the straining of the remoteness test has reached a new height since 'unexpected' and 'unforeseeable' are exactly synonymous. And so, it appears any risk may be foreseeable in the right circumstances. A risk is reasonably foreseeable even if it is 'very exceptional' or 'not a serious possibility' or 'slight' or 'unexpected'. Is it not fictitious to still talk about foreseeability when the word has been so denatured?

Tort lawyers might reply that the law of remoteness is more complex than pure foreseeability. They would be right. The case law has undercut the foreseeability test in a number of ways. To begin with, it is only necessary to foresee the broad category of damage, not the extent thereof,[237] nor the manner in which it materialises.[238] Next, the eggshell skull rule means that a victim's unusual susceptibility (e.g., a weak heart) is not considered too remote.[239] The final nail in the coffin is that a risk/benefit analysis is undertaken so that even a negligible risk does not justify inaction if it is easy to eliminate.[240] But this reply, while correct, would miss the point.

My point is that foreseeability is not what it is said to be. It is not a condition for recovery. The adumbrated qualifications do not rescue foreseeability. They emasculate it even further. They explain *how* the foreseeability test has been hollowed out of content. Foreseeability is a formal requirement that has no bite. It is a non-requirement. Hence the suspicion that it is a fiction.

3.9.2 *Is Remoteness in Negligence a Fiction?*

It would be unsafe to conclude that remoteness in negligence is a Hard Fiction. The first obstacle is the falsity requirement. Hard Fictions are barefaced in their falsity. We need to point to a definite contradiction with the physical world.

235 Ibid. [21] (Sedley LJ quoting Judge Bullimore).
236 Ibid. [23] (emphasis added).
237 *Hughes v Lord Advocate* [1963] AC 837 (HL) 845 (Lord Reid).
238 Ibid. 853 (Lord Morris), 855–6 (Lord Guest).
239 *Owens v Liverpool Corporation* [1939] 1 KB 394 (CA) 400–1 (Mackinnon LJ); *Smith v Leech Brain & Co Ltd* [1962] 2 QB 405 (HC) 415 (Lord Parker CJ).
240 *The Wagon Mound (No 2)* (n 218) 644; see also 642.

When we are dealing with degrees of probability at the lower end of the scale, it is hard to say with any conviction that a certain event is unforeseeable as opposed to foreseeable. This is because there is no bright line; it is a continuum.

Moreover, even if we accept that a particular gradation of foreseeability crosses the boundary into unforeseeability, how can we know that the judge is conscious of the falsity? The judge could just have a slightly different boundary. Both the falsity and consciousness requirements are difficult or impossible to fulfil. Remoteness in negligence is not a Hard Fiction.

On the other hand, the way the foreseeability test has been strained (arguably to extinction) does suggest a Soft Fiction. Are the three elements of the Soft Fiction (factual issue, unnatural interpretation, consciousness) present? Foreseeability is clearly a factual test. It is the reasonable man in a new guise: what 'the reasonable man should have foreseen'.[241] As has been argued earlier, at some length, the reasonable man test is factual.

The straining of foreseeability does amount to the imposition of an unnatural interpretation on a rule of law. Foreseeability may be a continuum, sure enough, but a foreseeability test under which any risk may be foreseeable (even a 'very exceptional' one) is a non-test. It should be remembered that here we are not seeking to establish unambiguous falsity but a strained interpretation. Interpreting the foreseeability test in *Koufos v C Czarnikow Ltd (The Heron II)* (1967), Lord Upjohn said that 'the tortfeasor is liable for any damage which *he can reasonably foresee* may happen as a result of the breach *however unlikely it may be*, unless it can be brushed aside as far fetched'.[242] If such an equivocation – which this author's mind is not subtle enough to comprehend – is not a strained interpretation, I do not want to know what is.

But are the judges conscious of the contrived nature of the reasoning? In my opinion, they must be. If cornered on the point, they would have to admit that they stretched the test beyond its ordinary meaning. A 'very exceptional' risk is by definition not a reasonably foreseeable risk. A risk is not foreseeable 'however unlikely it may be'. An *E coli* outbreak is not a reasonably foreseeable result of a defective container. Whatever the motives, this must be a conscious straining of the remoteness test. Remoteness in negligence is a Soft Fiction.

3.9.3 *Effect Classification*

This is the first New Fiction we have encountered that is not an Essential Fiction. Foreseeability is not the real conceptual reason for the result of the

[241] *The Wagon Mound (No 1)* (n 216) 426 (Viscount Simonds).

[242] [1969] 1 AC 350 (HL) 422.

cases. If the judges had decided the above cases on foreseeability alone, they would have reached a different result. They found the defendants liable for other reasons[243] – policy reasons or their inner sense of justice – and foreseeability had to be carried along. The judges had to say that the unlikely event was reasonably foreseeable – because that was the law and it generally made sense – so they did. Reasonable foreseeability is like the Auxiliary Fictions of ages past (e.g., the neck verse or finding in trover) – not the real reasons for the result of the case. Indeed, they masked the real reasons. It was just something that had to be said: lip service. Remoteness in negligence is an Auxiliary Fiction.

3.9.4 *Evaluation*

The aim of the fiction is to allow recovery where the damage is not reasonably foreseeable, but there are other reasons to hold the defendant liable. This can be seen in Lord Reid's speech in *The Wagon Mound (No 2)*:

> [T]he evidence shows that the discharge of so much oil onto the water must have taken a considerable time, and a vigilant ship's engineer would have noticed the discharge at an early stage. . . . The most that can be said to justify inaction is that he would have known that [the oil could ignite] in very exceptional circumstances. But that does not mean that a reasonable man would dismiss such a risk from his mind and do nothing when it was so easy to prevent it.[244]

As we have said, the fiction is Auxiliary, meaning it is not the real reason for the result of the case. In the above passage lurks the real reason. Lord Reid acknowledged that the risk was 'very exceptional' (read: not reasonably foreseeable), but thought the defendant's inaction was inexcusable, given how easy it was to solve the problem. The real reason for the result of the case, then, was that inaction was unreasonable, not that the risk was foreseeable. The aim of the fiction here, as elsewhere,[245] was to enable recovery in spite of the remoteness test, where there is an overpowering reason to do so.

To evaluate the fiction, we ask whether it is the best available means of achieving this aim. The alternative to the fiction is to adopt a new test that is more flexible or more nuanced. As it stands, the remoteness test is quite uncertain. As we have seen in the context of another Soft Fiction, *volenti*

243 These are explored in the next section (3.9.4).
244 *The Wagon Mound (No 2)* (n 218) 644; see also 642.
245 See, e.g., *Jolley v Sutton* (n 227) 1093 (Lord Hoffmann); *Page v Smith* [1996] AC 155 (HL) 170 (Lord Ackner).

non fit injuria, a strained argument is more uncertain than a plain falsehood. How are parties to know how much straining will be allowed in their case, if at all? How can parties predict whether the judge will effectively disapply the foreseeability criterion in their case or not? When judges knowingly play fast and loose with the law, the law is unpredictable. A result reached by twisted reasoning, even if it is a good result, is never a predictable result.

It is arguable, perhaps, that the foreseeability test is so eviscerated that it is consistent in its meaninglessness: it is never a barrier. Hence there is no uncertainty. But if this is true; if foreseeability is already dead, would it not be more sensible to accept its death rather than deny it? The law would then be officially changed so that foreseeability is no longer a *sine qua non* for remoteness.

The foreseeability test is either consistent in its fictitiousness, in which case there is no point keeping it; or it is inconsistent in its fictitiousness, in which case it is confusing. Either way, it is bad for the law. If the remoteness test in *The Wagon Mound (No 1)* has been found wanting by judges (who evaded it), it should be replaced; either with a multifactor test or a more nuanced test. The present response of the law – fudging – is beneath it. The Soft Fiction of remoteness in negligence ought to be abolished.

3.10 READING DOWN EXCLUSION CLAUSES

This is a practice I mentioned in the last chapter as an example of a Soft Fiction. I return to it now for classification and evaluation. It will be dealt with it in short order. A Soft Fiction is a factual issue decided by a consciously unnatural interpretation. I have already established that the meaning of a clause in a contract is a factual issue. As Lord Denning vividly described (or rather confessed) in *George Mitchell (Chesterhall) Ltd v Finney Lock Seeds Ltd* (1982), the courts consciously strained the meaning of exclusion clauses to an unnatural degree – so as to defeat them.[246] This *mea culpa*, a fine example of legal prose, was quoted at length in the last chapter. Some of these artificial constructions would be amusing if they were not authentic reasons for judgment. In *Webster v Higgin* (1948), to take one example, the exclusion clause read 'no warranty . . . is given or implied'. The Court seized upon the use of the present tense to conclude that the clause did not cover *pre*-contractual warranties.[247] So the practice of reading down exclusion clauses was a Soft Fiction before 1977.

[246] [1983] QB 284 (CA) 296–7.
[247] [1948] 2 All ER 127 (CA) 129 (Lord Greene MR), 130 (Evershed LJ).

Is this fiction still in existence? Lord Denning strongly implied that it was not extant at the time of writing, namely 1982. There is much to support this implication. Two years earlier, the House of Lords seemed to draw a line under the fiction. In *Photo Production Ltd v Securicor Transport Ltd* (1980), the Law Lords overturned Lord Denning himself for forcing an unnatural interpretation upon an exclusion clause.[248] In a speech echoed by his brethren, Lord Diplock stated:

> My Lords, the reports are full of cases in which what would appear to be very strained constructions have been placed upon exclusion clauses, mainly in what to-day would be called consumer contracts and contracts of adhesion. As Lord Wilberforce has pointed out, any need for this kind of judicial distortion of the English language has been banished by … the Unfair Contract Terms Act 1977. In commercial contracts negotiated between business-men capable of looking after their own interests … it is, in my view, wrong to place a strained construction upon words in an exclusion clause which are clear and fairly susceptible of one meaning only.[249]

In recent years, the courts have firmly rejected unnaturally restrictive interpretations of exclusion clauses. In *Transocean Drilling UK Ltd v Providence Resources plc* (2016), the Court of Appeal was unanimous that 'since the decision in *Photo Production* … the courts have recognised that artificial approaches to the construction of commercial contracts are to be avoided in favour of giving the words used by the parties their ordinary and natural meaning'.[250] Comments to the same effect were made in *Lictor Anstalt v Mir Steel UK Ltd* (2012),[251] *Persimmon Homes Ltd v Ove Arup and Partners Ltd* (2017)[252] and *Interactive E-Solutions JLT v O3B Africa Ltd* (2018).[253] In 2017, Professor Edwin Peel stated that 'the implementation of … [the Unfair Contract Terms Act 1977] … did see the passing of a particularly strained form of interpretation in which the courts persuaded themselves of an ambiguity which did not really exist'.[254]

Given the state of evidence, it is unlikely that the interpretation of exclusion clauses is still a Soft Fiction – at least as a widespread or condoned practice. I will therefore treat the fiction of reading down exclusion clauses as judicially abolished.

248 [1980] AC 827 (HL).
249 Ibid. 851 (Lord Diplock); see also 843 (Lord Wilberforce), 853 (Lord Scarman).
250 [2016] EWCA Civ 372, [2016] 2 All ER (Comm) 606 [14] (Moore-Bick V-P).
251 [2012] EWCA Civ 1397, [2013] 2 All ER (Comm) 54 [31]–[34] (Rimer LJ).
252 [2017] EWCA Civ 373, [2017] BLR 417 [56] (Jackson LJ).
253 [2018] EWCA Civ 62 [14] (Lewison LJ).
254 Edwin Peel, 'Contra Proferentem Revisited' [2017] LQR 6, 7.

Prior to its abolition, the fiction of reading down exclusion clauses was, obviously, a New Fiction. In terms of the Effect Classification, it was an Auxiliary Fiction. Judges employed unlikely interpretations – 'sophisticated refinements' per Lord Scarman[255] – not because they thought these interpretations were an objectively good way of understanding the exclusion clause. They resorted to this manipulation because, taking pity on the claimant, they did not want the clause to apply to the facts. Hence the fiction was not the real reason for the result of the case or a belief justifying the outcome. It was no more than a fig leaf, a means to an end – and an inelegant one at that.

All that remains now is to evaluate this bygone Soft Fiction (for didactic purposes that will become apparent in the next chapter). It is argued that it was right of the judges to abolish the fiction for the same reasons advanced for the abolition of the Soft Fictions in the first stage of the common intention constructive trust and remoteness in negligence. These arguments need not be repeated a third time. Fudging is no way to do law.

In conclusion, reading down exclusion clauses was a New Auxiliary Soft Fiction, which was rightly abolished circa 1980.

3.11 SUMMARY OF FINDINGS

Table 3.1 sets forth my conclusions regarding all the purportedly fictitious devices discussed in this book, in order of discussion.

3.12 CONCLUSION

The first chapter was history. The second chapter was theory. This third chapter was theory in practice. In it, the understanding we had acquired in the previous chapters was applied to contemporary fictions. I looked closely at a number of devices, determined whether they were fictitious, classified them and, for whatever it was worth, sentenced them to life or death. The results are tabulated below.

In the fourth and final chapter, I will attempt to extrapolate from my findings on individual fictions some general principles about all fictions. The point of this monograph is not simply to pass judgement on the value of this or that fiction, but to develop an 'Acceptance Test' that can be applied to any fiction.

[255] *Photo Production* (n 248) 853.

TABLE 3.1 *All fictions*

Device	Nature	Age	Effect	Recommendation: retain or abolish?
Dominus remisit curiam	Hard Fiction	Old	Jurisdictional	Already abolished
Vi et armis	Hard Fiction	Old	Jurisdictional	Already abolished
Geographical fictions	Hard Fiction	Old	Jurisdictional	Already abolished
Bill of Middlesex	Hard Fiction	Old	Jurisdictional	Already abolished
Writ of *quominus*	Hard Fiction	Old	Jurisdictional	Already abolished
Benefit of clergy	Hard Fiction	Old	Auxiliary	Already abolished
Pleading the belly	Hard Fiction	Old	Auxiliary	Already abolished
Common recovery	Hard Fiction	Old	Auxiliary	Already abolished
Trover	Hard Fiction	Old	Auxiliary	Already abolished
Ejectment	Hard Fiction	Old and New	Essential	Already abolished
Quasi-contract	Hard Fiction	Old and New	Essential	Already abolished
Corporation	Not a fiction	N/A	N/A	N/A
Trust (as such)	Not a fiction	N/A	N/A	N/A
Unsealed deed	Not a fiction	N/A	N/A	N/A
Reading down exclusion clauses	Soft Fiction	New	Auxiliary	Already abolished
Reasonable man	Not a fiction	N/A	N/A	N/A
Volenti non fit injuria	Soft Fiction	New	Essential	Abolish
Equity treats as done that which ought to be done	Hard Fiction	New	Essential	Retain
Estoppel	Hard Fiction	New	Essential	Retain
Single meaning rule	Hard Fiction	New	Essential	Abolish
Common intention constructive trust (subsistence stage)	Not a fiction anymore	New	Essential	Abolished
Common intention constructive trust (allocation stage)	Not a fiction	N/A	N/A	N/A
Remoteness in negligence	Soft Fiction	New	Auxiliary	Abolish

4

An Acceptance Test for Fictions

Lawyer, n. One skilled in circumvention of the law.

Ambrose Bierce[1]

4.1 INTRODUCTION

This chapter represents the culmination of this work. A long mathematical treatise may culminate in a short equation, whose neat simplicity stupefies us. Legal treatises do not usually reduce their subject to a pithy precept, nor are they known for neatness or simplicity. In this chapter, I will try to defy the odds and produce an algorithmic conclusion for the book – a flowchart – which contains all the knowledge we have accumulated. Needless to say, it will not approach the elegance (let alone the brilliance) of a scientific formula; but it will, it is hoped, be simple, concise and useful.

Having traced, described, defined, classified and evaluated fictions, it is now time to formulate a test to determine which fictions should be retained and which discarded. This test will be called the 'Retention Test'. I will also propose a slightly different 'Creation Test' for situations where a judge is considering creating a new fiction. At the end of this chapter, these two tests will be joined in one flowchart, depicting a single 'Acceptance Test' for fictions. The Acceptance Test will thus combine both the Retention and Creation Tests and embody the conclusion of this research project.

The great difficulty in developing an acceptance test for fictions is that no two fictions are alike. If the previous chapters have taught us anything, it is that each fiction has a unique history, function and context. How can we generalise from

[1] Ambrose Bierce, *The Enlarged Devil's Dictionary* (Ernest Jerome Hopkins ed, Gollancz 1967) 176.

one to all? How can we reduce this diversity of circumstance to a one-size-fits-all test that is simple, concise and useful?

The answer lies in classification. No two persons are alike, but it is possible to classify them by relevant characteristics. Fictions may also be classified according to key characteristics, many of which I have already identified. The Retention Test will thus take the following form: if a fiction presents characteristics X, Y and Z, retain it; if not, abolish it. The Creation Test will work in the same way, but one of the characteristics will be different. As long as the characteristics are not in themselves unclear, the test will meet the condition of being simple, concise and useful.

This Acceptance Test will be developed hereinbelow in three stages. First, I will ask what *kind* of test we want. Do we want a flexible or strict test? What degree of discretion will we permit? What general view of fictions will the test reflect? This first stage addresses the general nature and direction of the test.

The second stage is concerned with the motives for fictions. What role should a fiction's motive play in the Acceptance Test? Can we judge fictions by their motives? What are these motives?

Finally, I will attempt to generalise the conclusions about individual fictions from the last chapter. This third stage of extrapolation will give the test its content: what characteristics make up the test. Much of what will be said in this chapter has already been foreshadowed in the discussions of individual fictions in previous chapters. This chapter will connect the dots.

4.2 THE NATURE OF THE TEST: THE DEGREE OF DISCRETION

4.2.1 *Tests and Discretion*

Inasmuch as the Acceptance Test is the climax of this monograph, it will be helpful to pause and reflect on the nature of the Test. I have just said that we want a test that is simple, concise and useful. I looked with envy to the precision of equations. It is suggested that what sets apart scientific formulae and legal tests, making one exact and the other inexact, is discretion.[2] A scientific formula does not admit of discretion. A computer can apply it. It has a high predictive value. If we know the value of the variables, we can predict the answer with certainty.

[2] 'Discretion' here means the freedom to decide. A judge has discretion to the extent that the rules do not inexorably compel a result. Examples below will shed further light on this point. Having thus defined discretion, I accept Professor Dworkin's conception of judicial discretion as not merely subjective, but based on principle, practice and systemic coherence: Ronald Dworkin, *Law's Empire* (Hart 1986) 400–13.

Not so with most legal tests. To be sure, a few legal tests leave no scope for discretion. The test for the age of majority is an example. Assuming the person can prove his date of birth (which is a matter of evidence, not law), the judge has no discretion in deciding whether he is a minor. This is a decision a computer can make. But most legal tests are not like that. Most legal tests involve some degree of post-factual discretion. The discretion is post-factual in the sense that the judge (let alone different judges) may justifiably reach different conclusions on the same agreed facts. This is why we cannot replace judges with supercomputers.[3] Legal tests are less predictable than their scientific counterparts because they are usually discretionary.

Importantly for our Acceptance Test, legal tests vary in the width of their discretion. I can crudely[4] divide this spectrum of discretion into four segments: (i) no discretion, (ii) narrow discretion, (iii) wide discretion and (iv) unfettered discretion. Below are examples of each category.

4.2.1.1 No Discretion

An example of a test that involves no discretion is, as we have seen, the age of majority. The judge does not consider how mature the person actually is (mentally, intellectually, emotionally) but simply checks whether the person has attained the age of eighteen.[5] The judge has no influence over the result. The result is entirely predictable. Another example of a test involving no discretion is s 9 of the Wills Act 1837, which specifies the formalities required for a valid will.[6]

4.2.1.2 Narrow Discretion

An example of a narrow-discretion test is found in s 1 of the Contracts (Rights of Third Parties) Act 1999:

3 Even Professor Dworkin, who argued that discretion, properly exercised, was not merely subjective, conceded, 'No electronic magician could design from my arguments a computer program that would supply a verdict'; ibid. 412.

4 It is conceded that this division is not precise in the sense that the boundaries are not bright lines. Since my purpose is to identify a general width for the Acceptance Test, a precise classification for all cases is not necessary.

5 Family Law Reform Act 1969, s 1.

6 The requirement in sub-s (b) that the 'testator intended by his signature to give effect to the will', may in an exceptional case involve a modicum of discretion, but in the vast majority of cases the situation is clear.

(1) Subject to the provisions of this Act, a person who is not a party to a contract (a 'third party') may in his own right enforce a term of the contract if –

(a) the contract expressly provides that he may, or
(b) subject to subsection (2), the term purports to confer a benefit on him

(2) Subsection (1)(b) does not apply if on a proper construction of the contract it appears that the parties did not intend the term to be enforceable by the third party.

The influence the judge has on the result lies in deciding whether a term 'purports to confer a benefit' and whether the parties 'did not intend the term to be enforceable by the third party'. While there will always be marginal cases,[7] in the ordinary run of cases it will be clear whether a term appears to confer a benefit. Once this is decided, the judge construes the contract to see if there is a contrary overall intention. On the whole, the judge is largely constrained by the facts of the case. He is more constrained than free. Now it is true that the facts themselves are commonly in dispute and the judge exercises discretion in deciding them. However, we are concerned with *degrees* of discretion. The judge has influence over the result, but this influence is greater than in (i) (no discretion) and smaller than (iii) or (iv) (wide or unfettered discretion). In cases of narrow discretion, the result is fairly predictable. A lawyer would normally be able to advise a client with a high degree of confidence.

Other examples of a narrow-discretion test include s 1 of the Law Reform (Frustrated Contracts) Act 1943 (empowering the court to make an allowance for benefits received under a frustrated contract) and the test for repudiation – 'evince an intention no longer to be bound by the contract'.[8]

4.2.1.3 Wide Discretion

An example of a wide-discretion test is the tripartite test for whether a duty of care exists at common law:

7 Such a case was *Dolphin Maritime & Aviation Services Ltd v Sveriges Angfartygs Assurans Forening* [2009] EWHC 716 (Comm), [2010] 1 All ER (Comm) 473, where a third party's commission was deemed 'incidental' to the parties' intentions and thus not recoverable under the Act: [74]–[77] per Christopher Clarke J.

8 *Freeth v Burr* (1873–74) LR 9 CP 208 (CP) 213 (Lord Coleridge CJ); approved in *Heyman v Darwins* [1942] AC 356 (HL) 362 (Viscount Simon LC), 379 (Lord Wright).

> What emerges is that, in addition to the *foreseeability of damage*, necessary ingredients in any situation giving rise to a duty of care are that there should exist ... a relationship ... of '*proximity*' or '*neighbourhood*' and that the situation should be one in which the court considers it *fair, just and reasonable* that the law should impose a duty.[9]

Here all three (highlighted) elements of the test are vague, in what seems to be an order of increasing vagueness. Even if the first two elements can be considered clear enough,[10] the third element is so open-ended and devoid of identifiable content that the judge exercises almost complete influence over the outcome of the test. Whatever the facts, or the first two elements, the judge can always say a duty of care would not be 'fair' on the facts. The judge is more free than constrained. It may even be said that the judge is not constrained by any objective fact. This makes the result hard to predict. Considering this test will only ever be called upon in hard or novel cases, it is of little help.

Other examples of a wide-discretion test include s 61 of the Trustee Act 1925 (which empowers the court to relieve trustees from personal liability) and the multifaceted test for rescission of gifts in equity.[11]

4.2.1.4 Unfettered Discretion

An example of an unfettered-discretion test is Rule 3.1(2)(a) of the Civil Procedure Rules 1998 which says that the 'court may ... extend or shorten the time for compliance with any rule, practice direction or court order'. Here the judge is totally unconstrained. His influence over the result is complete.

Another example of an unfettered-discretion test is Rule 3.1(3) of the same Rules, which provides: 'When the court makes an order, it may ... make it subject to conditions, including a condition to pay a sum of money into court.'

It may be said, with good reason, that even a test that is not explicitly fettered by any consideration cannot be exercised arbitrarily. Orders made pursuant to the above Rules are subject to appeal and irrational orders will be overturned. Thus an order setting the trial date for the next visitation of Halley's Comet will be quashed. So even an 'unfettered' discretion is not absolutely unfettered. When I say 'unfettered', I really mean that the test is subject to only minimal rationality.

9 *Caparo Industries v Dickman* [1990] 2 AC 605 (HL) 617–18 (Lord Bridge).

10 My examination of remoteness cases in the last chapter suggests that foreseeability is anything but clear.

11 *Pitt v Holt* [2013] UKSC 26, [2013] 2 AC 108 [128] (Lord Walker).

4.2.2 *Choosing the Width of the Discretion*

In which category of discretion should we place our Acceptance Test? I certainly do not wish it to be an unfettered-discretion test. That will be self-defeating. The whole point of this chapter is to provide guidance (at the very least) as to which fictions to accept. A conclusion that judges or legislators 'may' create or retain fictions is pointless.[12]

In the context of fictions, a wide-discretion test will be almost as pointless as an unfettered-discretion test. A conclusion along the lines of 'fictions should be accepted if they are just and reasonable' does not offer any real guidance and merely begs the question. It will be an admission that it is not possible to articulate concrete conditions for the acceptance of fictions.

A no-discretion test will be very handy but is, alas, impossible. The field of legal fictions is too complex for a test that involves no discretion whatsoever. We have seen in the last chapter that the evaluation of fictions involves weighing arguments and alternatives. This is the stuff of discretion. A test which precludes discretion must be ruled out.

And so, by elimination, we are left with narrow discretion. This means our Acceptance Test will allow a measure of discretion but, hopefully, contain this discretion within meaningful boundaries. It should not be a free-wheeling discretion. Thus the challenge we face in formulating the Acceptance Test is to make sure the discretion is narrow.

4.3 THE NATURE OF THE TEST: THE GENERAL APPROACH

4.3.1 *The Possible Approaches*

An Acceptance Test for fictions requires a general approach to fictions. It is perhaps surprising that, having discussed fictions at such length, one should still struggle to answer the question 'What is your general view of fictions?' But it is right that I should consider this question now. We can arrive at an informed view after the discussion, not before the discussion.

Let us suppose that we have to design a legal system from scratch. What would be our attitude to fictions? Four attitudes are realistically possible. First, we can decree that no fictions be allowed. This is the zero-tolerance attitude. Second, we can adopt the more nuanced stance that fictions will be avoided but not banned. This attitude may be described as fiction minimisation.

[12] For the avoidance of doubt, I am not concerned here with fictions which give judges unfettered discretion, but with the pointlessness of advising judges that they have unfettered discretion in choosing which fictions to retain – which is no advice at all.

Third, we can positively encourage fictions. This may be called fiction maximisation. Fourth, we need not care whether a device is fictitious. This is indifference.

Each of these attitudes implies a basic view of legal fictions. The zero-tolerance approach implies that fictions are never legitimate. The fiction-minimisation approach implies that fictions are generally bad but sometimes necessary: a necessary evil. The fiction-maximisation approach implies that fictions are fundamentally good. The indifferent approach implies that it does not matter whether a device is fictitious or not, just as the day of the week on which the device entered English law does not matter.

But before we decide which view to adopt, one thing is clear: we must have *a* view. Just as we cannot design a city without some basic assumptions about what is good for a city to have, we cannot design a legal system without some basic assumptions about what is good for a legal system to have.

4.3.2 *The Champions of the Various Approaches*

Almost all people who have thought about the subject take either the zero-tolerance view or the fiction-minimisation view, explicitly or implicitly.[13] This means that most commentators agree that fictions are bad in themselves and differ only in the strength of the medicine that they prescribe.

These two schools of thought are ably represented by Jeremy Bentham and William Blackstone respectively. It is worth remarking that the careers of these two men were intertwined. Bentham attended Blackstone's famous lecture series in Oxford in the 1760s as a sixteen-year-old.[14] Both men were unsuccessful barristers who made their mark as academics.[15] Bentham's very first mark

[13] In addition to the writers specifically discussed below, adherents of zero tolerance include John Austin, *Lectures on Jurisprudence*, vol 2 (Robert Campbell ed, 5th edn, John Murray 1885) 610; Henry Sumner Maine, *Ancient Law* (Murray 1930) 34; Jeremiah Smith, 'Surviving Fictions' (1917) 27 Yale LJ 317, 154; see also the authors quoted in Michael Lobban, 'Legal Fictions before the Age of Reform' in LFTP, 216–17. Adherents of fiction minimisation include Oliver R Mitchell, 'Fictions of the Law: Have They Proved Useful or Detrimental to Its Growth?' (1893) 7 Harvard LR 249, 264–5; Lon L Fuller, *Legal Fictions* (Stanford University Press 1967) 20–2; Pierre JJ Olivier, *Legal Fictions in Practice and Legal Science* (Rotterdam University Press 1975) 111, 150–1; RA Samek, 'Fictions and the Law' (1981) 31 U Toronto LJ 290, 313; K Scott Hamilton, 'Prolegomenon to Myth and Fiction in Legal Reasoning, Common Law Adjudication and Critical Legal Studies' (1988) 35 Wayne LR 1449, 1470; Douglas Lind, 'The Pragmatic Value of Legal Fictions' in LFTP, 106; James Lee, 'Fictions in Tort' in LFTP, 272; see also the authors quoted in Lobban (n 13) 214–15.

[14] Richard A Posner, 'Blackstone and Bentham' (1976) 19 The Journal of Law and Economics 569, 569.

[15] Ibid.

upon the world, A *Fragment on Government*,[16] published in 1776, was a withering criticism of Blackstone and the common law. In the preface, Bentham said of his erstwhile teacher that 'the welfare of mankind, were inseparably connected with the downfall of his works'[17] – no less. Severe and hyperbolic as these remarks may be, nothing in the common law exasperated Bentham more than legal fictions. That *enfant terrible* of English law castigated fictions with such vituperation that, it is fair to assume, he outdid any other critic of fictions in history. The following selection will suffice:

> [L]egal fiction [is] . . . the most pernicious and basest sort of lying – lying by or with the concurrence and support, as well as for the profit, of the judge . . . By the help of this instrument of fraud and extortion . . . a tissue of absurdities, which have no more natural connexion with it than a chapter out of the adventures of Baron Munchausen, or the tales of Mother Goose.[18]
>
> It affords presumptive and conclusive evidence of intellectual weakness, stupidity, and servility, in every nation by which the use of it is quietly endured.[19]
>
> [T]he pestilential breath of Fiction poisons the sense of every instrument it comes near.[20]
>
> It has never been employed but to a bad purpose. It has never been employed to any purpose but the affording a justification of something which otherwise would be unjustifiable.[21]
>
> [A] wilful falsehood, having for its object the stealing legislative power, by and for hands which could not, or durst not, openly claim it.[22]
>
> It affords presumptive and conclusive evidence of moral turpitude in those by whom it was invented and first employed.[23]
>
> Fiction of use to justice? Exactly as swindling is to trade.[24]

If Bentham was the iconoclast, Blackstone spoke for tradition and pragmatism. At all events, he struck a more conciliatory tone:

16 Jeremy Bentham, *A Comment on the Commentaries and a Fragment on Government* (JH Burns and HLA Hart eds, Clarendon Press 2008).
17 Ibid. 394.
18 Jeremy Bentham, *Rationale of Judicial Evidence*, vol 2 (Rothman 1995) 687.
19 Charles Kay Ogden and Jeremy Bentham, *Bentham's Theory of Fictions* (Routledge 2013) cxvii.
20 Bentham, *A Fragment on Government* (n 16) 411 fn [r].
21 Ogden and Bentham (n 19) cxvi.
22 Jeremy Bentham, *The Works of Jeremy Bentham*, vol 1 (John Bowring ed, William Tait 1843) 243.
23 Ogden and Bentham (n 19) cxvii.
24 Jeremy Bentham, *Rationale of Judicial Evidence*, vol 4 (n 18) 300.

> And these fictions of law, though at first they may startle the student, he will find upon farther consideration to be highly beneficial and useful: especially as this maxim is ever invariably observed, that no fiction shall extend to work an injury; its proper operation being to prevent a mischief, or remedy an inconvenience, that might result from the general rule of law.[25]

Earlier still, circa 1675, Sir Matthew Hale took a similarly pragmatic approach:

> [T]hough fictions be a shew of something that is not, yet there is scarce any well-ordered law, nay not even the Civil law, but hath its fictions. For they are but expedients without injuring anybody to bring men to their rights.[26]

Professor Baker was probably right when he said that Hale's view was representative of the profession.[27] It is a refrain of this book that English lawyers were pragmatic people. Fictions did not scare them.

Though these statements by Blackstone and Hale look quite positive, indeed seeming to exalt fictions ('highly beneficial and useful'), they should not be mistaken for defences of fiction maximisation. Blackstone and Hale said that fictions could do some good in certain circumstances, not that they should be encouraged generally for their own sake. It is just a more upbeat way of saying that they are a necessary evil – which is fiction minimisation.

Since Bentham's time, academic opinion has become more nuanced[28] but judicial opinion has reversed, with judges having come round to the Benthamite point of view. In an influential case of the 2000s, Lord Nicholls sounded remarkably like Roscoe Pound[29] exactly one hundred years before: 'I would like to think that, as a mature legal system, English law has outgrown the need for legal fictions.'[30] Sir Terence Etherton, recently Master of the Rolls, reflected the *zeitgeist* in these extra-judicial remarks from 2008:

> The use of a fiction in modern times to legitimise legal analysis is unsatisfactory. It brings to mind the former theory that the law of quasi-contract rests on an implied promise on the part of the recipient third party to repay, which has now been completely exploded. Fictions prevent the coherent development

25 3 Bl Comm 43.

26 Matthew Hale, 'A Disquisition Touching the Jurisdiction of the Common Law and Courts of Admiralty' in MJ Prichard and DEC Yale (eds), *Hale and Fleetwood on Admiralty Jurisdiction*, vol 108 (Selden Society 1992) 24.

27 LTB, 48.

28 n 13.

29 Roscoe Pound, 'Spurious Interpretation' (1907) 7 Columbia LR 379, 382–3, quoted in Chapter 2 in this book, in the text to n 112.

30 *OBG Ltd v Allan* [2007] UKHL 21, [2008] 1 AC 1 [229].

> of the law in accordance with principle, and indicate an immaturity of legal development.[31]

Whatever decline in popularity or acceptability the fiction may have suffered, it is still the case that almost all commentators fall into one of two schools of thought: the Benthamite school (zero tolerance) or the Blackstonian school (fiction minimisation). Nobody, to my knowledge, supports the fiction-maximisation view. Professor Louise Harmon summed up the situation as follows:

> Most of the participants in the historical debate expressed varying degrees of toleration for the legal fiction ... none of the participants gave the legal fiction his unqualified support. There may have been recognition of its utility, but certainly no thunderous applause. Indeed, even those who thought the legal fiction had its time and place seemed somewhat embarrassed by it.[32]

If this is still true, and I believe it is, it means that virtually no one thinks fictions are good in themselves. I will shortly consider why this is so.

The indifferent view is largely overlooked. It is all-too-often assumed that fictions are either good or bad and that we must have some strong opinion about them. Few pause to consider the possibility that legal fictions do not make a difference either way; that they are simply unimportant *as fictions*. It is therefore welcome that a 2015 collection of essays on legal fictions, titled *Legal Fictions in Theory and Practice*, goes against the grain of the scholarship: 'There seems to be little enthusiasm [among the contributors to the publication] for saying that fictions, in themselves, are either good or bad – instead, like other techniques, they are liable to be abused, but also to be put to good use ... there is evaluative complexity here.'[33]

This book may signal a shift in opinion towards indifference, though it must be said that the very publication of the book suggests otherwise. At any rate, a truly indifferent approach to fictions means not simply that some can be good and some bad, but that it does not matter whether something is a fiction or not. Laws can be good or bad. That does not make law a matter of indifference. Put this way, true indifference to fictions is rare indeed.

[31] Terence Etherton, 'Constructive Trusts: A New Model for Equity and Unjust Enrichment' (2008) 67(2) CLJ 265, 279 (footnotes omitted).

[32] Louise Harmon, 'Falling Off the Vine: Legal Fictions and the Doctrine of Substituted Judgment' (1990) 100 Yale LJ 1, 3.

[33] Maksymilian Del Mar, 'Introducing Fictions: Examples, Functions, Definitions and Evaluations' in LFTP, xxvi.

The state of the scholarship may be summarised as follows. The positions of fiction maximisation and (true) indifference command no following to speak of. The positions of zero-tolerance and fiction minimisation have enough disciples to be called schools of thought. The latter outnumbers the former by a significant margin.[34] The Blackstonians have had the upper hand since 1900 (at the latest) – and probably throughout history. While this is not a democratic decision, and the arguments of the minority have to be taken on their merits, it is significant that academic opinion weighs decidedly on the side of fiction minimisation.

4.3.3 *Choosing an Approach*

So, in designing a hypothetical legal system, what will be our basic view or default position on fictions? In the previous chapter, I made two general observations about the default position. I said, first, that we would always prefer truth to fiction, all things being equal. I grounded this position in the axiomatic superiority of truth over falsehood. If we stop preferring truth to falsehood, all rational discourse will end. I shall call this preference for truth the 'Default Position'.

But I also said, later in the same chapter, that we should not hasten to rationalise the law from the above, given the evolutionary and practical nature of the common law; and not least because of the unintended consequences that might follow. If it works, don't fix it. This is a conservative disposition. I shall call this second observation 'the Conservative Argument'.

These two observations are, on their face, incompatible. The view that truth should always trump fiction (all other things being equal) (the Default Position) represents a bias against fictions: the fiction must justify itself. The view that the common law should not be disturbed unless there is a good reason for doing so (the Conservative Argument) represents a bias in favour of existing fictions: it is the removal of a fiction that must be justified, not its existence. How can these views be reconciled? Another way to phrase the question is: who bears the onus of proof, the proponents or opponents of a fiction?

On closer reflection, the Default Position and the Conservative Argument are not inconsistent. This is because of the bracketed qualification that the Default Position only applies *all other things being equal*. That is to say, the anti-fiction bias has effect only if all other factors have been *neutralised*. Economists make ample use of this qualification in the form of the shorter

[34] n 13.

Latin phrase *ceteris paribus* ('other things equal'). If I say that, *ceteris paribus*, I prefer pasta to pizza, it does not mean that I always choose pasta over pizza. For example, the higher the price of pasta relative to pizza, the more likely I am to choose pizza. My preference for pasta holds true when the prices of pasta and pizza are equal – that is, when price is *neutralised*.

So it is with fictions. When all other factors are neutralised, we always prefer truth to fiction. But there will be situations where we will prefer fiction to truth because of some preponderant circumstance. One such circumstance may be that the fiction is entrenched in the law and undoing it will require a wholesale remaking of an area of law. I was swayed by this consideration in the context of the vendor-purchaser constructive trust. Indeed, this situation is just what the Conservative Argument is about. We refrain from disturbing an established system unless there is some special justification for doing so.

Now we see that the two observations are not incompatible. The Conservative Argument – that we should be slow to disturb entrenched fictions – is simply one of the factors that may sway us in deciding whether to depart from the Default Position. It will not be decisive. In evaluating the single meaning rule, I took into account the disturbance that might result from the abolition of the fiction, but recommended abolishing it anyway (because the injustice of the fiction outweighed the potential disturbance).

And so, I do have a basic bias against fictions – fictions do have to justify themselves – but one way of doing so is through the Conservative Argument. It is now apparent that of the four approaches to fiction – zero tolerance, fiction minimisation, fiction maximisation, indifference – I adopt the second. I believe fictions are a necessary evil. As Lon Fuller put it, fictions were 'something of which the law ought to be ashamed, and yet with which the law cannot, as yet, dispense'.[35]

I can arrive at this conclusion also by elimination. In the last chapter, I concluded that some New Fictions deserved to live. That rules out zero-tolerance. Fiction maximisation would contradict my basic, indeed axiomatic, preference for truth over falsehood (Default Position) – even when other things *are* equal. Indifference would also fundamentally contradict this tenet because it would mean I do not esteem truth and recoil from falsehood. The only attitude that remains is fiction minimisation. Whether we judge existing or novel fictions, this will be our guiding principle.

So far I have decided two things about the Acceptance Test: the discretion must be narrow and the guiding principle will be fiction minimisation.

[35] Fuller (n 13) 2.

4.4 MOTIVES FOR FICTIONS

4.4.1 *Motives in Context*

In building an Acceptance Test, layer by layer, what account shall we take of the fiction's motive? Should we judge a fiction by the motivations of its creator? Can we really unearth these motivations? 'This inquiry will, of necessity, lead us into a conjectural field. One can scarcely conceive of a more complex and speculative problem than that of human motives',[36] said Fuller, and valiantly threw himself into the attempt. I shall do the same; for, as Fuller realised, 'a fiction becomes understandable only when we know why it exists, and we can know that only when we know what actuated its author'.[37]

In the *Symposium*, Plato says that the motive of love ennobles otherwise ignoble things:

> Consider, too, how great is the encouragement which all the world gives to the lover; . . . in the pursuit of his love the custom of mankind allows him to do many strange things, which philosophy would bitterly censure if they were done from any motive of interest, or wish for office or power. He may pray, and entreat, and supplicate, and swear, and lie on a mat at the door, and endure a slavery worse than that of any slave – in any other case friends and enemies would be equally ready to prevent him, but now there is no friend who will be ashamed of him and admonish him, and no enemy will charge him with meanness or flattery; the actions of a lover have a grace which ennobles them.[38]

Descending to the world of earthly fictions, might it be that a noble motive ennobles an otherwise ignoble fiction? Can we undermine any rule if the cause is just?

It may perhaps be recalled that I have already mentioned motives in a number of contexts. In the first chapter, I attributed each Old Fiction to one of two broad motives: justice or convenience. In the second chapter, it was argued that motives should not form part of the *definition* of legal fiction. In the third chapter, I implicitly dealt with motives when identifying the aim of each New Fiction. This fourth chapter is an attempt to generalise my previous findings. I will offer, first, a general account of the motives for fictions;

36 Ibid. 49.
37 Ibid. 49–50.
38 Plato, *Symposium*, 182d-183b; alternatively: RM Hare and DA Russell (eds), *The Dialogues of Plato* (Benjamin Jowett tr, Sphere Books 1970) 196.

and, second, an answer to the question whether a fiction is justified by its motives. It will be contended that, unlike the lover's actions, a fiction is justified by its efficacy in achieving its aim, not by its motives. This does not mean that the question of why fictions exist is unimportant. I delve into it presently.

4.4.2 *Motives in the Literature*

Whereas the definition of fiction has provoked voluminous academic discussion, '[t]here has never appeared to be much debate as to the reasons why the law has resort to fictions'.[39] John Austin found it 'extremely difficult to determine, why subordinate judges … have so often accomplished their object through the medium of fictions'.[40]

Many writers simply assume or assert a motive, often one that suits their thesis. Bentham thus posited nefarious motives, namely deceit or subversion of the law.[41] Maine, who saw fictions as a stage in the early development of the law, and now obsolete, wrote: 'It is not difficult to understand why fictions in all their forms are particularly congenial to the infancy of society. They satisfy the desire for improvement, which is not quite wanting, at the same time that they do not offend the superstitious disrelish for change which is always present.'[42]

Similarly self-serving was Hale's choice of motive – justice – which fitted nicely with his defence of fictions as promoting justice. For him, fictions were motivated by a desire 'to accommodate judicial proceedings and the just recovery of Men's Rights'.[43]

The truth is that most scholars, of whom the last-mentioned few are illustrative, did not approach motives as an issue in its own right. The motive was implicit or secondary in their analysis.

One thinker stands out in this regard. The most systematic study of the motives behind legal fictions is Lon Fuller's, who devoted a third of his Depression-era trilogy of articles to the issue.[44] He saw the motive question as key, indeed *the* key, to understanding fictions.[45] Where others understood

[39] John Gwilliam, 'Legal Fictions – A Critical Analysis' (1975) 8 Victoria U Wellington LR 452, 452.
[40] John Austin, *Lectures on Jurisprudence*, vol 2 (n 13) 609.
[41] See text to n 22.
[42] Maine (n 13) 33.
[43] Hale (n 26) 24.
[44] Fuller (n 13) ch 2; originally LL Fuller, 'Legal Fictions' (1930–1) 25 Illinois LR 513.
[45] Fuller (n 13) 49–50.

motives through their view of fictions, Fuller sought to understand fictions through their motives.

Fuller begins his analysis of motives with an arch-motive, the most general and inclusive that can be articulated:

> Speaking for the moment in the most general terms, the purpose of any fiction is to *reconcile a specific legal result with some premise or postulate*. Where no intellectual premises are assumed, the fiction has no place. An autocrat, deciding disputes upon the basis of instinct or selfish interest, and feeling no compulsion to explain his decisions . . . would have no occasion to resort to fiction. A premiseless law would be a fictionless law – if it could be called law at all.[46]

This overarching raison d'être for the legal fiction has won wide acceptance and the even-greater accolade of no opposition. John Gwilliam and James Stoneking, for instance, recycle Fuller's words almost verbatim.[47]

Having stated the arch-motive, Fuller offers the most comprehensive typology hitherto of specific motives for fictions. Below is an overview, necessarily incomplete, of this typology. After introducing each of Fuller's motives, I will advert to other legal thinkers who found the motive persuasive. In this way, Fuller's typology will give structure to the literature.

4.4.2.1 Motive of Policy

'In short, a judge, fully conscious that he is changing the law, chooses . . . to deceive others into believing that he is merely applying existing law.'[48] Many scholars, before and after Fuller, saw this as the pre-eminent motive. Bentham, we know, was certain this was the driving force behind fictions. Austin described it as a pragmatic tactic: 'By accomplishing the change through a fiction, [judges] rather eluded the existing law, than formally annulled it: they preserved its integrity to appearance, although they broke it in effect', wishing thereby 'to conciliate . . . the friends or lovers of the law which they really annulled.'[49] Austin added for good measure: 'By covering the innovation with a decent lie, he treated the abrogated law with all seemly respect, whilst he knocked it on the head.'[50]

46 Ibid. 51 (emphasis added).
47 Gwilliam (n 39) 462; James B Stoneking, 'Penumbras and Privacy: A Study of the Use of Fictions in Constitutional Decision-Making' (1984) 87 West Virginia LR 859, 864.
48 Fuller (n 13) 57.
49 Austin, vol 2 (n 13) 609–10.
50 Ibid.

Peter Smith, whose wide conception of fictions we encountered in the second chapter, argued that fictions were secretly used to advance normative goals.[51] Jeremiah Smith, of like mind, thought that the primary motive for fictions (by the early twentieth century) was '[t]o conceal the fact that judges, by their decisions, are making or changing the substantive law'.[52] Baker, explicitly channelling Maine, was of the same view: 'The object of fictions is that they allow the operation of the law to change without any outward alteration in the rules.'[53] Oliver R Mitchell, in the *Harvard Law Review* of 1893, put the point starkly: 'A legal fiction is a device which attempts to conceal the fact that a judicial decision is not in harmony with the existing law. The *only use and purpose*, upon the last analysis, of any legal fiction is to nominally conceal this fact that the law has undergone a change at the hands of the judges.'[54]

The alert reader may have noticed that Fuller's statement that the judge sets out to deceive others contradicts Fuller's refrain that fictions do not deceive anyone.[55] To be sure, Fuller is careful enough to discount this motive: '[I]t is a little difficult to see how the supposed deceit could actually succeed. Bentham and Austin were not fooled by it.'[56] Perhaps Fuller sees the deception of others as a motive that exists but is ineffective.

My take on this motive of policy is somewhat different. The deception, if it exists, lies in concealing the real reasons for the decision, not in concealing the change in the law. The fiction thus serves as a thin veneer for policy arguments. The fictions previously examined showcase this motive in action. The real reason for lowering the remoteness bar in negligence was, probably, the concern about easily rectifiable harm that was left to fester for no good reason. In the cases, the policy reason, whatever it was, was masked by fictitious reasonable foreseeability. Similarly, the real reason for backtracking on the agreement requirement in *volenti* was the lack of sympathy for extremely reckless claimants. The policy reason in those cases was cloaked as an implied agreement to forgo compensation.

With respect to geographical fictions, the policy reasons for hearing foreign cases were pragmatic, but they were not discussed. The record simply misstated the place, which avoided the issue altogether, preventing the true reasons from rising to the surface. The non-traversable allegation of *vi et*

51 Peter J Smith, 'New Legal Fictions' (2006) 95 Georgetown LJ 1435, 1489.

52 Smith, '*Surviving Fictions*' (n 13) 147–8.

53 LTB, 35; Maine (n 13) 32–3. In fairness to Baker, judging by his statements elsewhere, he would probably not go so far as to say that judges sought to *deceive*.

54 Mitchell (n 13) 262 (emphasis added).

55 Fuller (n 13) 5–6.

56 Ibid. 57–8.

armis, too, kept the reader of the rolls in the dark about the real reasons for expanding the jurisdiction of the King's Bench.

And thus the motive of policy consists, according to this re-interpretation of Fuller, in *covering up*: not the change in the law itself, but the reasons for the change. Judges use fictions to cover up policy arguments. Fuller's name for this motive ('motive of policy') is more apt than he imagined.

4.4.2.2 Motive of Emotional Conservatism

If the judge who is motivated by policy wishes to deceive others (per Fuller), the judge driven by emotion deceives himself.[57] Fuller uses the term 'self-deception',[58] which again flies in the face of his conviction that fictions do not deceive. Fuller's general drift, though, indicates that the judge is not so much deluded as concerned to preserve the stability and authority of the old law, to which he is emotionally attached: 'I call this the motive of emotional conservatism because it proceeds, not from any clearly formulated theory of the process of law making, but from an emotional and obscurely felt judgment that stability is so precious a thing that even the *form* of stability, its empty shadow, has a value.'[59] This is reminiscent of Maine's disparaging 'superstitious disrelish for change'[60] or Austin's sneer about avoiding 'offence to the lovers of things ancient',[61] only that here the judge himself is the lover of ancient things.

It should be said, in view of the patronising tone of some writers, that emotional conservatism is not just nostalgia or fear of change. Stability and predictability have a value in any system, let alone one which has to be obeyed by millions. Moreover, the objectivity – and hence legitimacy – of the legal system depends on the fact that judges regard themselves as largely bound by existing law, and change it only rarely and incrementally. A judge who dismisses existing law and forms as mere tradition misunderstands his high office. It is therefore rational for a judge to be change-averse – to be 'emotionally conservative'.

4.4.2.3 Motive of Convenience

It is easier to misdescribe the facts than to re-open basic concepts and re-write textbooks.[62] As we saw in the last chapter, in the context of the vendor-

57 Fuller (n 13) 58.
58 Ibid.
59 Ibid.
60 Maine (n 13) 33.
61 Austin (n 13) 610.
62 Fuller (n 13) 59–63.

purchaser constructive trust, overhauling an area of law is a daunting task with unintended consequences. Few are the brave who would undertake it, let alone in the context of adjudicating a particular dispute. Fuller borrows an illustration from Rudolf von Jhering, a German jurist of the nineteenth century:

> [A] taxing board has had schedules printed in which . . . because the article was not at the time known, a column or heading for an article . . . is lacking. In order to avoid the necessity of reprinting the whole schedule they provide that the article shall be brought under one of the existing columns; that lignite, for example, shall be regarded as hard coal.[63]

Even Bentham, who usually prefers wicked motives, agrees 'love of ease, or say aversion to labour' is a possible incentive for fictions.[64]

But convenience is not merely a matter of time-saving. As Professor Peter Birks explained, *legal* convenience was uppermost in the minds of plaintiffs' lawyers:

> When the action for money paid was fictionalized, why did it happen? No rule of law actually prevented counsel from devising an honest form of action. But a new pattern would have encountered an instant demurrer. And the demurrer would have had to be met with novel uncertain arguments. Experiments of that kind cannot be made at a client's expense.[65]

The oft-trodden route is also relatively risk-free. The accommodation of the new inside the old, by way of fictions, was of course the *modus operandi* of the Old System. It continues to this day, albeit less stridently since the forms are not so rigid. Fuller said it well: 'Lawyers will not have to change their concepts – they need only change the content of these concepts.'[66]

Side by side with legal convenience, we find linguistic convenience. Fuller, later in his work, talks of 'abbreviatory fictions', whose function is to avoid circumlocution.[67] These can be de-fictionalised by expanding the shorthand. He names corporate personhood as an example.[68] He presumably means that instead of enumerating the rights and obligations of corporations, it is easier to

63 Fuller (n 13) 60.
64 Ogden and Bentham (n 19) cxix.
65 Peter Birks, 'Fictions Ancient and Modern' in Neil MacCormick and Peter Birks (eds), *The Legal Mind* (Clarendon Press 1986) 100–1.
66 Fuller (n 13).
67 Ibid. 81–3.
68 Ibid. 82.

make the analogy with humans, which holds good for most purposes. Kelsen argued that all legislative fictions are in fact mere abbreviations.[69] Convenience therefore comes in many guises: practical, legal, linguistic – to name a few.

4.4.2.4 Motive of Intellectual Conservatism

This is Fuller's most original – and interesting – motive:

> A judge may adopt a fiction, not simply to avoid discommoding current notions [motive of convenience], nor for the purpose of concealing from himself [motive of emotional conservatism] or others [motive of policy] the fact that he is legislating, but merely because he does not know how else to state and explain the new principle he is applying.[70]

Fuller's chosen name of intellectual conservatism is perhaps inapt. It implies the judge creates the fiction to conserve some intellectual dogma. The sense conveyed by Fuller's exposition is that the judge *feels in his bones*, but cannot articulate, in a legally acceptable way, the rightness of the new principle. He is at a loss. Fuller – always quotable – said more generally that 'the fiction is the cement which is always at hand to plaster together the weak spots in our intellectual structure'.[71] How true in this context. 'Intellectual weakness' is a less kind but more accurate description of this motive.

4.4.2.5 Institutional Constraints

Fuller observes that some fictions may be invoked by 'mere habit'.[72] Bentham similarly speaks of 'Aversion to depart from accustomed habits'.[73] Baker concurs, pointing to comments by Scroggs CJ concerning the use of *indebitatus assumpsit* for the profits of a usurped office:[74]

> If this were now an original case, we are agreed it would by no means lie. . . . But because judgments have been upon it, and that on solemn arguments, and many judgments – though some passed *sub silencio*, yet others have been debated and settled . . . we are therefore willing to go the same way.[75]

69 Hans Kelsen, 'On the Theory of Juridic Fictions' (Christoph Kletzer tr) in LFTP, 10.
70 Fuller (n 13) 63.
71 Ibid. 52.
72 Ibid. 87.
73 Bentham, *Works of Jeremy Bentham*, vol 3 (n 22) 274.
74 LTB, 54 fn 80.
75 *Howard v Wood* (1688) 2 Shower KB 21, 89 ER 767 (KB) 769.

Force of habit is not a motive for fictions but a reason for their spread and persistence. Habit can never explain the first use of a fiction. At most, habit is a motive for not abolishing fictions.

Allied to the notion of habit is the doctrine of precedent. John Gwilliam and Peter Smith say *stare decisis*, by which an *ad hoc* creative solution to a hard case is replicated and entrenched, has a role in the proliferation of fictions.[76] Precedent brings us to an important factor in the generation of fictions, which is surprisingly inconspicuous in Fuller. Peter Smith has called it 'institutional and professional constraints'.[77] Any system which professes objectivity and predictability values stability. As Robert Samek says, 'Starting off with the motive of keeping the law stable, the obvious conservative strategy is to hide any changes that are made by stretching the old concepts to accommodate the new. … For any given system, a certain level of energy is necessary to overcome these forces and to break the stable state.'[78]

In his analysis of the process by which the law changes, Professor Paul Mitchell stressed the importance of apparent historical continuity. Judgments include extensive discussion of previous decisions and are written so as 'to legitimize subsequent statements about what the law is, by making the past consistent with, and, indeed, appear to lead inevitably to, an assertion about the present'.[79] Shackled by precedent and wary of the stigma of judicial activism, judges find in fiction the lesser evil. Roscoe Pound goes so far as to say: 'When justice must be administered within the four corners of a rigid code or by means of a body of customary law which has attained fixity … the only resource in the absence of legislative revolution, from which men shrink, is to find by interpretation the needed rules.'[80]

In an unreferenced quotation attributed to John Bouvier, Sidney Miller has the French-American lexicographer speak in the same terms: 'Courts, confined to the administration of existing rules, and lacking power to change them, have frequently avoided injustice by assuming in behalf of justice, that the actual facts are different from what they really are.'[81] John Orth observes that it is the very nature of rules that creates the need for their evasion by fiction:

76 Gwilliam (n 39) 461; Smith, 'New Legal Fictions' (n 51) 1486–8.
77 Smith, 'New Legal Fictions' (n 51) 1473.
78 Samek (n 13) 315.
79 Paul Mitchell, 'Patterns of Legal Change' (2012) 65 CLP 177, 179.
80 Roscoe Pound, *Interpretations of Legal History* (CUP 1923) 131.
81 Sidney T Miller, 'The Reasons for Some Legal Fictions' (1910) 8 Michigan LR 623, 624 fn 4.

> The Rule of Law, humanity's best effort so far to produce justice on a regular basis, requires rules, but because of their rigidity and generality, rules can produce injustice in individual cases. Making and changing rules is the very definition of legislation, but the legislature is constrained to make rules with only prospective effect, and in any event the legislature is not in permanent session and cannot be expected to address every imaginable (and unimaginable) contingency. The judges have responded from time immemorial with fictions and constructions of one sort or another.[82]

The point made by these commentators is that sometimes judges use fictions because the system leaves no other avenue for justice or reform. We know that under the sclerotic Old System fiction was often the only way to reform the law.

Compounding external constraints is the judges' own professional culture. As Peter Smith says, 'Lawyers are socialized to view the legal system as a distinct system with a distinct set of norms, and they tend to guard that system from challenges to its norms.'[83] Pierluigi Chiassoni understands fictions chiefly as a means of overcoming institutional constraints – including legal culture – in reforming bad rules.[84] There can be no doubt that institutional constraints are an important motive for the creation of legal fictions.

4.4.2.6 Greed

This last motive on our list is startling at first sight. It is likely, however, that some of the Jurisdictional Fictions of the Tudor era were motivated, in part, by the commercial interests of court officials. The judges of the three royal courts in Westminster were paid out of, and in proportion with, the business of their respective court. A busy courtroom meant high revenues. Courts had a financial incentive to attract plaintiffs and from the late fifteenth century actively competed for litigation. They did so mainly by offering more efficient or plaintiff-friendly procedures for various actions and by encroaching on the jurisdiction of fellow courts.[85] Fictions were weapons in this trade war. The two great fictions of the day, the bill of Middlesex and the writ of *quominus* were, we recall, Jurisdictional Fictions. The former effectively extended the jurisdiction of the King's Bench to include debt and the former

82 John V Orth, 'Fact & Fiction in the Law of Property' (2007) 11 Green Bag 65, 79.
83 Smith, 'New Legal Fictions' (n 51) 1473.
84 Pierluigi Chiassoni, *Interpretation without Truth* (Springer 2019) 192–3, 200.
85 IELH, 47–57.

enlarged the jurisdiction of the Exchequer to include wholly-private debt claims. John Hill Burton, in an introduction to a collection of Bentham's works, wrote:

> The origin of this class of fictions was of the most sordid character – the judges and other officers of court being paid by fees, a trade competition for jurisdictions took place; each court trying to offer better terms to litigants, than the others, and adopting the fictions as a means of accomplishing this object.[86]

Bentham himself did not miss this opportunity to take a swipe at legal fictions:

> King's Bench stole business from Common Pleas: Common Pleas stole it back again from King's Bench. Falsehood, avowed falsehood, was their common instrument. [King's Bench] let off one lie; [Common Pleas] answered it by another. The battle is in all the books ... Unwilling to be left behind, Exchequer stole with both hands at once, stole from both its neighbours.[87]

It is telling that by 1700 the three common-law courts in Westminster Hall had 'near parity of jurisdiction'.[88]

It is important, however, not to overstate the role of profiteering in the development of fictions – even those fictions intimately connected with it. There must have been other reasons why these procedural fictions appeared in the Tudor era and not in the preceding centuries. Court functionaries were probably not greedier in the sixteenth century than in the fourteenth. Lucre alone cannot be a full explanation, even if it was one of the motives. Baker cautioned against attributing changes in the law to 'avarice': 'The officials who benefited from changes in the legal system are seen rather as having reacted productively to forces outside their control.'[89]

Needless to say, the pecuniary motive for fictions is not relevant today.

4.4.2.7 A Disagreement about Terminology: The Two True Motives

Fuller's account of motives is illuminating and original. It is accepted here, subject to the minor reservations already expressed and the following disagreement. At the risk of pedantry, it seems that something in the terminology has

86 Bentham, *Works of Jeremy Bentham*, vol 1 (n 22) 41.
87 Bentham, *Rationale of Judicial Evidence*, vol 4 (n 18) 307–8.
88 IELH, 58.
89 JH Baker, 'English Law and the Renaissance' (1985) 44 CLJ 46, 50.

gone awry. Sadly, that small but important slippage has affected the understanding of motives.

The words 'motive', 'motivation', 'reason' and 'cause' are synonymous in the thesaurus sense and interchangeable in many contexts. But shades of meaning can be crucial. If I miss the bus because my meeting ran overtime, the meeting was the reason for my missing the bus, but not the motive for it. On a moment's reflection, it is obvious that I had no motive whatsoever for missing the bus: I wanted to catch it. 'Reason' and 'motive' are not the same. While 'reason' is simply a matter of causation, 'motive' implies a deep-seated source of *inducement*; indeed 'a contemplated end the desire for which influences … a person's actions'.[90] The meeting did not induce me to miss the bus, though it did cause it.

Institutional constraints like precedent or statute are thus not motives for using fictions, though they are reasons for doing so. The judge who uses a fiction to dodge an old rule is not *motivated* by institutional constraints. He is motivated by the desire to reach a just result. The constraints are like my meeting: it caused me to miss the bus, but it did not motivate me to miss it.

Now it is plain that it is senseless to say that a judge was motivated by a desire to deceive others (motive of policy), let alone to deceive himself (emotional conservatism). No sane judge is motivated by a desire to deceive. The need to hide the reasons for the decision may be a reason for using a fiction, but it cannot possibly be the motive for it. Deception, if it exists, is a by-product, not a motive. The motive must be something like justice, or convenience, or (formerly) gain.

It will also be seen that Fuller's motive of intellectual conservatism (which I re-christened 'intellectual weakness') is in truth no motive at all. A judge cannot be motivated by not knowing what to say. That is a hindrance: the opposite of a motivation. Intellectual weakness is a reason for fictions, certainly – but not a motive. True current motives there are only two: justice and convenience.

It is possible to subdivide these two motives in search of greater specificity, but the temptation should be resisted. The opacity of fictitious reasoning makes the discovery of motives empirically unsound. Beyond deducing some broad motive (justice or convenience) from the end result, or clues in the judgment, the exercise is entirely speculative. We can say with sufficient confidence that what actuated the judges to stretch remoteness in negligence or the *volenti* defence was their sense of justice. But we cannot say much more. We have no window into men's souls. It is better to confine ourselves to what

90 Oxford English Dictionary, www.oed.com/view/Entry/122712, accessed 24 January 2016.

we know than to presume to speak on behalf of others. Nowadays there are two motives for creating legal fictions, namely justice and convenience.

4.4.2.8 Summary of Motives

Table 4.1 reproduces Table 3.1, containing all the fictions discussed in this work, with the addition of a column for motive.

4.4.3 *Motives and the Acceptance Test*

What role, if any, should motives play in the Acceptance Test? Should we discriminate on the basis of motive? It seems to me that both justice and convenience (the motives I have identified) are legitimate motives. Justice is indisputably legitimate, being the supreme aspiration of the legal system. Convenience, whether practical, legal or linguistic, is perhaps not as lofty a goal as justice, but any system is allowed to, and indeed should, take convenience into account. If a fiction reduces costs and risks, if it saves us the trouble of re-conceiving entire areas of law and re-writing textbooks, if it avoids prolixity, then it has positive value. The Acceptance Test will not disqualify a fiction because of motive.

Should a motive save a fiction from abolition? That is the Plato-inspired question with which I began this inquiry into motives. The answer must be no. Whether the motive is justice or convenience, the law only has the benefit of the sought-after justice or convenience if the fiction succeeds in furthering justice or convenience. I will judge fictions by how effectively they achieve their aims (which is some specific instantiation of justice or convenience). If a fiction is pursued for the sake of justice or convenience, and there is no justice or convenience, there should be no fiction. The way to hell, the trite saying goes, is paved with good intentions. What counts is the result, not the intentions. The Acceptance Test will reflect this: fictions will be judged by their efficacy in achieving their aims, not by their original motives.

Philosophers will not fail to detect a utilitarian or consequentialist approach in the last paragraph – and, concomitantly, a rejection of virtue ethics. Fictions are to be judged by their consequences, not by the virtue of their motives. Some readers may prefer one ethical philosophy to the other. I do not presume to say which is better in general. I only say that, *in this context*, the utilitarian approach is appropriate because fictions are themselves a means to an end and no more. No one invents fictions for their own sake. If a fiction is a means, it should be evaluated *as a means* – that is, as a way to attain some other aim. Hence the utilitarian evaluation.

TABLE 4.1 *All fictions with motives*

Device	Nature	Age	Effect	Motive	Recommendation: retain or abolish?
Dominus remisit curiam	Hard Fiction	Old	Jurisdictional	Convenience	Already abolished
Vi et armis	Hard Fiction	Old	Jurisdictional	Justice	Already abolished
Geographical fictions	Hard Fiction	Old	Jurisdictional	Justice	Already abolished
Bill of Middlesex	Hard Fiction	Old	Jurisdictional	Convenience	Already abolished
Writ of *quominus*	Hard Fiction	Old	Jurisdictional	Convenience	Already abolished
Benefit of clergy	Hard Fiction	Old	Auxiliary	Justice	Already abolished
Pleading the belly	Hard Fiction	Old	Auxiliary	Justice	Already abolished
Common recovery	Hard Fiction	Old	Auxiliary	Justice	Already abolished
Trover	Hard Fiction	Old	Auxiliary	Justice	Already abolished
Ejectment	Hard Fiction	Old and New	Essential	Convenience	Already abolished
Quasi-contract	Hard Fiction	Old and New	Essential	Justice	Already abolished
Corporation	Not a fiction	N/A	N/A	N/A	N/A
Trust (as such)	Not a fiction	N/A	N/A	N/A	N/A
Unsealed deed	Not a fiction	N/A	N/A	N/A	N/A
Reading down exclusion clauses	Soft Fiction	New	Auxiliary	Justice	Already abolished
Reasonable man	Not a fiction	N/A	N/A	N/A	N/A
Volenti non fit injuria	Soft Fiction	New	Essential	Justice	Abolish
Equity treats as done that which ought to be done	Hard Fiction	New	Essential	Justice	Retain

TABLE 4.1 *(continued)*

Device	Nature	Age	Effect	Motive	Recommendation: retain or abolish?
Estoppel	Hard Fiction	New	Essential	Justice	Retain
Single meaning rule	Hard Fiction	New	Essential	Convenience	Abolish
Common intention constructive trust (subsistence stage)	Not a fiction anymore	New	Essential	Justice	Already abolished
Common intention constructive trust (allocation stage)	Not a fiction	N/A	N/A	N/A	N/A
Remoteness in negligence	Soft Fiction	New	Auxiliary	Justice	Abolish

4.5 ANALYSIS OF PREVIOUS RESULTS

The Acceptance Test for fictions will be based on the results collated in previous chapters. As stated above, the Acceptance Test will be made up of a Retention Test (for existing fictions) and a Creation Test (for fictions about to be created).

This section brings together all our conclusions with a view to gleaning general insights and principles. In particular, I will focus on the correlations between different classifications and the correlations between classifications and results. The results analysed in this section are tabulated in Table 4.1. The reader may find it convenient to refer back to that table. It sets out every fiction discussed in this work and classifies it by nature, age, effect and motive. The last column records the recommendation as to the fiction's preservation.

It is argued below that the classification of a given fiction gives us important signals, sometimes decisive indications, as to whether the fiction should live or die.

4.5.1 *The Correlation between Nature and Recommendation*

The Nature Classification includes two classes: Hard Fictions and Soft Fictions. A Hard Fiction is a factual issue consciously decided irrespective of the facts. A Soft Fiction is a factual issue decided by a consciously unnatural interpretation of the law. 'Recommendation' indicates whether a fiction should be retained.

We have identified fourteen Hard Fictions. Of these, eleven have already been abolished (the Old Fictions). Two I have marked for retention (Equity treats as done that which ought to be done, estoppel) and one for abolition (single meaning rule). No necessary relationship can be inferred from this. The fact that not all Hard Fictions are marked for abolition (or retention) means the 'hardness' of the fiction (viz the Nature Classification) cannot, on its own, contain the answer to the question whether to retain or abolish a given fiction.

We have identified four Soft Fictions in total: (i) *volenti non fit injuria*, (ii) the inference in the first stage of the common intention constructive trust, (iii) remoteness in negligence and (iv) reading down exclusion clauses. I have found all four to be deserving of abolition ((ii) and (iv) are already abolished). This is a more promising result. There is a perfect correlation between the classification of Soft Fiction and the recommendation: a 100% abolition rate. Of course, the sample is rather small. We cannot *deduce* that because four Soft Fictions should be abolished, *all* Soft Fictions should suffer the same fate. At the most, we may have an *inference*.

If we could, however, demonstrate by logical argument that there is something about Soft Fictions that makes them deserving of abolition, then we would have something more than an inference: we would have a principle. It is such general principles that will be the building blocks of the Acceptance Test.

So is it a coincidence that all the Soft Fictions we have examined were marked for abolition – or is there a reason for this apparent correlation? I suggest it is not a coincidence. There is good reason why Soft Fictions all deserve to be abolished, and precisely *because* they are Soft Fictions. It is submitted that the Soft Fiction is unworthy of our legal system as a matter of principle as well as of practice. The argument from principle will be presented first.

4.5.1.1 The Principled Argument against Soft Fictions

A Soft Fiction is a factual issue decided by a consciously-unnatural interpretation of the law. To speak plainly, it is bad reasoning, a fudge, so much so that even the judge is unconvinced (hence conscious of the unnatural interpretation). To embrace Soft Fictions is to embrace bad reasoning. To accept Soft Fictions is to give up on a common-sense interpretation of the law and to condone casuistry. As noble as the motives for Soft Fictions may be – and doubt not they are – a bad argument is a bad means to achieve even a good end. A bad debating point is bad even if one agrees with the speaker's position. A bad argument discredits its maker. A Soft Fiction discredits the law.

But are not Hard Fictions just as discreditable as Soft Fictions? Why am I so hard on Soft Fictions and so soft on Hard Fictions (several of which I want to keep)? First of all, even if Hard Fictions were as bad as Soft Fictions, that would not exonerate the Soft Fictions (though it would reveal a double standard).

More to the point, Hard Fictions are not as bad. Though it may seem counterintuitive that the Soft Fiction should be more discreditable than the Hard Fiction, so it is. The totally fictional plot of Wuthering Heights is not discreditable. But a consciously flawed argument in a book, whether fiction or non-fiction, would bring the writer into discredit. To say that cats are to be treated as dogs is not discreditable. But to argue in a judgment, with apparent seriousness, that cats should be construed to mean dogs – that 'cat' really means 'dog' – *is* discreditable. The former does not offend reason; the latter degrades it. To twist the truth is worse than to step outside it. He who steps outside the truth does not trample on it. That is why the contrived applications of *volenti* are worse than the hardest of Hard Fictions; because they have the appearance of truth, the claim of truth.

A Hard Fiction is not a bad argument: it is not an argument at all. A thing that is patently false, like Wuthering Heights or geographical fictions or the maxim that Equity treats as done that which ought to be done, is just pure fiction; 'an open and avowed pretense'.[91] But a contrived interpretation is not pure fiction; it is still an interpretation, indeed a legally valid one. It professes to be sound legal reasoning when it is not. The problem with the Soft Fiction is that it purports to be true. As Fuller said more generally, 'A fiction becomes wholly safe only when it is used with a complete consciousness of its falsity.'[92] In sum, the Hard Fiction is safe because it asks us to suspend disbelief; the Soft is unsafe because it attempts to deceive us.[93]

4.5.1.2 The Practical Argument against Soft Fictions

If the principled argument against Soft Fictions is that bad reasoning is reprehensible, the practical argument against Soft Fictions is that bad reasoning is unpredictable. Let us take a judge whose policy is to reach what she considers the morally correct outcome – even at the price of bending the rules. The key word is 'bending', not 'breaking'. This judge would baulk at utter impossibilities like London in Minorca or female clergy (in the seventeenth century), but would gladly suffer a very wide definition of agreement when she wants to deploy the *volenti* defence. The judge I have imagined, it will be understood, favours Soft Fictions and rejects Hard Fictions.

A judge who has a proclivity for Soft Fictions is inherently unpredictable – because we do not know which rules she will bend, when, and to what extent. I have argued before that the rule 'Cats are deemed to be dogs for the purposes of pet tax' is more certain than the rule 'The definitions of some pets can be strained for the purposes of pet tax.' A black-letter judge may sometimes issue unjust decisions, but she cannot be accused of unpredictability. A judge who treats rules as provisional or negotiable, and moreover stoops to consciously unsound reasoning, is less likely to issue unjust decisions (at least according to her own lights). But she is less predictable. All depends on her personal conception of justice.

This unpredictability may be seen in the case law of one of the Soft Fictions I have discussed, the first stage of the common intention constructive trust (while it existed, in the pre-*Kernott* days). In many cases, the courts were willing to strain the facts and 'infer' a common intention on questionable evidence – or even contrary to the evidence (e.g., *Eves v Eves* (1975) and *Grant v Edwards* (1986)[94]). But the courts were not always so accommodating. They were not willing to

91 Fuller (n 13) 80.

92 Ibid. 10.

93 This contrast between suspension of disbelief and deception was helpfully suggested by Professor Richard Nolan in his capacity as my PhD examiner.

94 [1975] 1 WLR 1338 (CA); [1986] Ch 638 (CA) respectively.

stretch the facts in *Buggs v Buggs* (2003),[95] where the facts were more favourable to the claimant woman than in *Eves v Eves* or *Grant v Edwards*. In the opinion of the judge in *Buggs*, the evidence was insufficient to establish a common intention, despite his findings that 'it was recognised by all three parties that the [property] should belong to the [claimant's] household'; that 'the members of that household acted to their detriment'; and that the claimant 'made a strong contribution to the family's welfare in financial as well as personal terms'.[96]

Nor were the courts ready to infer a common intention in *Burns v Burns* (1983), where the claimant shared the property with the defendant for seventeen years;[97] nor in *Carley v Smith* (1980), described by Lawton LJ as 'a sad story';[98] nor even in *Springette v Defoe* (1992) – because the common intention was held independently by the cohabitants rather than expressly discussed.[99]

To conclude, because the Soft Fiction was bad reasoning as opposed to a transparent rule of law, it was applied inconsistently. The first stage of the common intention constructive trust is a testament to the unpredictability of Soft Fictions.

The Hard Fiction, it is interesting to note, is impervious to the charge of unpredictability. There was no unpredictability in geographical fictions and there is no unpredictability in estoppel. Treating cats as dogs is fictitious but not unpredictable. It is a transparent rule. We know exactly how to treat cats. The certainty of transactions is unperturbed by Hard Fictions. If the law is to change, as it sometimes must, let it be done transparently.

But the problem with the Soft Fiction is not just that it undermines certainty. It also distorts the real reasons for the decision. The consciously flawed argument is a smokescreen for policy-driven decision-making (as discussed earlier in this chapter). We have seen this in the Soft Fiction of remoteness in negligence. Again, if a decision is grounded in policy, let it be done transparently and openly debated.

This is the double-headed argument for the proposition that all Soft Fictions should be abolished. It is *unprincipled* and *uncertain* to use bad arguments. We have succeeded in establishing a correlation between the Nature Classification (Hard/Soft) and the recommendation (retain/abolish). The Acceptance Test will reflect the conclusion that only Hard Fictions should be accepted. This is the first question in the algorithm:

95 [2003] EWHC 1538 (Ch), [2004] WTLR 799.
96 Ibid. [36], [49]–[50] (Nicholas Davidson QC).
97 [1984] Ch 317 (CA) 327–33 (Fox LJ), 335 (May LJ).
98 [1980] Lexis Citation 217 (CA) [3], [12]–[20] (unnumbered) (Lawton LJ).
99 (1992) 24 HLR 552 (CA) 557 (Dillon LJ), 558 (Steyn LJ), 560 (Sir Christopher Slade).

is the fiction Hard or Soft? If Soft, abolish; if Hard, move on to the next question.

4.5.2 *The Correlation between Age and Recommendation*

Since Old Fictions are by definition defunct, they are strictly speaking irrelevant to the Acceptance Test. We will never have to apply the test to decide whether an Old Fiction should remain. It will nonetheless be instructive to see whether the Acceptance Test, if applied to Old Fictions, produces sensible results.

4.5.3 *The Correlation between Effect and Recommendation*

The Effect Classification has three classes: Jurisdictional, Auxiliary and Essential. Jurisdictional Fictions only affect the choice of court. Auxiliary Fictions are merely formal and do not affect the conceptual foundation of an action. Essential Fictions go to the heart of an action and represent the real reason for the decision.

Table 4.1 lists five Essential Fictions for which there is a recommendation. The recommendation is to retain two (Equity treats as done that which ought to be done, estoppel) and abolish three (*volenti non fit injuria*, single meaning rule, the inference in the first stage of the common intention constructive trust). The last is already abolished, but I propose to use the evaluation of it for didactic purposes. Table 4.1 lists two Auxiliary Fictions for which there is a recommendation (remoteness in negligence, reading down exclusion clauses). The recommendation is to abolish both. There are no Jurisdictional Fictions with a recommendation. Those are all Old Fictions that have already been abolished. In the paragraphs below, I will argue that only Essential Fictions should be retained. This conclusion is consistent with, but not necessitated by, the above findings.

A fiction that is not Essential has, by definition, nothing to do with the reasons for the result of a case. It is meaningless text or legal lip service. In other words, it is superfluous. There seems to be no good reason to perpetuate meaningless text. Non-essential fictions can be removed without affecting the basis of the action. It is astounding just how cleanly the Old Jurisdictional and Auxiliary Fictions were removed by the Common Law Procedure Act 1852. One day they were there; the next day they were gone. Nobody missed them. Nobody mourned them. That was the ultimate proof of their superfluity. Old Essential Fictions, as we have seen, could not be got rid of so easily. They formed the basis of actions and alternatives had to be provided, lest claimants should find themselves without a remedy. I described in the first chapter how Parliament had to establish a new statutory code for ejectment, because ejectment was an Essential Fiction. The abolition of non-Essential Fictions was not attended by such problems – or indeed any problems.

One would struggle to explain why a device that is useless and superfluous should be preserved for eternity. Occam's Razor should trim these unnecessary propositions. How much more is the razor needful when the useless device in question is a fiction? If the Default Position is to avoid fictions (unless there is some ground for accepting them), it seems that *ex hypothesi* superfluous fictions cannot hope to justify themselves.

The wisdom of this policy may be seen in the fiction of remoteness in negligence. It is an Auxiliary Fiction. We have looked at cases where recovery was allowed, although the risk was not reasonably foreseeable. The chestnut of reasonable foreseeability was recited for form, taking centre stage in judgments, while the real reasons hid behind the curtain. How much better would it have been if judges had not had to say the words 'reasonably foreseeable' when the risk was clearly not so? If we no longer need to say '*vi et armis*' in every action for trespass, why should we have to say 'reasonable foreseeability' in every action for negligence?

In conclusion, it has been argued that only Essential Fictions should be retained. The Acceptance Test now has two conditions: to be retained, the fiction must be Hard and Essential.

4.5.4 *The Role of Justice in the Acceptance Test*

We continue with our analysis of previous results. The aim is to extrapolate from these results an Acceptance Test for all fictions. By this stage in the construction of the test, I have argued for the abolition of all non-Essential Fictions and all Soft Fictions. The *volenti* fiction is dead. The remoteness fiction in negligence is dead. What is left? It remains to examine previous results relating to fictions that are both Hard and Essential. Were all of them accepted? The fiction of the single meaning rule is both Hard and Essential. Yet I concluded that it should be abolished. It is clear then that the Acceptance Test will disapprove of at least some fictions that are both Hard and Essential. The reason I decided that the single meaning fiction should be abolished was the injustice it produced. This suggests that justice has a role to play in the Acceptance Test.

This is hardly surprising. Justice is one of the two motives for creating fictions. It has been so from an early date. Consistently, justice has also proved to be a check on fictions. Judges have refused to apply a fiction, even a generally recognised fiction, in circumstances when it was seen to undermine justice. Lord Mansfield CJ said in *Lane v Wheat* (1783) that '[f]ictions are allowed against all the king's subjects for the furtherance, but never for the hindrance, of justice'.[100] Edward Coke insisted that '*semper in fictione juris subsistit aequitas*' (in legal fictions equity always exists). The phrase occurs, with slight variations, in three of his reports and in his *Commentary upon Littleton*.[101] Justice thus controls the scope of a fiction.

We should not depart from this consistent historical position. If a fiction is responsible for injustice, it cannot be condoned. We use fictions, reluctantly, because they help us reach a desirable outcome. There is no reason to defend a fiction which brings about an undesirable outcome – and injustice is axiomatically undesirable. A fiction that, like Frankenstein's monster, turns on its maker to become an instrument of mischief has lost its justification for existence. The Acceptance Test, in addition to disallowing Soft and non-Essential Fictions, should bar a fiction that creates or exacerbates injustice.

But here we run into a problem. Justice is subjective. No two people have the same understanding of it. Using justice as a criterion in the Acceptance Test would make it vague and unpredictable. It would be too redolent of those unhelpful tests quoted earlier in this chapter, which refer to what is 'just and reasonable'. If I were to adopt a vague injustice condition, the Acceptance Test would be a wide-discretion test rather than a narrow-discretion test. This is not the type of test I have pursued.

What is the solution? How do we protect the law from unjust fictions but at the same time preserve the predictability of the Acceptance Test? More specifically, how do we reduce the scope of the discretion in relation to the justice condition from wide to narrow? The solution I propose here is to adopt a more stringent injustice criterion for the disqualification of a fiction: not simply 'injustice' but 'Manifest Injustice'. 'Manifest' is defined herein as 'non-debatable'. Hence, Manifest Injustice is less disputable than simple injustice. An Acceptance Test referring to Manifest Injustice could be sufficiently certain. The difference between simple injustice and Manifest Injustice will be explained and exemplified presently.

Reasonable people hold diametrically opposed views on what is just and unjust. One man's justice is another man's injustice. Some people believe in low taxes. They tend to see taxation as inherently predatory – as a confiscation of hard-earned income by the state, a disincentive for entrepreneurship and a punishment for success. Other people favour high taxes. They tend to see

[100] (1783) 1 Doug 314 (KB), cited in LTB, 54 fn 82.
[101] LTB, 55 fn 83.

taxation as inherently salutary – as a way to reduce inequality, fund public services and share widely the resources of society. Both groups tolerate a degree of taxation. But the first group sees *high* taxes as unjust, whereas the second group sees *low* taxes (on high earners) as unjust. Their respective views of justice, in this respect, are diametrically opposite. Yet it is not possible to say that one group is objectively in error. Who is to say what the correct tax rate is? Correct in terms of what? There is no common premise. Even conclusive empirical studies by economists (an unlikely prospect) would avail us nothing because the disagreement is about *goals* and *values*, not means. That is to say, the disagreement is about the relative importance of such things as equality and freedom and reward (which is a value judgment). It is not about how best to achieve either of these (which is an empirical question). From the perspective of an objective judge, there is no way to settle this difference of opinion. Indeed, courts refuse to rule on political questions as a matter of policy.[102] The rate of taxation is an example of debatable injustice (i.e., non-Manifest).

Let us now, to further elucidate the concept, consider an example of debatable injustice in the law. The Supreme Court has recently reaffirmed a rule of law, the justice of which is debatable. In *MT Højgaard A/S v E.ON Climate & Renewables UK Robin Rigg East Ltd* (2017),[103] a builder contracted to build wind farms according to designs. The wind farms were built faithfully to the designs, but failed shortly after installation. It later transpired that the designs had been flawed. No wind farm built to them was ever going to work. The Court had to determine who bore the liability for the failure: the builder or the client. It was held, following a line of cases, that in hard cases such as this English law generally visited liability on the builder.[104] Broadly, this is because the builder is primarily engaged to build something that works. The designs are secondary. So it is the builder who bears the risk of faulty designs.

Now this rule of law is open to the charge of injustice. It may be argued that the builder's obligation is to build *to the designs*, not contrary to them. The builder (or its insurer) should not incur liability for performing the contract. It is the commissioner of the work who should bear the risk of commissioning something that does not work.

102 For example, the 'public benefit' test (for charitable trusts) will not be satisfied by a political goal: 'because the Court has no means of judging whether a proposed change in the law will or will not be for the public benefit'. See *Bowman v Secular Society Ltd* [1917] AC 406 (HL) 442 (Lord Parker).

103 [2017] UKSC 59, [2017] Bus LR 1610.

104 Ibid. [44] (Lord Neuberger P); *Cammell Laird & Co Ltd v Manganese Bronze & Brass Co Ltd* [1934] AC 402 (HL) 425 (Lord Wright).

However one looks at it, this is a question that does not admit of an easy answer. Both options seem to carry a degree of injustice. The court must choose between plague and cholera. It is not possible to say, beyond reasonable disagreement, which outcome is less unjust. This is an example of debatable injustice in the law (i.e., non-Manifest).

There are many things whose justice is debatable. Tax is one of them. Liability for flawed designs is another. The voting age is yet another. However, there are many things whose justice is not at all debatable. These include bribery, deceit, wanton violence – to name a few. These are things that no right-minded person would defend.

It is, of course, a fact of history that what we regard as self-evidently wrong has not always been so regarded. Slavery is an example. But where the consensus has reversed – as in the case of slavery – the injustice of such a practice may be regarded as being beyond debate *in this day and age*. It is therefore possible for a judge to regard certain things as objectively unjust (not merely as illegal[105]).

The purpose of this exercise is to demonstrate that it is possible to distinguish between two types of injustice: debatable and non-debatable. For our purposes, non-debatable injustice is Manifest and debatable injustice is not Manifest.

By stating that the Acceptance Test will disallow fictions which cause Manifest Injustice, I am setting the bar high. Only the kind of injustice that reasonable people do not disagree on will trigger the exclusion. I do so to ensure that the Acceptance Test is of narrow discretion and not wide discretion. The test is of narrow discretion because (i) all the cases where there is no hint of injustice clearly do not trigger the exclusion, (ii) all the cases where it is debatable whether there is injustice do not trigger the exclusion (i.e., there is no need to determine whether there really is injustice) and (iii) only cases of indisputable injustice trigger the exclusion. True, the decision maker still exercises discretion in deciding whether the case is one of debatable or non-debatable injustice, but this level of discretion is small and acceptable. I never said we should allow no discretion at all. I said we should allow narrow discretion.

Thus if the trigger for the exclusion of a fiction is that it causes Manifest Injustice, the decision maker has a narrow discretion. By acting only on Manifest Injustice, we sidestep or neutralise the uncertainty which is immanent in the whole justice question. The problem of uncertainty is solved.

105 This following point is beyond the scope of this work, and nothing here rests on it, but there is probably an almost-perfect overlap between the things that are Manifestly Unjust and the things that are illegal. The oft-cited exception is conjugal infidelity. The author cannot think of other exceptions.

It may be urged against me that in seeking certainty, I oversimplify and paper over a complex question. I do not deny that the solution proposed above avoids a complex question. Indeed, that is its aim. But I say it is better than the alternative. I also draw encouragement from the view expressed by Lord Neuberger P in *FHR European Ventures LLP v Cedar Capital Partners LLC* (2014). There, the Supreme Court had to determine, after years of confusion and disagreement between courts, the legal treatment of bribes taken by agents. The President, with whom the Court agreed, said:

> The respondents' formulation of the Rule has the merit of simplicity: any benefit acquired by an agent as a result of his agency and in breach of his fiduciary duty is held on trust for the principal. On the other hand, the appellant's position is more likely to result in uncertainty. ... Clarity and simplicity are highly desirable qualities in the law. Subtle distinctions are sometimes inevitable, but in the present case, as mentioned above, there is no plainly right answer, and, accordingly, in the absence of any other good reason, it would seem right to opt for the simple answer.[106]

In the context of justice, too, there is no plainly right answer. So it is right, I submit, to opt for the simple answer.

In avoiding uncertainty, however, I have exposed myself to an objection from another quarter. If only Manifest Injustice is a reason to abolish a fiction, it follows, uncomfortably, that ordinary injustice is apparently fine. Are we really content to accept fictions that cause *any* injustice?

This counter-argument misapprehends the distinction between Manifest Injustice and non–Manifest Injustice. For our purposes, if the injustice is not Manifest, we cannot really know whether there is injustice at all (because reasonable people disagree). So this counter-argument puts the cart before the horse. It assumes that a thing is unjust when we do not have the liberty to make precisely this assumption.

It has been wisely said that '[t]he lawyer cannot afford to adventure himself with philosophers'.[107] We cannot base a test on a criterion which is an intractable philosophical debate in itself. It is frankly not for this project, or indeed the legal system, to arbitrate philosophical questions of justice. The author of this work, or even a judge, is no better arbiter of such questions than the next person. Given the courts are ill-equipped to dabble in philosophy, and in view of the desirability of certainty, the law should remain as objective

106 [2014] UKSC 45, [2015] AC 250 [35].

107 *HMS London* [1914] P 72 (Prob Div & Adm) 78 (Evans P), quoting Sir Frederick Pollock on causation.

as possible and respond only to Manifest Injustice. This is what I have proposed.

Let us now apply the criterion of Manifest Injustice to one of our own fictions. In the previous chapter, I came to the view that the single meaning rule should be abolished. That was because the rule caused 'injustice'. The injustice consisted in allowing people to make statements that are defamatory in the eyes of the reasonable man in the absence of any defence. We can now see that such an outcome would constitute Manifest Injustice. There is a consensus that a person should not have her reputation destroyed due to a false accusation. Nobody would consider being traduced as a criminal or as a crook or as an incompetent as just.

It is true that I canvassed several arguments in favour of the fiction and allowed that one of them (the chaos argument) had merit. But this does not mean that the injustice of the fiction is debatable and hence non-Manifest. These arguments in support, even if accepted as valid, did not challenge the injustice itself: that a person could have their reputation destroyed due to a false accusation. To say that removing the fiction would make litigation more expensive is not the same as disputing the injustice caused by the fiction. The injustice of the single meaning rule is not debatable. Ergo it causes Manifest Injustice, and its abolition is consistent with our developing Acceptance Test.

To conclude this section, the Acceptance Test will disallow fictions that cause Manifest Injustice. Adding this condition to the conditions I have already identified, the Acceptance Test reads as follows: retain a fiction if it is Hard, Essential and does not cause Manifest Injustice; otherwise, abolish it.

4.5.5 *The Role of the Conservative Argument in the Acceptance Test*

In a recent decision of the Supreme Court, Lord Hodge observed that '[o]ne of the attractions of English law as a legal system of choice in commercial matters is its stability and continuity'.[108] There is much to be said for stability, continuity and (I take the liberty to add) predictability in a system that has to be obeyed by millions. Since my Acceptance Test, if adopted, will spell change for the law (by abolishing some fictions), it behoves me to bear in mind Lord Hodge's implied admonition.

This Conservative Argument, as I have called it above, is that judges should be change-averse. Why change the law if we do not have to? Why sow disorder if there is no compelling reason to change the law? This argument found its strongest expression by the pen of Sir Edward Coke:

[108] *Wood v Sureterm Direct Ltd* [2017] UKSC 24, [2017] 2 WLR 1095 [15].

> The laws of England consist of three parts, the common law, customs, and Acts of Parliament: for any fundamental point of the ancient common laws and customs of the realm, it is a maxim in policy, and a trial by experience, that the alteration of any of them is most dangerous; for that which hath been refined and perfected by all the wisest men in the former succession of ages, and proved and approved by continual experience to be good and profitable for the commonwealth, cannot without great hazard and danger be altered or changed.[109]

In our context, the Conservative Argument means that we should be change-averse as regards the future of fictions. Given the organic nature of the common law; the risk of unintended consequences; and the importance of stability, continuity and predictability; we should think twice before abolishing a fiction – if we can live with it. We should not seek precipitately to change the law from above in pursuit of theoretical purity or utopia.

It must be stressed, once more, that the Conservative Argument is not decisive. Nor should we read Coke to be saying that the common law must never change – only that it cannot be changed 'without great hazard'. The Conservative Argument is not an argument for no change. It is an argument for caution, for a *presumption* of no change for established law.

The Conservative Argument is not new in this book. It was first put forward in the last chapter and then considered earlier in this chapter. I concluded that while the Default Position was to prefer truth over fiction (all other things being equal), one of the arguments that could sway a decision maker in favour of retaining an entrenched fiction was the Conservative Argument.

It follows that the Acceptance Test ought not to treat existing and novel fictions as if they were the same. Heedful of the Conservative Argument, and Lord Hodge's counsel, we should be more tolerant of established fictions than of newly-proposed fictions. In other words, the Acceptance Test must set a higher bar for new fictions compared with existing fictions.

And so, when we have an *existing* fiction (that is Hard and Essential), we will disturb the law (by abolishing the fiction) only for a sufficiently good reason. We already know what to call such a sufficiently good reason: Manifest Injustice.

If I were to adopt a lesser bar, then even fictions that are Hard, Essential and give rise to no Manifest Injustice would effectively have to show that there is no non-fictitious solution. This would contradict the Conservative Argument: instead of changing the law only for a compelling reason, we would have a system where the law must change *unless* there is a compelling reason not to

109 Edward Coke, *The Selected Writings and Speeches of Sir Edward Coke*, vol 1 (Steve Sheppard ed, Liberty Fund 2003) 95.

change it. This would make every existing fiction debatable and cause much needless instability. There are too many problems in the law as it is for us to busy ourselves with changes for which there is no compelling reason.

Of course, the Conservative Argument has no application where a judge is considering creating a new fiction – as may be required to resolve a hard case. In this situation, the Default Position reigns supreme. Fiction should be absolutely the last resort. The proponent of the fiction must point to a compelling reason for its creation. The proponent must show that the fiction is the *only* practical way to avoid Manifest Injustice.

The Acceptance Test has now split into two tests – or sub-tests: one for existing fictions and one for novel fictions: a Retention Test and a Creation Test.

4.6 THE RETENTION TEST

We have, at last, arrived at the full statement of the Retention Test: *a fiction should be retained if it is Hard, Essential and does not cause Manifest Injustice*. It will be recalled that the capitalised terms mean the following:

> A Hard Fiction is a factual issue consciously decided irrespective of the facts. It is to be contrasted with a Soft Fiction, which is a factual issue decided by a consciously unnatural interpretation of the law.
>
> An Essential Fiction is a fiction which represents the real basis for the result of the case. It is to be contrasted with a Jurisdictional Fiction, which merely determines the court in which the action is heard; and an Auxiliary Fiction, which amounts to no more than lip-service, meaningless text or verbal flourish.
>
> Manifest Injustice is an outcome which all reasonable people would agree is unjust.

4.7 THE CREATION TEST

4.7.1 *Background and Statement*

This monograph has mostly focussed on fictions that are or were in our law. I have not directed attention to the fictions that are yet to be. The demise of the Old System has all but removed the need to create New Fictions. The judicial fashion is decidedly anti-fiction.[110] But fashions have been known to change,

[110] *OBG Ltd v Allan* (n 30) (Lord Nicholls); *Forsyth-Grant v Allen* [2008] EWCA Civ 505, [2008] 2 EGLR 16 [45] (Toulson LJ).

and even today, it cannot be ruled out that a judge, finding herself between a rock and a hard place, may be tempted by this old friend of her predecessors, the fiction. And so, as we bring to an end our examination of fictions of the past and present, we should look ahead to the fictions of the future. What guidance can this work give to a judge or policy maker who is considering creating a legal fiction?

It might be said that the Creation Test should not differ from the Retention Test. If we conclude that a fiction should be retained, is it not implied that it was right to create it in the first place? No; at least not in every case. This is because the Conservative Argument (let sleeping dogs lie) does not apply to fictions not yet created. One cannot conserve the non-existent. Hence, the deference that should be shown to established fictions has no place here. In the absence of such toleration, and remembering our basic bias against fictions (the Default Position), the Creation Test should be more stringent than the Retention Test.

Such a test has already been foreshadowed. I now state the Creation Test fully: *a fiction should be created if it is Hard, Essential and the only practical way to avoid Manifest Injustice*. The defined terms have the same meaning as in the Retention Test.

What, it may be asked, is the role of convenience in the Creation Test? We know that convenience may justify the retention of an existing fiction. Indeed, that is a major element of the Conservative Argument. The Retention Test implicitly takes the convenience of retention into account by setting the bar for abolition quite high.

Does the Creation Test make no allowance for convenience? It is conceivable that an inconvenience may be so oppressive that it amounts to Manifest Injustice. But then, of course, the condition of Manifest Injustice would be satisfied. There is therefore no problem. In any event, such cases must be exceptional. A new fiction should only be created to avoid an obviously unjust *outcome*.

At the risk of repetition, and for the abundance of clarity, the Creation Test is more stringent than the Retention Test. Whereas the Retention Test demands of a fiction that it cause no Manifest Injustice (a negative filter), the Creation Test allows a fiction only in order to avoid Manifest Injustice (a positive filter). The latter reflects the basic bias against fiction; the former our tolerance of existing law expressed in the Conservative Argument. It is the Conservative Argument, therefore, that justifies the difference between the two tests.[111] Certain existing fictions we will tolerate for the sake of stability and convenience, but new fictions we will allow only as a last resort.

[111] To paraphrase Professor Richard Nolan, my PhD examiner.

4.7.2 *The Application of the Creation Test*

The Creation Test, as its name suggests, applies only where there is not a fiction in existence. This may occur if there is some technical or institutional barrier to a non-fictitious solution. An example of such a situation is where an Act of Parliament has an unintended and perverse consequence. Since the judge is unable to disapply the Act, the only way to achieve a just and sensible outcome is to create a legal fiction. This difficult choice – whether to create a new fiction – will be seen to advantage in the juxtaposition of two cases: *Barnett v French* (1980),[112] where a fiction was rightly created as a last resort; and *Fairchild v Glenhaven Funeral Services* (2002),[113] where a fiction was wisely eschewed.

4.7.2.1 *Barnett v French*: A Fiction Rightly Created

This case is a prime example of legislation with a perverse effect. Some background for this curious case is necessary. When motor vehicles became common in the early twentieth century, so did traffic accidents. Parliament responded by regulating the use of motor vehicles and visiting criminal liability on offenders. Relevantly to our purposes, the Lights on Vehicles Act 1907 (now wholly repealed) enjoined 'every person who shall cause or permit any vehicle to be in any street' to install headlamps.[114] The Act also fixed a penalty for default.[115] Aware that many vehicles were owned by the Crown, and mindful of the legal impossibility of prosecuting the Crown for permitting unroadworthy vehicles to be on the road, Parliament made special provision for vehicles in the service of the Crown. It was provided that the relevant government department shall nominate an official, who would automatically (without personal fault) assume criminal liability under the Act.[116] This scapegoating provision was presumably intended to ensure that the government was not above the law. In time, this mode of application to Crown vehicles was extended to numerous traffic offences.[117]

For many years, public authorities did not nominate their officials to answer for traffic violations. Prosecuting authorities did not insist on such nominations.[118] The law was not enforced. But this long honeymoon ended at just the wrong time for a certain HG Barnett, functionary of the Department of the Environment. As a senior civil servant, he was nominally responsible for

112 [1981] 1 WLR 848 (QB).
113 [2002] UKHL 22, [2003] 1 AC 32.
114 s 1.
115 s 2.
116 s 5(4).
117 See, e.g., Road Traffic Act 1972, s 188(8).
118 *Barnett v French* (n 112) 852 (Donaldson LJ).

a fleet of 3,500 vehicles. In May 1979, one of those vehicles was found to have a flat tire. Barnett, the Department's nominee, was charged under the Road Traffic Act 1972,[119] into which the scapegoating mechanism had been incorporated.[120] He was convicted at first instance and appealed to the Court of Appeal. Donaldson LJ took pity on the bureaucrat, who, 'In the nature of things . . . can have no personal control over . . . vehicles, which are distributed all over the country.'[121]

But how was the man's 'legitimate grievance' to be redressed, given the unambiguous force of the statute?[122] 'Solely because of the position which he holds, he is at risk of becoming the citizen with the longest record of motoring convictions ever known.'[123]

After canvassing other options, the Court of Appeal finally settled on a fiction. It was important for the Court to fulfil the legislative purpose, while avoiding collateral casualties: 'If Parliament's obvious intentions are to be fulfilled, what is required is "a person" who will stand in the shoes of the department for the purposes of criminal proceedings, but who cannot be prejudiced personally by performing this very important function.'[124]

Donaldson LJ, delivering the judgement of the Court, thought 'it would be a grave reflection on the flexibility and ingenuity of a common law system if what is essentially a procedural problem were to be accepted as insoluble'.[125] Happily, Donaldson LJ found a solution in one of the Old Fictions I described in the first chapter:

> A little over 300 years ago a not dissimilar problem arose in connection with proceedings for the recovery of land . . . Mr. John Doe came to the rescue, sometimes assisted by Mr. Richard Roe. These two gentlemen were conceived, in an intellectual rather than a biological sense, about the year 1656, and are said to have been the brain children of Rolle C.J. . . .
>
> So far as we know, John Doe's services to the law have thus far been confined to the civil jurisdiction of the courts and he has never been called upon to serve the Crown. However, we see no reason why he should be unable or unwilling to assist the courts with this new problem. . . .
>
> If a 'natural' person is to be nominated, it is clear that only John Doe, Richard Roe or one of his relations fills the bill. John Doe would have been

119 s 40.
120 s 188(8).
121 *Barnett v French* (n 112) 850.
122 Ibid. 850.
123 Ibid. 850.
124 Ibid. 853.
125 Ibid. 853.

> particularly well qualified in the instant case since the Department of the Environment is known to its intimates as 'DoE'. Pending any change in the law, we can see no legal, constitutional or ethical objection and very real and practical advantages if government departments were to nominate John Doe. . . .
>
> Of course, the name John Doe is not unknown in real life, but we do not think that any confusion could arise between the departmental John Doe and any others. For the purposes of criminal records, people with the same name are usually distinguished by their date of birth and John Doe's is 'circa 1657'. We trust that our suggestion will not lead to John Doe acquiring any considerable criminal record, but if he does it will be for the government department concerned and not for John Doe to offer an explanation and he will have the consolation of having yet again rendered a signal service to the law.[126]

The case of *Barnett v French* is a clever and justifiable creation of a legal fiction. It conforms with the Creation Test. It is a Hard Fiction because the existence of John Doe as nominee is factual, clearly false and knowingly so. It is an Essential Fiction because the nomination is the doctrinal basis for the outcome. It is also the only practical way to avoid Manifest Injustice, being the conviction of an innocent man.

Appropriately, the judges did not hastily opt for fiction but carefully assessed other alternatives. For example, the incorporation of a company, 'Crown Defendants Ltd', was ruled out because 'there would be considerable difficulty in drafting the company's principal objects'.[127] Another solution was that the Department would only nominate people actually culpable. Interestingly, the Court rejected this solution because it would have involved the Department trying the issue of guilt. The scapegoating, we remember, was automatic: the nominee was *deemed* responsible.[128] Other solutions were also considered.[129] Obvious to remark, the Court could not change the statute, which required a nomination. Fiction was the only practical way to avoid Manifest Injustice while fulfilling Parliament's intention: a conviction was recorded against a government nominee, but no innocent people were harmed in the process. The government nominee was in any event nominally guilty rather than guilty for personal fault. He was nominally guilty because the Crown could not be. What did it matter that the nominal person was not a real person? The nominee was just a substitute for the Crown anyway. This was an acceptable creation of a legal fiction.

126 Ibid. 853–4.
127 Ibid. 853.
128 Road Traffic Act 1972, s 188(8).
129 *Barnett v French* (n 112) 852.

4.7.2.2 *Fairchild v Glenhaven Funeral Services*: A Fiction Rightly Avoided

This case, concerning the scourge of asbestos, was a hard case *par excellence*. Asbestos is a fibrous material, used in construction. Inhalation of the fibres may cause mesothelioma, an incurable cancer of the lung. It is understood that, while longer exposure to asbestos increases the risk of contracting the disease, the disease is not caused by the *accumulation* of exposure (as sunburn is caused by cumulative exposure to the sun) but by a particular intake of fibres (as road injuries are caused by a particular accident, not by cumulative exposure to the road).[130] This medical fact was crucial in the instant case because the claimants had all been exposed to asbestos in the service of several employers. It was found that all employers breached their duty of care by exposing the claimants to asbestos, but there was no way of knowing which of the negligent employers exposed each claimant to the specific fibres that caused the disease.

This was a seemingly insurmountable difficulty,[131] for it had been a cardinal rule of causation (of physical harm) that the claimant must prove that the harm would not have occurred but for the defendant's tort.[132] Two previous cases had made inroads into that principle.[133] Crucially, however, these did not involve multiple potential tortfeasors. The civil standard of proof is the balance of probabilities. While it was clear that one of the several employers must have been responsible for the deadly exposure, the probability that any single employer was responsible was less than 50 per cent (or just unknowable). If the Court did not retreat from the cardinal rule, all defendants would get off scot-free. The House of Lords was confronted with a judicial Sophie's Choice: sell out or fall into disrepute. Either way, the English law of causation could not survive as it stood.

In the event, the House of Lords chose what most people would accept as the lesser evil. It created a narrowly circumscribed exception for mesothelioma cases of this sort. Under this 'modified approach to proof of causation',[134] it was sufficient for the claimants to prove that each employer had materially increased the risk of illness.[135]

130 *Fairchild* (n 113) [7] (Lord Bingham).

131 Indeed, in the case under consideration, the High Court and the Court of Appeal dismissed the claim: *Fairchild v Glenhaven Funeral Services Ltd* (HC, 1 February 2001) (reversed); *Fairchild v Glenhaven Funeral Services Ltd* [2002] 1 WLR 1052 (CA) (reversed).

132 *Barnett v Chelsea and Kensington Hospital Management Committee* [1969] 1 QB 428 (QB) 438–9 (Neild J); *Fairchild* (n 113) [8]–[9] (Lord Bingham).

133 *Bonnington Castings Ltd v Wardlaw* [1956] AC 613 (HL) 620 (Lord Reid); *McGhee v National Coal Board* [1973] 1 WLR 1 (HL) 6 (Lord Wilberforce), 8–9 (Lord Simon), 12 (Lord Salmon).

134 *Fairchild* (n 113) [2] (Lord Bingham).

135 Ibid. [2], [34] (Lord Bingham), [42] (Lord Nicholls), [47] (Lord Hoffmann), [108] (Lord Hutton), [158] (Lord Rodger).

Importantly for our purposes, the House of Lords toyed with the idea of solving the evidentiary problem (proof of causation) with a legal fiction. Instead of formally changing the law to fit the case, the Appellate Committee could have simply 'inferred' or imputed proof of probability, or downright 'found' it on the facts. It would not have been the first time such a thing was done. But the House expressly rejected this option:

> Lord Wilberforce … wisely deprecated resort to fictions and it seems to me preferable, in the interests of transparency, that the courts' response to the special problem presented by cases such as these should be stated explicitly. I prefer to recognise that the ordinary approach to proof of causation is varied than to resort to the drawing of legal inferences inconsistent with the proven facts.[136]

It is submitted that their Lordships were right. This decision is consistent with the Creation Test. A strained inference would have been a Soft Fiction, which is anathema to both Retention and Creation Tests. A clear factual finding in defiance of the factual uncertainty would have been a Hard Fiction. Even so, it would not have been the *only* practical way to solve the problem. So much is proved by the result of the case. A narrow exception was created in lieu of a fiction. More than a decade after that momentous decision, no negative consequences have been discerned. *Fairchild* illustrates how the Creation Test could correctly prevent the creation of fictions.

We can see that the Creation Test will only be satisfied where there is some constraint which prevents the judge from changing the law. Without wishing to limit the scope of the Creation Test, the constraint may take the form of legislation (as we have seen in *Barnett v French*), binding precedent or impracticality.

It is difficult to see how the Creation Test can ever be satisfied when the decision of whether to create a fiction is made by legislators. Parliament is sovereign, meaning it faces no technical or institutional barriers (except its own procedures, which can themselves be changed by Parliament[137]).

4.8 THE ACCEPTANCE TEST

Now that both the Retention and Creation Tests have been articulated, it is possible to merge them into a single flowchart. This flowchart, shown in Table 4.2, is the Acceptance Test.

136 Ibid. [35] (Lord Bingham); see also, to the same effect, [65] (Lord Hoffmann); [150] (Lord Rodger).

137 *R (Jackson) v Attorney General* [2005] UKHL 56, [2006] 1 AC 262 [81] (Lord Steyn).

4.9 HARD CASES

It is one thing to espouse a principled approach in theory. It is quite another thing to follow it in practice. In hard cases, especially, it is easier said than done. What is a judge to do when faced with a hard case (one to which existing law offers no just answer)? The purpose of this section (4.9) is to clarify how the flowchart should be used in such a predicament.

Let us return to *Eves v Eves* (1975), the case concerning the common intention constructive trust, where the man tricked the woman into thinking that she could not own the house because she was too young. We recall that the trust could only arise if the parties had an actual, provable intention to share ownership. This made *Eves v Eves* a hard case. There was no actual intention so, according to law, no trust. But this lack of intention had been induced by deception. The law seemed to lead to an unjust result. The judges (Lord Denning MR, Browne LJ and Brightman J) overcame this problem by straining the law (a Soft Fiction) to find an actual common intention in the man's dishonest conduct and the woman's subsequent contributions to the property. Thus a Soft Fiction was used to avoid an unjust result in a hard case.

The problem for my thesis is that the Acceptance Test does not allow the judges to do this. Soft Fictions are never 'allowed'. So what were the judges in *Eves v Eves* supposed to do without Soft Fictions in their armoury? Were they to deny the woman any share in the house (as the trial judge, Pennycuick V-C, had done[138])?

No, they need not have. It seems that *Barnett v French* (the hard case about attributed traffic violations) shows us the way. As the flowchart in Table 4.2 already indicates, the solution to hard cases is Hard Fictions.[139] The injustice in *Barnett v French* was avoided by a Hard Fiction: attributing the offences to a fictional person. It would have been better, in the author's opinion, if the judges in *Eves v Eves* had stated clearly that they knowingly found an intention irrespective of the facts (by definition a Hard Fiction). That would have flagged the inadequacy in the law and invited a higher court to do one of three things: embrace the fiction, change the law to obviate the fiction, or reinstate the original law (whereby no trust arises). A Soft Fiction serves only to bury the problem in obfuscatory reasoning, filling the law with ambiguity, contradiction and doubt. *Eves v Eves* is an example of the general point that hard cases should be resolved (in the last resort) through Hard Fictions.

[138] *Eves v Eves* (HC, 10 April 1974).

[139] Only when the Hard Fiction is a last resort, as reflected in the flowchart.

TABLE 4.2 *Flowchart of Acceptance Test*

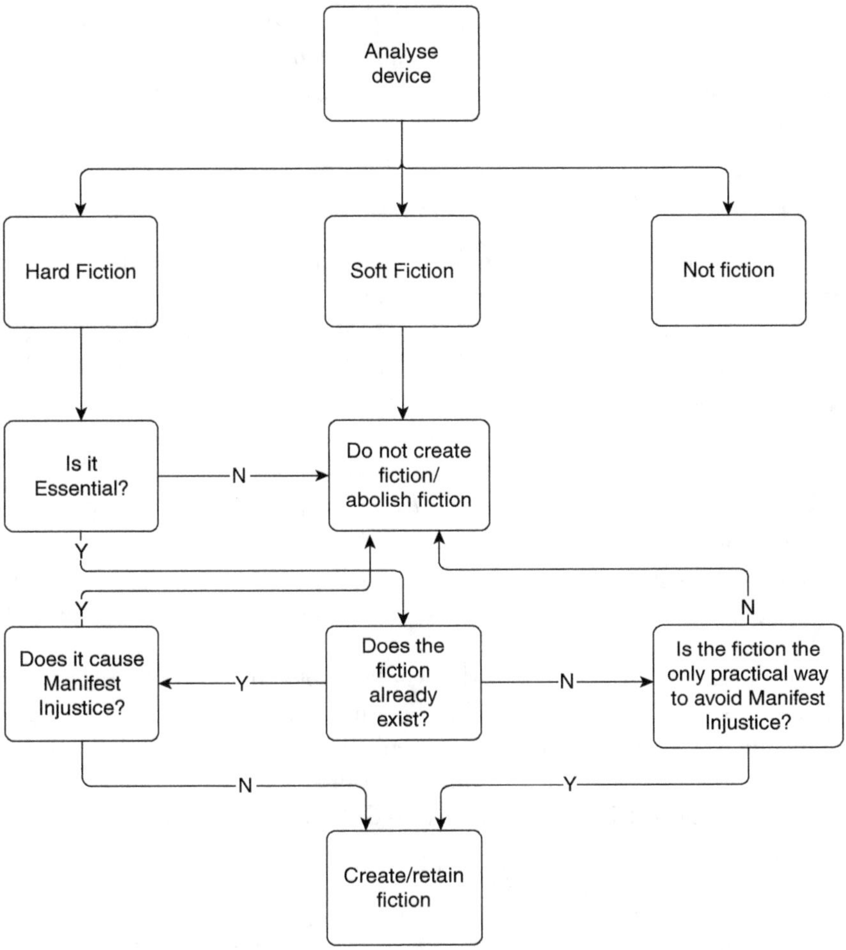

Key
Hard Fiction: A factual issue consciously decided irrespective of the facts
Essential Fiction: A fiction which represents the real basis for the result of the case
Manifest Injustice: An outcome which all reasonable people would agree is unjust

There is more to be said about the fiction *as a signal* that reform is necessary, and indeed as a *bridge* to reform. I add, by the way, that my original draft of these lines, written in early 2019, ended with the wish that other scholars should take up this idea as a subject of future research. I am therefore happy to discover that Maksymilian Del Mar has not waited for my exhortation and independently pursued this avenue of inquiry, with impressive results, in his 2020 book *Artefacts of Legal Inquiry*.[140]

The aim of this section (4.9) is to explain how the Acceptance Test should apply to hard cases. The answer is simple enough. The flowchart applies as it is, without a gloss, without deviation.

4.10 CONCLUSION

The introduction to this chapter promised an Acceptance Test in three stages. At stage one, I asked what kind of test was needed. The answer was a test of narrow discretion, aiming at fiction minimisation. At stage two, I scrutinised the motives for fictions, only to conclude that there were fewer motives than commonly supposed – justice and convenience – and that both were legitimate justifications for fictions. At stage three, I inferred the variables in the Acceptance Test from my previous analyses of fictions.

The previous chapter was *specifically* prescriptive in that it considered a number of specific fictions and recommended retention or abolition. This chapter offers a *general* prescription. It presents a pair of tests, the Retention and Creation Tests, united in an Acceptance Test, in flowchart form, which can be applied to any fiction.

The flowchart in Table 4.2, and this whole chapter, may be reduced to three propositions: (i) the only acceptable fictions under any circumstances are Hard and Essential; (ii) no fiction should be retained unless it is Hard, Essential and does not cause Manifest Injustice; and (iii) no fiction should be created unless it is Hard, Essential and the only practical way to avoid Manifest Injustice.

140 Maksymilian Del Mar, *Artefacts of Legal Inquiry* (Hart 2020) ch 5, esp 258, 263.

General Conclusion

This monograph grew out of a PhD dissertation, submitted to the University of Cambridge in 2018. It was titled *Deus ex Machina*. The Latin phrase literally means 'God from a machine'. It described a device of ancient Greek stagecraft. At the end of a play, with the plot seemingly at an impasse, a god would descend onto the stage and solve all the problems. Apparently introduced by Aeschylus (died 456 BC), this miraculous *dénouement* was achieved by a crane which lowered an actor dressed as the deity. Hence 'God from a machine'.[1]

Despite the reputation of its supposed inventor, *deus ex machina* is now a byword for creative inadequacy. It has come to mean any abrupt and convenient intervention serving to rescue a hopeless situation. It is in this wide sense that the phrase may be applied to legal fictions. Unable to resolve a case in conformity with the facts and accepted rules, the judge, like the playwright, gives up, as it were. She summons a higher power to abolish both facts and rules – and produce a happy ending. *Deus ex machina*.

* * *

The story of legal fiction in England may be retold in brief. Fictions have been in use in the common law almost since its inception in the second half of the twelfth century. At that time, fictions were essentially *procedural*, existing mostly in the form of a non-traversable pleading, but also as withdrawn pleadings, collusion or bad evidence. Regardless of their mode of operation, fictions had one of three effects on the law around them. Some were what I called Jurisdictional, affecting only the choice of court. Others were Auxiliary, to wit, meaningless text. Still others were Essential, meaning they

[1] Chris Baldick, *Oxford Dictionary of Literary Terms* (4th edn, OUP 2015); Thomas G Chondros et al., '"Deus-Ex-Machina" Reconstruction in the Athens Theater of Dionysus' (2013) 67 *Mechanism and Machine Theory* 172, 172.

changed the substance of the action and formed the basis of the decision. Fiction-making was then, as now, motivated primarily by justice and convenience.

Fictions multiplied and flourished, especially from the late fifteenth century, owing to the ossification of the forms of action and the ever-mounting burdensomeness of the process. Fiction was sometimes the only way to reform the law – and in many cases did. Some of the old common law's most recognisable actions – trover, ejectment, money had and received – were based on fictions.

Inevitably, the backlash came. The nineteenth century, for most a romantic age, was for the law an age of reason. The Old System with its antiquated writs and fictions was rationalised in a series of legislative reforms. In this new order, fictions supposedly had no place. Parliament gave them marching orders. After many years' good service, it seemed they were dishonourably discharged. The old and the weak, the Jurisdictional and Auxiliary Fictions, obeyed. However, the strong – the Essential Fictions – had been deeply embedded in doctrine, and were not successfully cashiered. They survived the great Victorian rationalisation. Some of these, like quasi-contract, were individually replaced later. Others, like estoppel, are still with us.

After these shocks, English law welcomed the new century shorn of forms and formality. As the law changed, so did the fictions. No longer immanent in the procedure of the courts, fictions ceased to be statements that could not be proved or disproved. For this reason, they were not even obviously fictions. As the fiction became more elusive and more arguable, its scope grew and diversified.

It became necessary, for me, to distinguish between Hard Fictions, Soft Fictions and non-fictions. For which purpose I reviewed the intellectual history of the fiction. I defended the fiction, according to my ability, from the overly sceptical on one side and the overly credulous on the other. As already stated, the definitions I settled upon do not profess to be correct in an absolute sense – for no conception of fiction is correct absolutely. They are, it is argued, analytically superior because they avoid the problems of other definitions. This precise understanding of the fiction in the modern law was a gateway to a rigorous evaluation of current fictions. Furthermore, it enabled the fulfilment of the undertaking declared in the General Introduction.

* * *

The General Introduction to this work counted three shortcomings in the literature concerning legal fictions. First, it alleged, there was confusion regarding the definition. Seemingly irreconcilable views prevented any consensus from coalescing around one concept of the fiction. I have sought to dispel the confusion and cement a consensus by distinguishing between Hard Fiction and Soft Fiction. This solution preserves analytical precision while acknowledging the versatility of the device. Still, this is not a free-for-all: both types of fiction recognised here have clear boundaries and exclude some uses of the term.

Second, the General Introduction complained that the treatment of fictions in the literature was either too abstract or too particular. This book deals with twenty-five specific fictions, but also paints an overall picture of the role of the legal fiction as a device in private law. It is at once general and specific. It uses specific fictions to reach conclusions about fictions in general.

The third deficiency identified in the General Introduction was that the literature was too thin on practical advice. This monograph makes specific recommendations regarding a number of surviving fictions. These recommendations, along with other useful information, may be seen in Table 4.1. Most importantly, the Acceptance Test for all fictions is a practical answer to a practical problem. It is presented as a flowchart in Table 4.2.

* * *

Finally, the General Introduction foretold a 'new system for dealing with legal fictions'. Let it be re-capitulated here. It consists, first and foremost, in a precise understanding of the concept of the legal fiction (the Nature Classification: Hard Fiction, Soft Fiction, non-fiction); secondarily, in distinguishing between Essential Fictions, which inform the decision and may still have a role to play in the last resort, and Jurisdictional and Auxiliary Fictions, which have no rational role or justification (the Effect Classification); and of the other elements of the Acceptance Test, which complete this new system for dealing with legal fictions.

This Acceptance Test is the answer to the core question which has driven this project from the beginning: *Which fictions should we accept and which reject?* It is the thesis of this book.

Bibliography

Accomando C, *The Regulations of Robbers: Legal Fictions of Slavery and Resistance* (Ohio State University Press 2001)

Anonymous, 'Lessons from Abroad: Mathematical, Poetic, and Literary Fictions in the Law' (2002) 115 Harvard LR 2228

Arnold MS, 'Law and Fact in the Medieval Jury Trial: Out of Sight, Out of Mind' (1974) 18 AJLH 267

Austin J, *Lectures on Jurisprudence or the Philosophy of Positive Law* (Robert Campbell ed, 5th edn, John Murray 1885)

Bailey SJ, 'Warranties of Land in the Thirteenth Century' (1944) 8 CLJ 274

Baker JH, 'New Light on Slade's Case' (1971) 29 CLJ 213

'The Use upon a Use in Equity 1558–1625' (1977) 93 LQR 33

'English Law and the Renaissance' (1985) 44 CLJ 46

'The Three Languages of the Common Law' (1997) 43 McGill LJ 5

The Law's Two Bodies (OUP 2001)

An Introduction to English Legal History (5th edn, OUP 2019)

Baker JH and Milsom SFC, *Sources of English Legal History: Private Law to 1750* (2nd edn, Butterworths 2010)

Baldick C, *Oxford Dictionary of Literary Terms* (4th edn, OUP 2015)

Baloch TA, *Unjust Enrichment and Contract* (Hart 2009)

Bentham J, *The Works of Jeremy Bentham, Published under the Superintendence of His Executor, John Bowring* (John Bowring ed, William Tait 1843)

Rationale of Judicial Evidence (Rothman 1995)

A Comment on the Commentaries and a Fragment on Government (JH Burns and HLA Hart eds, Clarendon Press 2008)

Biancalana J, *The Fee Tail and the Common Recovery in Medieval England 1176–1502* (CUP 2001)

Bierce A, *The Enlarged Devil's Dictionary* (Ernest Jerome Hopkins ed, Gollancz 1967)

Birks P, 'Fictions Ancient and Modern' in Neil MacCormick and Peter Birks (eds), *The Legal Mind: Essays for Tony Honoré* (Clarendon Press 1986)

Black HC, *Black's Law Dictionary* (Bryan A Garner ed, 10th edn, West Group 2000)

Blackstone W, *Commentaries on the Laws of England* (Clarendon Press 1765–9)

Blatcher M, *The Court of King's Bench 1450–1550* (Athlone Press 1978)

Bowen (Lord), 'Progress in the Administration of Justice during the Victorian Period', *Select Essays in Anglo-American Legal History*, vol 1 (Little, Brown and Company 1907)
Braithwaite J, 'The Origins and Implications of Contractual Estoppel' [2016] LQR 120
Brereton PLG, 'Equitable Estoppel in Australia: The Court of Conscience in the Antipodes' (Australian Law Journal Conference: Celebrating Eighty Years, Sydney, 16 March 2007)
Campbell K, 'Fuller on Legal Fictions' (1983) 2 Law and Philosophy 339
Carter JW, 'Discharge as the Basis for Termination for Breach of Contract' [2012] LQR 283
Chiassoni P, *Interpretation without Truth* (Springer 2019)
Chico V, 'Known Unknowns and Unknown Unknowns: The Potential and the Limits of Autonomy in Disclosure of Genetic Risk' (2012) 28 Professional Negligence 162
Chondros TG et al., '"Deus-Ex-Machina" Reconstruction in the Athens Theater of Dionysus' (2013) 67 Mechanism and Machine Theory 172
Clapp JE, *Webster's Dictionary of the Law* (Random House 2000)
Coke E, *The First Part of the Institutes of the Lawes of England: Or, a Commentarie upon Littleton* (London 1628)
The Selected Writings and Speeches of Sir Edward Coke (Steve Sheppard ed, Liberty Fund 2003)
Coleman D (ed), *Hume: Dialogues Concerning Natural Religion* (CUP 2007)
Cooke E, *The Modern Law of Estoppel* (OUP 2000)
de Haas E and Hall GDG (eds), *Selden Society: Early Register of Writs* (Bernard Quaritch 1970)
de Saussure F, *Course in General Linguistics* (Charles Bally, Albert Sechehaye and Albert Riedlinger eds, Wade Baskin tr, McGraw-Hill 1966)
de Zulueta F, *The Institutes of Gaius* (Clarendon Press 1953)
Defoe D, *The Fortunes and Misfortunes of the Famous Moll Flanders* (David Blewett ed, Penguin 1989)
Del Mar M, *Artefacts of Legal Inquiry* (Springer 2020)
'Introducing Fictions: Examples, Functions, Definitions and Evaluations' in Maksymilian Del Mar and William Twining (eds), *Legal Fictions in Theory and Practice* (Springer 2015)
'Legal Fictions and Legal Change in the Common Law Tradition' in Maksymilian Del Mar and William Twining (eds), *Legal Fictions in Theory and Practice* (Springer 2015)
Del Mar M and Twining W (eds), *Legal Fictions in Theory and Practice* (Springer 2015)
Dickens C, *The Pickwick Papers* (James Kinsley ed, OUP 1986)
Donaldson I, *Ben Jonson: A Life* (OUP 2011)
Douglas S, 'The Nature of Conversion' [2009] CLJ 198
Dworkin R, *Law's Empire* (Hart 1986)
Dymond A, 'Inference and Imputation: Cases after Jones v Kernott' (2016) 19 Journal of Housing Law 57
Etherton T, 'Constructive Trusts: A New Model for Equity and Unjust Enrichment' (2008) 67(2) CLJ 265
'The Legitimacy of Proprietary Relief' (2014) 2 Birkbeck Law Review 59
Fifoot CHS, *History and Sources of the Common Law: Tort and Contract* (Stevens 1949)

Finch H, *Law, or a Discourse Thereof* (n.p. 1759)
Frank J, *Law and the Modern Mind* (Bretano's 1930)
Friedmann D, 'The Performance Interest in Contract Damages' (1995) 111 LQR 628
Fuller LL, 'Legal Fictions' (1930–1) 25 Illinois LR 363
'Legal Fictions' (1930–1) 25 Illinois LR 513
'Legal Fictions' (1930–1) 25 Illinois LR 877
Legal Fictions (Stanford University Press 1967)
Gardner S, 'Equity, Estate Contracts and the Judicature Acts: Walsh v Lonsdale Revisited' (1987) 7 OJLS 60
'Rethinking Family Property' (1993) 109 LQR 263
Gardner S and MacKenzie E, *An Introduction to Land Law* (Hart 2015)
Glanvill R, *Treatise on the Laws and Customs of the Kingdom of England* (c 1189)
Goh N, 'Non-Reliance Clauses and Contractual Estoppel: Commercially Sensible or Anomalous?' [2015] JBL 511
Goudkamp J, *Tort Law Defences* (Hart 2013)
Gove PB (ed), *Webster's Third International Dictionary of the English Language Unabridged* (Könemann 1993)
Gray JC, *The Nature and Sources of the Law* (2nd edn, Macmillan 1921)
Gray K and Gray SF, *Land Law* (7th edn, OUP 2011)
Gustafsson H, 'Fiction of Law' (2010) 41 Rechtstheorie 319
Gwilliam J, 'Legal Fictions – A Critical Analysis' (1975) 8 Victoria U Wellington LR 452
Hale M, *The History of the Pleas of the Crown* (London 1736)
Hale M, 'A Disquisition Touching the Jurisdiction of the Common Law and Courts of Admiralty ... ' in MJ Prichard and DEC Yale (eds), *Hale and Fleetwood on Admiralty Jurisdiction*, vol 108 (Selden Society 1992)
Hall GDG (ed), *The Treatise on the Laws and Customs of England Commonly Called Glanvill* (Nelson 1965)
Hamilton KS, 'Prolegomenon to Myth and Fiction in Legal Reasoning, Common Law Adjudication and Critical Legal Studies' (1988) 35 Wayne LR 1449
Handley KR, 'Reinventing Estoppel in the Privy Council' [2014] LQR 370
Hare RM and Russell DA (eds), *The Dialogues of Plato* (Benjamin Jowett tr, Sphere Books 1970)
Harmon L, 'Falling Off the Vine: Legal Fictions and the Doctrine of Substituted Judgment' (1990) 100 Yale LJ 1
Harpum C, Bridge S and Dixon M, *The Law of Real Property* (8th edn, Sweet & Maxwell 2012)
Harris P and McCartney E, 'The Harm of Legal Fictions' [2015] Construction LJ 195
Hastings M, *The Court of Common Pleas in Fifteenth Century England* (Cornell University Press 1947)
Hayward A, 'Common Intention Constructive Trusts and the Role of Imputation in Theory and Practice' (2016) 3 The Conveyancer and Property Lawyer 233
Hedley S, 'Implied Contract and Restitution' (2004) 63(2) CLJ 435
Herbert AP, *More Uncommon Law* (Methuen 1982)
Hoffmann (Lord), 'Anthropomorphic Justice: The Reasonable Man and His Friends' (1995) 29 The Law Teacher 127
Holdsworth W, *A History of English Law*, vol 1 (AL Goodhart and HG Hanbury eds, 7th edn, Methuen, Sweet & Maxwell 1969)

Holmes OW, *The Common Law* (Belknap Press 2009)
Howarth D et al., *Hepple and Matthews' Tort Law* (7th edn, Hart 2015)
Hudson J, *The Oxford History of the Laws of England*, vol 2 (1st edn, OUP 2012)
Ibbetson DJ, 'Assumpsit and Debt in the Early Sixteenth Century: The Origins of the Indebitatus Count' (1982) 41 CLJ 142
'Sixteenth Century Contract Law: Slade's Case in Context' (1984) 4 OJLS 295
A Historical Introduction to the Law of Obligations (OUP 1999)
Jacob G, Tomlins TE and Granger TC, *The Law-Dictionary: Explaining the Rise, Progress, and Present State, of the English Law*, vol 1 (4th edn, Clarke 1835)
Jaffey AJE, 'Volenti Non Fit Injuria' (1985) 44 CLJ 87
Jones MA (ed), *Clerk & Lindsell on Torts* (22nd edn, Sweet & Maxwell 2018)
Junor G, 'Vicarious Liability – Redefined?' (2016) 24 SLT 125
Kelsen H, 'On the Theory of Juridic Fictions: With Special Consideration of Vaihinger's Philosophy of the As-If' in Maksymilian Del Mar and William Twining (eds), Christoph Kletzer (tr), *Legal Fictions in Theory and Practice* (Springer 2015)
Kerr RM, *An Action at Law: Being an Outline of the Jurisdiction of the Superior Courts of Common Law, with an Elementary View of the Proceedings in Personal Actions and in Ejectment* (2nd edn, William Henry Bond 1855)
Kidner R, 'The Variable Standard of Care, Contributory Negligence and Volenti' (1991) 11 Legal Studies 1
Kletzer C, 'Kelsen on Vaihinger' in Maksymilian Del Mar and William Twining (eds), *Legal Fictions in Theory and Practice* (Springer 2015)
Knauer NJ, 'Legal Fictions and Juristic Truth' (2010) 23 St Thomas LR 1
Langbein JH, 'The Later History of Restitution' in WR Cornish et al. (eds), *Restitution: Past, Present and Future* (Hart 1998)
Lee J, '"And the Waters Began to Subside": Imputing Intention under Jones v Kernott' (2012) 5 Conveyancer and Property Lawyer 421
'Fictions in Tort' in Maksymilian Del Mar and William Twining (eds), *Legal Fictions in Theory and Practice* (Springer 2015)
Lind D, 'The Pragmatic Value of Legal Fictions' in Maksymilian Del Mar and William Twining (eds), *Legal Fictions in Theory and Practice* (Springer 2015)
Lobban M, 'Legal Fictions before the Age of Reform' in Maksymilian Del Mar and William Twining (eds), *Legal Fictions in Theory and Practice* (Springer 2015)
Maine HS, *Ancient Law* (first published in 1861, Murray 1930)
Maitland FW, *The Forms of Action at Common Law* (AH Chaytor and WJ Whittaker eds, CUP 1965)
McBride NJ, 'Duties of Care – Do They Really Exist?' (2004) 24 OJLS 417
McBride NJ and Bagshaw R, *Tort Law* (6th edn, Pearson 2018)
McCrudden C, 'Legal Research and the Social Sciences' [2006] LQR 632
McFarlane B, Hopkins N and Nield S, *Land Law: Text, Cases and Materials* (3rd edn, OUP 2015)
Mee J, 'Joint Ownership, Subjective Intention and the Common Intention Constructive Trust' [2007] Conveyancer and Property Lawyer 14
Miller JA, 'Liars Should Have Good Memories: Legal Fictions and the Tax Code' (1993) 64 U Colo LR 1
Miller ST, 'The Reasons for Some Legal Fictions' (1910) 8 Michigan Law Review 623

Millett P, 'Bribes and Secret Commissions' (1993) 1 Restitution Law Review 7
Milsom SFC, 'Trespass from Henry III to Edward III: Part I General Writs' (1958) 74 LQR 195
Historical Foundations of the Common Law (2nd edn, Butterworths 1981)
Mitchell OR, 'Fictions of the Law: Have They Proved Useful or Detrimental to Its Growth?' (1893) 7 Harvard LR 249
Mitchell P, 'Patterns of Legal Change' (2012) 65 Current Legal Problems 177
Mitchell P, *A History of Tort Law 1900–1950* (CUP 2015)
Munday R, *Evidence* (8th edn, OUP 2015)
Murphy J, 'A Legal Fiction? Pt 1' (2015) 165 New Law Journal 13
Naniwadekar M, 'The Application of the Single Meaning Rule to Cases Other than Defamation' [2010] International Company and Commercial Law Review 408
Nolan RC, 'Equitable Property' (2006) 122 LQR 232
Oakley AJ, *Constructive Trusts* (3rd edn, Sweet & Maxwell 1997)
Ogden CK and Bentham J, *Bentham's Theory of Fictions* (Routledge 2013)
Oldham JC, 'On Pleading the Belly: A History of the Jury of Matrons' (1985) 6 Criminal Justice History 1
Olivier PJ, *Legal Fictions in Practice and Legal Science* (Rotterdam University Press 1975)
Orth JV, 'Fact & Fiction in the Law of Property' (2007) 11 Green Bag 65
O'Sullivan J, 'In Defence of *Foakes v. Beer*' (1996) 55 CLJ 219
'Remoteness of Damage in Concurrent Liability Cases', *The Joint TECBAR / PNBA Lecture, Inner Temple Hall* (2014), http://pnba.co.uk/wp-content/uploads/2014/05/Dr-Janet-OSullivan-Paper-29-April-2014.pdf
O'Sullivan & Hilliard's The Law of Contract (9th edn, OUP 2020)
Palmer RC, *English Law in the Age of the Black Death, 1348–1381* (University of North Carolina Press 1993)
Partington A (ed), *Oxford Dictionary of Quotations* (4th rev edn, OUP 1996)
Pawlowski M, 'Imputing a Common Intention in Single Ownership Cases' (2015) 29 Trust Law International 3
Peel E, 'Contra Proferentem Revisited' (2017) 133 LQR 6
Peel E and Goudkamp J, *Winfield and Jolowicz on Tort* (19th edn, Sweet & Maxwell 2014)
Petroski K, 'Legal Fictions and the Limits of Legal Language' in Maksymilian Del Mar and William Twining (eds), *Legal Fictions in Theory and Practice* (Springer 2015)
Piska N, 'Intention, Fairness and the Presumption of Resulting Trust after *Stack v Dowden*' (2008) 71 MLR 120
Pollock F, 'Has the Common Law Received the Fiction Theory of Corporations?' (1911) 27 LQR 219
Pollock F and Maitland FW, *The History of English Law before the Time of Edward I*, vol 1 (2nd edn, CUP 1968)
Posner RA, 'Blackstone and Bentham' (1976) 19 Journal of Law and Economics 569
Pound R, 'Spurious Interpretation' (1907) 7 Columbia Law Review 379
Interpretations of Legal History (CUP 1923)
Prichard MJ, 'Scott v. Shepherd (1773) and the Emergence of the Tort of Negligence', *The Selden Society Lectures 1952–2001* (Selden Society 2003)
Prichard MJ and Yale DEC, 'Introduction' in MJ Prichard and DEC Yale (eds), *Hale and Fleetwood on Admiralty Jurisdiction*, vol 108 (Selden Society 1993)

Quinn M, 'Fuller on Legal Fictions: A Benthamic Perspective' [2013] International Journal of the Law in Context 466

Rastell J, *Les Termes de La Ley* (first published 1527, J Johnson 1812)

Ross A, 'Legal Fictions' in Graham Hughes (ed), *Reason, Law, and Justice: Essays in Legal Philosophy* (University of London Press 1969)

Russell B, *The Problems of Philosophy* (2nd edn, OUP 2001)

Samek RA, 'Fictions and the Law' (1981) 31 U Toronto LJ 290

Samuel G, 'Is Law a Fiction' in Maksymilian Del Mar and William Twining (eds), *Legal Fictions in Theory and Practice* (Springer 2015)

Schauer F, 'Legal Fictions Revisited' in Maksymilian Del Mar and William Twining (eds), *Legal Fictions in Theory and Practice* (Springer 2015)

Scott A, 'Ceci n'est pas une Pipe: The Autopoietic Inanity of the Single Meaning Rule' in Andrew T Kenyon (ed), *Comparative Defamation and Privacy Law* (CUP 2016)

Simons KW, 'Assumption of Risk and Consent in the Law of Torts: A Theory of Full Preference' (1987) 67 Boston University Law Review 213

Simpson AWB, 'The Introduction of the Action on the Case for Conversion' (1959) 75 LQR 364

A *History of the Land Law* (2nd edn, Clarendon Press 1986)

A *History of the Common Law of Contract: The Rise of the Action of Assumpsit* (Clarendon Press 1987)

Simpson JA and Weiner ESC (eds), *The Oxford English Dictionary* (2nd edn, Clarendon Press 1989)

Smith J, 'Surviving Fictions' (1917) 27 Yale LJ 147

'Surviving Fictions' (1917) 27 Yale LJ 317

Smith PJ, 'New Legal Fictions' (2006) 95 Georgetown LJ 1435

Sparkes P, 'Ejectment: Three Births and a Funeral' in Maksymilian Del Mar and William Twining (eds), *Legal Fictions in Theory and Practice* (Springer 2015)

Stephen HJ, A *Treatise on the Principles of Pleading in Civil Actions* (Joseph Butterworth & Son 1824)

Stern S, 'Legal Fictions and Exclusionary Rules' in Maksymilian Del Mar and William Twining (eds), *Legal Fictions in Theory and Practice* (Springer 2015)

Stoneking JB, 'Penumbras and Privacy: A Study of the Use of Fictions in Constitutional Decision-Making' (1984) 87 W Va LR 859

Sugarman SD, 'Assumption of Risk' (1997) 31 Valparaiso University Law Review 833

Swadling W, 'The Vendor-Purchaser Constructive Trust' in Simone Degeling and James Edeman (eds), *Equity in Commercial Law* (Lawbook Co 2005)

'The Fiction of the Constructive Trust' (2011) 64 Current Legal Problems 399

'Constructive Trusts and Breach of Fiduciary Duty' [2012] Trust & Trustees 985

Turner PJ, 'Understanding the Constructive Trust between Vendor and Purchaser' (2012) 128 LQR 582

Vaihinger H, *The Philosophy of 'As If': A System of the Theoretical, Practical and Religious Fictions of Mankind* (CK Ogden tr, 2nd edn, Routledge & Kegan Paul 1965)

Varga C and Szájer J, 'Presumption and Fiction: Means of Legal Technique' [1988] Archiv für Rechts- und Sozialphilosophie 168

Virgo G, 'Restitution of Void Loans' (2010) 69 CLJ 447

'Profits Obtained in Breach of Fiduciary Duty: Personal or Proprietary Claim?' (2011) 70 CLJ 502

The Principles of Equity & Trusts (2nd edn, OUP 2016)
Waters DWM, *The Constructive Trust* (Athlone Press 1964)
Watts P, 'Bribes and Constructive Trusts' (1994) 110 LQR 178
'*Tyrrell v Bank of London* – An Inside Look at an Inside Job' (2013) 129 LQR 527
Whayman D, 'Remodelling Knowing Receipt as a Gains-Based Wrong' (2016) 7 JBL 565
Williston S, 'Liability for Honest Misrepresentation' (1910) 24 Harvard LR 415
Witting C, *Street on Torts* (14th edn, OUP 2015)

Index

For EU product safety concerns, contact us at Calle de José Abascal, 56–1°,
28003 Madrid, Spain or eugpsr@cambridge.org.

www.ingramcontent.com/pod-product-compliance
Lightning Source LLC
LaVergne TN
LVHW011812200926
848484LV00005B/1156

* 9 7 8 1 3 1 6 5 1 9 4 7 9 *